A Daily Walk Through the New Testament

Thomas E. Dewlen

Preface

This book came into being through a message preached at the Assemblies of God church in Medaryville, Indiana on January 1, 2017. At that time, we began a year-long journey through the New Testament, a journey which lead first to a blog, and, ultimately, to this book. We hope that you will join us for a prayerful, year-long walk through every chapter in the New Testament. It is important that we don't just read through the Word of God, as we would any other book (for it is **not** just any other book), but that we pray through it, hiding it in our hearts, and allowing the Holy Spirit to apply it to our lives. Much of what you read will not be new to you, but it is our hope and prayer that you will be encouraged to "dig deeper" in the Word of God for yourself, and in the process, be drawn closer to the God of the Word!

I would like to give special thanks to the following people: my mother, Naomi Dewlen, who first encouraged me to read and study God's Word; my wife, Linda Dewlen, and my daughter, Laura Dewlen Quirindongo, without whose help nothing would have been accomplished around here over the years; and thanks to the church family at Medaryville, who have come faithfully for over twenty-five years as we have studied the Word and worshiped the Savior together.

Most of all, thanks to the One who has given us His Word, the One Who is the Word come in human flesh, our Lord Jesus Christ! To know Him is to know life! His prayer for you, as you begin this journey is found in John 17:17, "Sanctify them through Thy truth. Thy Word is truth."

Blessings,
Pastor Tom

Read Matthew 1

Matthew 1:1 The book of the generation of Jesus Christ, the son of **David**, the son of **Abraham**.

Does anyone enjoy reading the lengthy lists of names in the Bible? Probably not! But, they are *all* there for a purpose. The New Testament begins with the genealogy of Jesus Christ. Israel's king must not be a foreigner, He must be a Jew, a descendant of Abraham (Deuteronomy 17:15), He must also be a descendant of King David (Psalm 89:35-37). Jesus fulfilled both of those qualifications. He is both Savior *and* King (Matthew 1:21, Matthew 2:2)! Is He *your* Savior (Romans 10:13)? Is He *your* King (Matthew 6:10)? Begin this walk through the New Testament making certain that he is both.

Old Testament genealogies rarely mentioned the names of women or Gentiles. Matthew 1 reminds us that God's plan includes both men **and** *women*, both Jews **and** Gentiles (Galatians 3:28). The Holy Spirit directed Matthew to include the names of four Gentile women. Tamar was a Canaanite (Matthew 1:3, Genesis 38); Rahab was a former prostitute (Matthew 1:5, Joshua 2); Ruth was a Moabite who became a follower of the Lord (Matthew 1:5, Ruth 1:16); Bathsheba is not even mentioned by name. She had been the wife of Uriah the Hittite and was the one with whom David committed adultery (Matthew 1:6, 2nd Samuel 11-12). We all have a past, we all have a story, but through the grace of God, we can all become part of the family (Ephesians 2:19, 2 Corinthians 5:17)! What about you, have you received Him (John 1:12) and become a part of the family of God Ephesians 2:19)?

6

Read Matthew 2

Matthew 2:1 Now when Jesus was born in Bethlehem of Judaea in the days of Herod the king, behold, there came wise men from the east to Jerusalem,

The wise men are mysterious. We are never told their number, only that they came from the east, probably modern-day Iraq. We are never told that they were kings. We are never told their names. We are never told *how* they knew to follow the star. We **are** told that they longed to see the King, so that they could worship Him (Matthew 2:2). Their trek to Bethlehem covered *at least* 1,000 miles and must have taken them through perils that we probably cannot even imagine. Still, they did not stop until they could bow down and worship Him (Matthew 2:11).

I pray that we are all on the same kind of spiritual journey. We have as our goal seeing the Lord Jesus Christ (Matthew 5:8, 1st John 3:1-3). We are not promised an easy road on that journey (Matthew 7:14, Acts 14:22), but we **are** promised His presence (Hebrews 13:5) and His power (Acts 1:8). When we see **HIM**, all that we suffered on the journey will be worth it (Romans 8:8). Let's determine, by His power, to stay faithful until we see Jesus!

It will be worth it all, when we see Jesus,
 It will be worth it all, when we see Christ,
One glimpse of His dear face, all sorrow will erase,
So bravely run the race 'till we see Christ.[1]

Through many dangers, toils and snares, I have already come, His grace has brought me safe thus far, and grace will lead me home.[2]

---

[1] "When We See Christ," Esther Kerr Rusthoi
[2] "Amazing Grace," John Newton.

Read Matthew 3

Matthew 3:1-2 In those days came John the Baptist, preaching in the wilderness of Judaea, And saying, Repent ye: for the kingdom of heaven is at hand.

John the Baptist was Jesus' cousin. His preaching prepared people for the coming of Jesus, the Messiah. The first word we hear from John's mouth is "Repent!" Interestingly, that is also the first word we hear from Jesus as He begins His earthly ministry (Matthew 4:17). God's will is that all people everywhere repent (Acts 17:30, 2nd Peter 3:9). It means to have a change of heart, to turn around and walk another way. Repentance is essential to salvation (Luke 13:3, Acts 2:38). John would not baptize those who did not show evidence of having repented (Matthew 3:8).

Those whom John baptized were anticipating the first appearance of Jesus. We are looking forward to His *Return* (Hebrews 9:28)! His Second Coming is imminent; He could come at any moment. Our motto should be like that of the US Coast Guard, Semper Paratus, Always Prepared (Matthew 24:44)! I pray the Holy Spirit helps us to have a contrite and humble heart until that day (Psalm 34:18, Psalm 51:17, Isaiah 57:15). Today, I recognize my great spiritual need; without **HIM** I can do nothing (Matthew 5:3, John 15:5).

Jesus, oh Jesus
Do you know Him today
Please don't turn Him away
Oh Jesus, my Jesus
Without Him how lost I would be
Without Him how lost I would be[3]

---

[3] "Without Him," Mylon LeFevre.

Read Matthew 4

Matthew 4:4 But he answered and said, It is written, Man shall not live by bread alone, but by every word that proceedeth out of the mouth of God.

It is interesting that the *first* place the Holy Spirit led Jesus after He was baptized was a place of testing (Matthew 4:1). We will also face times of testing and temptation in our lives (James 1:2-3). Those great tests will often come after great victories. Jesus was tempted in *every* way that *we* are, yet *He* never sinned (Hebrews 4:15).

He overcame in all the ways that Adam and Eve failed in the Garden of Eden, overcoming the lust of the flesh, the lust of the eyes, and the pride of life (1 John 2:15-17). Notice what He used to resist Satan's deception. He always used the Truth, the Word of God. Each time He was confronted with a Satanic attack, He countered with the Word, usually quoting the Book of Deuteronomy. We can use the *same* powerful sword against the enemies' attacks (Ephesians 6:17)!

Because *He* overcame temptation, He can help us when *we* are tempted (Hebrews 2:18). Just as in the example He gave us, we can apply the unchanging Word of God. In studying the Word, we become His disciples (John 8:31), and can walk in freedom (John 8:32). The Word will help us to grow in our faith (Romans 10:17), so that we can quench all the fiery darts the adversary throws our way (Ephesians 6:16).

As we walk through the New Testament together, let's make the words of Psalm 119:11 our daily prayer.

Thy word have I hid in mine heart, that I might not sin against thee.

Read Matthew 5

Matthew 5:3 Blessed *are* the poor in spirit: for theirs is the kingdom of heaven.

Matthew 5-7 is often called Jesus' Sermon on the Mount. As you read these chapters you will be struck by just how much you need **HIM!** That is a good thing. You may recognize the first few verses of chapter five as something called the Beatitudes or Blessings. Some call them the "Beautiful Attitudes." They all point to a complete reliance on Him.

Being poor in spirit has far less to do with the condition of our bank accounts than it does the condition of our hearts. It means that we recognize our own *spiritual* poverty outside of His salvation. We cannot receive the riches of that salvation, until we confess just how spiritually bankrupt we are without Him (1 John 1:8-10)!

In the Book of Revelation Jesus writes to a backslidden church, one that He describes as lukewarm (Revelation 3:16). The attitude of that church shows us the *opposite* of what it is to be poor in spirit. They said, "We are rich and increased with goods and have need of nothing (Revelation 3:17). The one who is poor in spirit says, "Without Him, I can do nothing (John 15:5)!

May God help us to be "poor in spirit," knowing that the true riches come from Him (Ephesians 1:18).

I need thee every hour,
Most gracious Lord;
No tender voice like thine
Can peace afford.
I need thee, O I need thee;
Every hour I need thee;
O bless me now, my Savior,
I come to thee.[4]

---

[4] "I Need Thee," Annie S. Hawks

Read Matthew 5:38-6:15

Matthew 6:9 After this manner therefore pray ye: Our Father which art in heaven, Hallowed be Thy Name.

The words of the Lord's prayer are very familiar to most of us. Jesus gave the same kind of teaching to His disciples on another occasion, when they asked, "Lord, teach us to pray." (Luke 11:1). That lets us know that prayer can be learned. We can all pray "better" than we are now.

Prayer is the privilege of all those who are God's children. We *become* His children when we are born again (John 1:12). That new relationship gives us bold access to our Father's throne (Hebrews 4:16). Our Father provides well for His children, but He has commanded us many times to ask (Matthew 7:7, Matthew 7:11, Matthew 18:19, Matthew 21:22, John 14:14, John 15:7, John 15:16, John 16:24, Ephesians 3:20, James 1:5, 1 John 3:22, 1 John 5:14-15).

James 4:2 says we "have not, because we ask not."

As we walk through the New Testament together let's make it our prayer too, "Lord teach *us* to pray!"

What a Friend we have in Jesus,
  All our sins and griefs to bear!
What a privilege to carry
  Everything to God in prayer!
O what peace we often forfeit,
  O what needless pain we bear,
All because we do not carry
  Everything to God in prayer![5]

---

[5] "What a Friend We Have in Jesus," Joseph M. Scriven.

Read Matthew 6:16-7:6

Matthew 6:33 But seek ye first the kingdom of God, and his righteousness; and all these things shall be added unto you.

Jesus summarized what He had just been teaching with these words about priorities. A priority is something that is more important than other things and that needs to be dealt with first. [6]

Making money must not be our priority, because no man can serve two masters (Matthew 6:19-24). In verse 29, He speaks of that one who has an 'evil eye,' a figure of speech speaking of one who is greedy and covetous (Proverbs 28:22). Someone once said, "Money is a wonderful servant, but a horrible master" Paul told a young preacher that the "*love* of money is the root of all evil."[7]

Often the things we worry about demonstrate our priorities. Jesus goes on to tell us that even our daily physical needs must not be our primary focus. Though the Word of God encourages responsibility (Proverbs 10:5, Proverbs 20:4) we must not be given over to worry about those things (Matthew 6:25). Our Father takes care of the birds and even the wildflowers, so He will certainly care for His children (Matthew 6:26-32). Remember, He provides daily bread for those who ask (Matthew 6:11)!

If *He* becomes our priority, putting the things of God first, we can rest assured that He will take care of the rest. Take Him at His Word!

'Tis so sweet to trust in Jesus,
Just to take Him at His Word
Just to rest upon His promise,
Just to know, "Thus saith the Lord!"
Jesus, Jesus, how I trust Him!
How I've proved Him o'er and o'er
Jesus, Jesus, precious Jesus!
Oh, for grace to trust Him more!

---

[6] https://www.**merriam-webster**.com/**dictionary**/**priority**
[7] 1 Timothy 6:10

Read Matthew 7:7 to 8:4

Matthew 7:13-14 Enter ye in at the strait gate: for wide *is* the gate, and broad *is* the way, that leadeth to destruction, and many there be which go in thereat: Because strait *is* the gate, and narrow *is* the way, which leadeth unto life, and few there be that find it.

A funeral was once held in a nearby community. The one conducting the service said something like this, "I know our dear sister is in heaven, for there are seven roads that lead there, and she surely must have found one of them." Perhaps the most dangerous false doctrine of our day is just that, the belief that all roads end up at the same place—heaven.

Jesus reminds us that the busy road, the road that most are traveling, will only lead to destruction, but there is another road, the road less traveled. That is the one we must take. Though Christians are sometimes accused of being narrow minded because of this, Jesus makes it very clear that there is only one way to the Father's House. He says, "I am the door of the sheep" and all who try to come in another way are "thieves and robbers!" (John 10:1). Perhaps His strongest words are in John 14:6, "I am *the* way, *the* truth, and *the* life: no man comes unto the Father, but by me."

That narrow road is not always easy, but the company is great. He will never leave or forsake you (Hebrews 13:5)!

Which road are *you* traveling today?

Read Matthew 8:5 to 8:27

Matthew 8:26-27 And he saith unto them, Why are ye fearful, O ye of little faith? Then he arose, and rebuked the winds and the sea; and there was a great calm. But the men marvelled, saying, What manner of man is this, that even the winds and the sea obey him!

Jesus was on the Sea of Galilee in a fishing boat with some of his disciples. Some of these men made their living fishing. They had seen many storms before, but this one was terrifying. They believed their lives were in danger. After all, the waves were coming up over the deck, likely filling the ship with water. The word Matthew used for the storm is *seismos*, it could also be translated as earthquake. This was no ordinary summer thunderstorm, but something of tsunami-like proportions!

Their fear turned to amazement as they saw the Lord's authority in action. The wind and waves obeyed His command. They still do! Remember today, if Jesus is with you in the boat, it's NOT going to sink. Have faith. Trust Him.

"Everything will be alright in the end. If it is not alright - It is not the end."[8]

---

[8] Pastor Phil Curtis, Franklin Assembly of God, Franklin, Indiana.

Read Matthew 8:28-9:13

Matthew 8:29 And, behold, they cried out, saying, What have we to do with thee, Jesus, thou Son of God? art thou come hither to torment us before the time?

Here Jesus encountered two demon-possessed men. They lived among the tombs, very fitting as they were held captive by an enemy who deals in death and destruction (John 10:10). Matthew describes them as fierce. This is from the same Greek word (chalepos) used to describe the *perilous* times in the last days (2nd Timothy 3). The fierceness, the violence, of these men instilled fear in those who passed by.

The demons, speaking from within these men, recognized Jesus as the Son of God. They also recognized that He was their Judge and the One who would one day consign them to their eternal destiny. Satan and his minions know that their time is short (Revelation 12:12), and they apparently know that eternal torment awaits them. Contrary to common thought, hell is *not* Satan's present headquarters. As of now, he is at work in this world (2 Corinthians 4:4). However, the lake of fire *will be* his eternal punishment (Matthew 25:41, Revelation 20:10), and it will only take one of God's holy angels to consign him to that place (Revelation 20:1-2).

Jesus conquered Satan on the cross, making an open show of him (Colossians 2:13-15) and has told us that we can resist him, steadfast in the faith (2nd Peter 5:8-9). If we resist him, he will flee from *us* (James 4:7)! If we have been born again, we are no longer living in Satan's dark kingdom, but we are living in God's kingdom of light (Colossians 1:13)! Glorious things are ahead for *that* kingdom!

Luke 10:19-20 19 Behold, I give unto you power to tread on serpents and scorpions, and over all the power of the enemy: and nothing shall by any means hurt you. 20 Notwithstanding in this rejoice not, that the spirits are subject unto you; but rather **rejoice, because your names are written in heaven.**

Read Matthew 9:14-34

Matthew 9:20-21 20 And, behold, a woman, which was diseased with an issue of blood twelve years, came behind *him*, and touched the hem of his garment: 21 For she said within herself, If I may but touch his garment, I shall be whole.

Jesus was on His way to raise the daughter of a certain ruler, when he encountered what some might have called an interruption, a woman with an issue of blood, a hemorrhaging that had continued to torment her for twelve years.[9] Her condition left her ceremonially unclean. Had they known, they would not have allowed her in a crowd like this, nor to have approached Jesus directly.   Perhaps she inched along the ground through the crowd, hoping to touch one of those four blue tassels, which were the hem of his garment.   That deliberate touch brought her an immediate healing.

Jesus healed in various ways.   Sometimes He laid hands on those who were sick (Matthew 8:1-3), He spoke the Word (Matthew 8:16), Sometimes His methods were very unusual (John 9:6) and He asked for some act of obedience (John 9:7).   This woman's healing was different still. She touched *Him* in faith. Nothing could deter her from touching Jesus.   I pray we all have the same kind of bold faith.

A woman tried many physicians, yet grew worse,
So to Jesus she came,
And when the crowd tried to restrain her,
She whispered these words through her pain.
Touching Jesus is all that matters, then your life will never be the same,
There is only one way to touch Him,
Just believe when you call on His Name.[10]

---

[9] If you would like more details about her story, read Mark 5:21-43 and Luke 8:43-48.
[10] "Touching Jesus," John Stallings.

Read Matthew 9:35-10:23

Matthew 9:36-38 But when he saw the multitudes, he was moved with compassion on them, because they fainted, and were scattered abroad, as sheep having no shepherd. Then saith he unto his disciples, The harvest truly *is* plenteous, but the labourers *are* few; Pray ye therefore the Lord of the harvest, that he will send forth labourers into his harvest.

Compassion has been defined as, "sympathetic pity and concern for the sufferings or misfortunes of others," but the Scriptures take it a step further, it includes being *moved* to do something about it. Jesus was moved with compassion as he saw the horrible lost condition of the multitudes. He is still moved with compassion over a lost world, not willing that any should perish (2nd Peter 3:9).

The lost all around us are compared to a harvest field, a harvest that could be lost unless the grain is brought in before the storm. The time for harvest is now (John 4:35). Former Assemblies of God Missions Director, Loren Triplett[11] once said, "You don't measure yourself by your success but by the unfinished task." How many have **yet** to hear?"

> There is peace and contentment in my Father's house today
> Lots of food on the table and no one is turned away
> There is singing and laughter as the hours pass by
> But a hush calms the singing as the Father sadly cries
>
> My house is full, but my field is empty
> Who will go and work for Me today
> It seems my children all want to stay around my table
> But no one wants to work my field
> No one wants to work my field[12]

---

[11] http://penews.org/News/Loren-Triplett-Dies
[12] "My House is Full," Lanny Wolfe.

Read Matthew 10:24-11:6

Matthew 10:31 Fear ye not therefore, ye are of more value than many sparrows.

Psalm 147 says that His understanding is infinite, He created the stars, numbered them, and gave them their names[13].   How many stars are there? It is estimated that there are five to ten times more stars in the universe than there are grains of sand on planet earth!   Is it any wonder that David was awestruck looking at the night sky?   It caused him to exclaim, "What is man that Thou art mindful of Him?"[14]   Who am I that the Creator would take notice of me?

He is infinite, but He cares about the small things in our lives.   Two sparrows were sold for a farthing, a trivial amount, but not one of them falls to the ground without the knowledge and care of the Creator[15].   He says that He knows the numbers of hairs on our heads[16].   Thinking about God's great knowledge of His Creation, David also marveled and said, "Such knowledge is too wonderful for me!" (Psalm 139:1-6).

How could such a Being care about me?   We know that He does—the cross will forever prove that!   Our value in His eyes is based on what He was willing to pay to redeem us, His own life blood (1 Peter 1:18-19).   Marvel at His creation today, and then rejoice that your Creator and Redeemer knows all about *you*!   Do you know Him (Jeremiah 9:23-24, Philippians 1:10)?

> Why should I feel discouraged, why should the shadows come,
> Why should my heart be lonely, and long for heav'n and home,
> When Jesus is my portion? My constant Friend is He:
> His eye is on the sparrow, and I know He watches me;
> His eye is on the sparrow, and I know He watches me.[17]

---

[13] Psalm 147:1-5
[14] Psalm 8:3-4
[15] Some sources give the value of the New Testament farthing (penny) as ½ of one US penny, a very small amount. The idea is that the Lord cares for things we think unimportant.
[16] He cares about every small detail in our lives.
[17] "His Eyes is on the Sparrow," Civilla D. Martin

Read Matthew 11:7-30

Matthew 11:28 Come unto me, all *ye* that labour and are heavy laden, and I will give you rest.

Jesus invites us to come to Him and find rest. If you are carrying a heavy load today, a load that is just too much for you, perhaps it is a burden you should not be bearing alone. Peter says, "Casting *all* your care upon Him, for He cares for you."[18] Think about it! Jesus says, "*My* yoke is easy, and my burden is light."

I am glad that my rest in Him is more than just a day of the week, it is a life of resting, trusting in what He has done for me (Hebrews 4:9-10). I rest in the finished work of Jesus on the cross. He said, "It is finished," and it is (John 19:30)! Now Jesus is *seated* at the Father's right hand, having completed His work on our behalf (Hebrews 1:3, Hebrews 10:12)! Rest in that! Trust in that!

Psalm 116:7-9 7 Return unto thy rest, O my soul; for the LORD hath dealt bountifully with thee. 8 For thou hast delivered my soul from death, mine eyes from tears, *and* my feet from falling. 9 I will walk before the LORD in the land of the living.

---

[18] 1 Peter 5:7

Read Matthew 12:1-21

Matthew 12:6 But I say unto you, That in this place is *one* greater than the temple.

They were hungry, walking through a grain field, and eating some handfuls of grain.[19] Of course, they were not stealing, this was allowed under the law.[20] The religious leaders, ever eager to accuse Jesus, rebuked them for working on the Sabbath.   They were probably accused of reaping, threshing, winnowing, and preparing food.   They had probably also walked further than the prescribed Sabbath day's journey (less than ½ a mile).

Jesus gave examples from the Scriptures, and He made two strong statements that sealed His right to do what He was doing.   He said, "I am greater than this temple[21] and "I am Lord of the Sabbath."[22]   These are amazing declarations in light of Leviticus 19:30, "You shall keep MY Sabbaths, and reverence MY sanctuary: I am the LORD." What was He saying?   The LORD Himself is standing in your midst and you do not recognize Him. Jesus had the right, because He was, and is, God.

He is Lord of the Sabbath, and Lord of the Temple, is He Lord of *your* life today?

Romans 10:9 That if thou shalt confess with thy mouth the Lord Jesus, and shalt believe in thine heart that God hath raised him from the dead, thou shalt be saved.

---

[19] Matthew 12:1
[20] Deuteronomy 23:25
[21] Matthew 12:6
[22] Matthew 12:8

Read Matthew 12:22-42

Matthew 12:36-37 But I say unto you, That every idle word that men shall speak, they shall give account thereof in the day of judgment. For by thy words thou shalt be justified, and by thy words thou shalt be condemned.

Words are powerful things. They can bring the sweetest comfort or the most intense pain (Proverbs 15:4). Just as the fruit of the tree indicates what kind of tree it is, our words indicate what we truly are (Matthew 12:33-34). Our words are a measure of the condition of our hearts!

The Bible is full of teaching about our words. Here are just a few examples: Proverbs 6:2, Proverbs 10:19, Proverbs 13:3, Proverbs 15:1, Proverbs 17:28, Proverbs 21:23, Proverbs 29:20, and James 3:2. The Lord warns us that the tongue can be like an out of control fire or a wild animal. It is something that no one can tame (James 3:8), no human being can tame it, that is. The Spirit of God will help us in this area, if we will but ask. Today, let's make our prayer the one that David prayed in Psalm 19:14.

Let the words of my mouth, and the meditation of my heart, be acceptable in thy sight, O LORD, my strength, and my redeemer.

Read Matthew 12:43-13:17

Matthew 13:16 But blessed *are* your eyes, for they see: and your ears, for they hear.

The disciples had questioned Jesus about His use of parables. His use of parables made the truth clearer to those who had hearts to receive, but those with self-satisfied, closed hearts only grew harder. Someone once said, "The same sun that softens wax will harden clay." If we receive His Word, we will be softened and changed. If we reject, our hearts will only become calloused and hard.

Like the disciples that spoke to Jesus, I want eyes that see and ears that hear what God is saying. Jesus said, "My sheep hear My voice."[23] Seven times we find the words, "He that hath an ear, let Him hear."[24] I will say "yes" to Him and to His Word! David's prayer in Psalm 25:4-7 is a good one for us to pray today.

Shew me thy ways, O LORD; teach me thy paths. Lead me in thy truth, and teach me: for thou *art* the God of my salvation; on thee do I wait all the day. Remember, O LORD, thy tender mercies and thy lovingkindnesses; for they *have been* ever of old. Remember not the sins of my youth, nor my transgressions: according to thy mercy remember thou me for thy goodness' sake, O LORD.

Open my eyes, Lord, I want to see Jesus,
To reach out and touch Him, and tell Him I love Him,
Open my ears, Lord, and help me to listen,
Open my eyes, Lord, I want to see Jesus.

---

[23] John 10:27
[24] Revelation 2:7, 11, 17, 29; Revelation 3:6, 13, 22.

Read Matthew 13:18-43

Matthew 13:22 He also that received seed among the thorns is he that heareth the word; and the care of this world, and the deceitfulness of riches, choke the word, and he becometh unfruitful.

Jesus had just taught them using a parable about a man sowing seeds. Some of the seeds fell on hard ground, where birds gobbled them up. Other seeds fell on stony, or shallow, ground. The seed sprouted quickly, but since its roots could not grow deeply, it dried up with the heat of the sun. Some seed fell among thorns and thistles, which smothered it. Some did fall on good ground, though, and produced an amazing harvest.

Jesus explained that the seed represents the Word of God. It is good seed! The soil is our hearts, how we *receive* the Word of God. A hardened heart will not see a harvest, nor will a heart that does not allow the word to grow deeply. We can even let other things choke out the effectiveness of the Word in our lives. Jesus mentions the cares of this world and the deceitfulness of riches, but there are many other things that we can allow to choke out the Word.

I pray that the Holy Spirit will break up the fallow ground of our hearts, so that the Word of God can sink deeply and produce a harvest (Jeremiah 4:3, Hosea 10:12). I pray He will help us to turn away from *anything* the devil may be using to choke out the Word in our lives.

Psalm 139:23-24 23 Search me, O God, and know my heart: try me, and know my thoughts: 24 And see if *there be any* wicked way in me, and lead me in the way everlasting.

Read Matthew 13:44-14:12

Matthew 13:44-46 Again, the kingdom of heaven is like unto treasure hid in a field; the which when a man hath found, he hideth, and for joy thereof goeth and selleth all that he hath, and buyeth that field. Again, the kingdom of heaven is like unto a merchant man, seeking goodly pearls: Who, when he had found one pearl of great price, went and sold all that he had, and bought it

Christ and His kingdom are like that hidden treasure, like that amazingly perfect and costly pearl—something of inestimable value. **Nothing** is of greater value than knowing God and living in His kingdom. Do you remember what we have been reading thus far? Jesus said that we must seek His kingdom *first,*[25] and that we must not allow spiritual thorns and thistles to choke out His Word in our lives.[26] Later, He asks, "What does it profit a man if he gains the whole world and loses his own soul?"[27] That is a question that we should all consider.

I once overheard a godly older Christian share these words with a new believer at his baptism, "It will not always be easy serving Jesus Christ, but it will *always* be worth it." Have you found that to be true? When we finally reach the other side, we will not regret anything that it may have cost us here.

> "Take up thy cross and follow Me,"
> I hear the blessed Savior call;
> How can I make a lesser sacrifice,
> When Jesus gave His all?[28]

---

[25] Matthew 6:33
[26] Matthew 13:22
[27] Mark 8:36
[28] "Take Up Thy Cross and Follow Me," A. H. Ackley

Read Matthew 14:13-36

Matthew 14:30-31 30 But when he saw the wind boisterous, he was afraid; and beginning to sink, he cried, saying, Lord, save me. 31 And immediately Jesus stretched forth *his* hand, and caught him, and said unto him, O thou of little faith, wherefore didst thou doubt?

Jesus sent His disciples on across the Sea of Galilee, while He spent time praying.   While crossing the dark sea, they encountered a terrifying storm and in the fourth watch, about three o'clock in the morning, Jesus came to them walking on the water.   At first, they superstitiously thought they might be seeing a ghost.   Some old sailors believed such appearances meant tragedy was near—death at sea.

What a relief it must have been to hear the voice of Jesus through the wind and waves.   Peter asked to leave the boat and come to Him and Jesus said, "Come!"   Peter's eyes were fixed on Jesus and in that moment, he did start walking to Jesus on the rough water. But, noticing the wind and waves again, and turning his eyes *from* Jesus, he began to sink.   I love that when Peter began to sink, Jesus took His hand. He has taken my hand many times!   Today, we will face various distractions. May the Lord help us to keep our focus where it needs to be.

> Turn your eyes upon Jesus,
> Look full in His wonderful face,
> And the things of earth shall grow strangely dim
> In the light of His glory and grace.[29]

---

[29] "The Heavenly Vision," Helen Howarth Lemmel

Read Matthew 15:1-28

Matthew 15:19-20 For out of the heart proceed evil thoughts, murders, adulteries, fornications, thefts, false witness, blasphemies: These are *the things* which defile a man: but to eat with unwashen hands defileth not a man.

The Jewish religious leaders took issue with Jesus and His disciples, because they did not follow their traditions about ritual handwashing before eating. This was not so much about hygiene, as it was about following human tradition.[30] These same leaders often broke God's direct commandments through their own traditional loopholes.[31] Their long-held traditions were wrongly given the same authority, or even more than, the Word of God.[32] Jesus made it clear. It is not what goes into a person that defiles them, unwashed hands, or the food that they eat, it is deeper than that, it comes from the heart.[33]

Though sin has outward manifestations (evil thoughts, murder, adultery, fornication, theft, lying, blasphemy, etc.), the root lies within the human heart. Jeremiah said, "the heart is deceitful above all things and desperately wicked."[34] David prays for God to know him, searching his heart[35], and we are told to *keep* our hearts with all diligence.[36] Let's all pray the words of Psalm 51:9-10 today.

Hide thy face from my sins, and blot out all mine iniquities. Create in me a clean heart, O God; and renew a right spirit within me.

---

[30] Matthew 15:1-2
[31] Matthew 15:3-6
[32] Matthew 15:7-9
[33] Matthew 15:15-20
[34] Jeremiah 17:9
[35] Psalm 139:23-24
[36] Proverbs 4:23

Read Matthew 15:29-16:12

Matthew 16:4 A wicked and adulterous generation seeketh after a sign; and there shall no sign be given unto it, but the sign of the prophet Jonas. And he left them, and departed.

The religious leaders asked Jesus to show them a sign from heaven, proving who He was. Of course, they were ignoring the many signs they had already witnessed in Jesus' life and ministry. They were more knowledgeable of the weather signs than they were of the Biblical signs that should have proved that He was their true Messiah.

They would receive no other sign than that of the prophet Jonah. He had already explained what that was in Matthew 12:39-41. Jonah's stint in the belly of the great fish was a picture of the three days and three nights Jesus would be in the grave before His resurrection. The ungodly pagans of Nineveh repented when the "resurrected" Jonah came preaching to them[37], but the religious crowd in "godly" Jerusalem would continue to reject their Messiah. Though they were very religious, Jesus calls them a wicked and adulterous generation!

The greatest sign this world has ever seen is the resurrection of Jesus Christ. Believing that Jesus died, and rose again, we repent of *our* sin and turn to Him in faith. Have you confessed the Lord Jesus Christ, and do you believe that He rose from the dead?

Romans 10:9-11 That if thou shalt confess with thy mouth the Lord Jesus, and shalt believe in thine heart that God hath raised him from the dead, thou shalt be saved. For with the heart man believeth unto righteousness; and with the mouth confession is made unto salvation. For the scripture saith, Whosoever believeth on him shall not be ashamed.

---

[37] Jonah 3

Read Matthew 16:13-17:8

Matthew 16:16 And Simon Peter answered and said, Thou art the Christ, the Son of the living God.

Some of the people were confused about Jesus' identity. Jesus asked, "Who do men say that I am?" Some thought He was some great man returned to earth—Elijah, Jeremiah, or one of the other prophets. Then came the critical question, a question that we must all answer. Jesus asked Peter, "But who do **you** say that I am?" Peter answered with a powerful confession of faith, "You are the Christ, the Son of the Living God." He is not "a" christ, but He is THE Christ, THE Son of THE Living God, THE unique Savior.

That confession of faith is the rock-solid foundation upon which the Lord's church is built. We must not build on any other foundation.[38] Jesus says that only the house built on the rock will withstand the storms.[39] Upon what foundation are you building *your* house today?

> My hope is built on nothing less
> Than Jesus' blood and righteousness;
> I dare not trust the sweetest frame,
> But wholly lean on Jesus' name.
> On Christ, the solid Rock, I stand;
> All other ground is sinking sand.[40]

---

[38] 1 Corinthians 3:11
[39] Matthew 7:24-25
[40] "The Solid Rock," Edward Mote.

Read Matthew 17:9-18:7

Matthew 18:1 At the same time came the disciples unto Jesus, saying, Who is the greatest in the kingdom of heaven?

This was not the only time the disciples had questions like this. Even the night before Jesus was crucified, they were arguing about which of them would be the greatest.[41] Jesus had taught them much about His coming kingdom, and they imagined they might well have high positions in that kingdom. Later before Pilate he insisted, "My kingdom is not of this world, or else my servants would fight."[42] Before He ascended to heaven, He promised the outpouring of the Spirit[43]. Even then His disciples assumed that it would mean the end of Roman domination. Perhaps this promised outpouring would make them great Spirit-filled military leaders as the Judges of Israel had been.[44]

Jesus, knowing their hearts, brought a little child into their midst and made a startling statement, "Except you be converted, and become as little children, you shall not enter into the kingdom of heaven."[45] Far from being the *greatest* in the kingdom of heaven, they would not even make it there without being converted and becoming like that little child--humble and trusting. We receive the gift of sonship when we are born again, receiving Jesus Christ. Are you a child of the King? If not, what's keeping you from receiving that gift today?

John 1:12 But as many as received **Him**, to them gave he power to become the sons of God, *even* to them that believe on his name:

---

[41] Luke 22:24
[42] John 19:36
[43] Acts 1:4-5
[44] Acts 1:6
[45] Matthew 18:3

Read Matthew 18:8-35

Matthew 18:21 Then came Peter to him, and said, Lord, how oft shall my brother sin against me, and I forgive him? till seven times?

Jesus gave clear teaching on how to deal with those who have sinned against us.   Often a relationship can be restored by going to that person one on one[46]. When possible, that should *always* be done first. If that does not settle the issue, then one or two other witnesses[47] should be brought, still with the idea of reconciliation. If that fails, only then is it to be brought before the church, the assembly of believers.[48]

It was in light of this teaching that Peter asked Jesus, "How often shall my brother sin against me, and I forgive him?   Till seven times?" Some of the Jewish rabbis suggested a limit of three times.   One might say, "Three strikes and you're out." Peter may have felt very generous, by suggesting more than twice that number. However, Jesus said, in effect, that we should be willing to forgive seventy-times seven— forgiveness with no limits.   If we are keeping tally marks, we are probably not really forgiving.   If this is the forgiveness that the Lord expects of His followers, how much greater must His forgiveness be toward those who repent.   It reminds us of Jesus' sobering words back in Matthew 6, "For if you forgive men their trespasses, your heavenly Father will also forgive you: but if you forgive not men their trespasses, neither will your Father forgive your trespasses."   May His love and mercy so fill us that we are able to pray His words from our hearts today.

Matthew 6:12 And forgive us our debts, as[49] we forgive our debtors.

---

[46] Matthew 18:15
[47] Matthew 18:16. These are witnesses, those who are aware of the circumstances, not those who have been unnecessarily brought into something that is none of their business.
[48] Matthew 18:17
[49] The little word "as" means "in the same way." We are asking the Lord to forgive us "in the same way" that we forgive those who sin against us.

Read Matthew 19:1-22

Matthew 19:3-6 The Pharisees also came unto him, tempting him, and saying unto him, Is it lawful for a man to put away his wife for every cause? And he answered and said unto them, Have ye not read, that he which made *them* at the beginning made them male and female, And said, For this cause shall a man leave father and mother, and shall cleave to his wife: and they twain shall be one flesh? Wherefore they are no more twain, but one flesh. What therefore God hath joined together, let not man put asunder.

The Jews in Jesus' day were divided over the issue of divorce. Some followed the teaching of the very strict Rabbi Shammai, who allowed divorce on very few grounds. Others followed the teaching of Rabbi Hillel, who was much looser in his interpretation. One could divorce his wife for an infraction as small as burning a meal!

The Pharisees who came to Jesus were not honest seekers, wanting to know the truth. Instead, they were trying to bring Him into their debate. "Can one put away his wife for *any* cause?" they asked. Jesus took them back to the very beginning; God Himself is the Creator of marriage, not human beings. By a divine miracle, two become one.

Marriage and the family, the very foundation of human society, are under attack. As Christians, we must do all we can to support the sanctity of marriage.

Today, let us pray specifically for our own marriages and the strengthening of every marriage in our church families.

Read Matthew 19:23-20:16

Matthew 19:23-24 Then said Jesus unto his disciples, Verily I say unto you, That a rich man shall hardly enter into the kingdom of heaven. And again I say unto you, It is easier for a camel to go through the eye of a needle, than for a rich man to enter into the kingdom of God.

A young man, usually known as the rich young ruler, came to Jesus asking, "What good thing shall *I* do that I may have eternal life?" Like most people in the world, he believed that salvation could be earned by what *he* did. He seems confident in his own righteousness, believing he had kept the commandments of God from his youth. Jesus, knowing his heart, made one statement that dashed this young man's hopes of ever getting to heaven because he was good enough. Jesus said, "If you want to be perfect, sell what you have and give to the poor." Unwilling to do that, he went away sorrowful. He did worship another god---money.

Jesus used this as a teaching moment. He told His disciples, "A rich man shall hardly enter into the kingdom of heaven." It would be easier for a camel to go through the eye of a needle than for a rich man to get to heaven. The disciples asked, "Who then can be saved?" Jesus said, "With man it is impossible, but with God all things are possible. The salvation of *any* of us impossible without a miracle, but He is still a miracle-working Savior! Praise God for the miracle of salvation today!

It took a miracle to put the stars in place,
It took a miracle to hang the world in space;
But when He saved my soul,
Cleansed and made me whole,
It took a miracle of love and grace![50]

---

[50] "It took a Miracle," John Peterson

Read Matthew 20:17-34

Matthew 20:24-28 24 And when the ten heard *it*, they were moved with indignation against the two brethren. 25 But Jesus called them *unto him*, and said, Ye know that the princes of the Gentiles exercise dominion over them, and they that are great exercise authority upon them. 26 But it shall not be so among you: but whosoever will be great among you, let him be your minister; 27 And whosoever will be chief among you, let him be your servant: 28 Even as the Son of man came not to be ministered unto, but to minister, and to give his life a ransom for many.

Earlier in Matthew, we read the disciples' questions about greatness, and Jesus' response to those questions. If they wanted to be truly great, they would need to become like little children[51]. By Matthew 20, it was the mother of two of the disciples, James and John, who was asking the questions. Could my two sons sit on either side of You, the place of honor, in Your kingdom? She believed she was looking out for the interests of her children, but the other ten disciples were, perhaps understandably, angry about this.

Jesus made it clear. In the kingdoms of this world greatness means the power to exert authority over others. That is not the case in God's kingdom. The ones who will be great in God's kingdom are those who serve. Jesus used the word minister (diakonos), one who waits on the needs of others, to describe a great one in the kingdom. He also used the word servant (doulos), a term for the humblest of servants. His example is our guide. He did not come to be ministered unto, but to minister and to give His life.

> Make me like you, Lord,
> Please make me like You.
> You are a servant
> Make me one too.
>
> Oh, Lord, I am willing.
> Do what you must do.
> To make me like you, Lord,
> Please make me like You [52]

---

[51] Matthew 18:1-6
[52] "Make Me Like You," Jimmy and Carol Owens

Read Matthew 21:1-22

Matthew 21:13 And said unto them, It is written, My house shall be called the house of prayer; but ye have made it a den of thieves.

It was Palm Sunday, Jesus' last trip to Jerusalem before the crucifixion. The temple was a busy place, with thousands of pilgrims in town preparing for the Passover. Many of them had traveled some distance and needed to exchange their foreign coins so they could purchase the required sacrifices. The currency exchange and selling of sacrificial animals in the temple had become a very lucrative, and probably crooked business, a business shared by priests and merchants. They would make a lot of money off the worshippers the week of Passover. Jesus saw this as a desecration of the *purpose* of the temple. He certainly had that right, because it was *His* house.

That beautiful temple was destroyed by the Romans in AD 70. Since that day, there has never been another Jewish temple in Jerusalem. It is not about places and earthly temples now. The Lord tells us that our bodies are the temple of the Holy Ghost.[53] What have I allowed in my body, His temple? His Temple is still to be a house of prayer!

Lord prepare me to be a sanctuary, Pure and holy, tried and true,
    With thanksgiving, I'll be a living, sanctuary for you.[54]

---

[53] 1 Corinthians 6:19-20.
[54] "Sanctuary," Randy Scruggs

Read Matthew 21:23-46

Matthew 21:44 And whosoever shall fall on this stone shall be broken: but on whomsoever it shall fall, it will grind him to powder.

Jesus is in Jerusalem where He will be rejected by His own people. There will be dire consequences for that rejection. The religious leaders of Jerusalem were the *builders* who rejected Jesus, the Chief Cornerstone. Because of that rejection the kingdom would be taken from them and given to others.

Jesus is the great rock, and there are two ways that we can respond to Him, with two different consequences. We can fall on that rock in brokenness and repentance and be saved. But, if we reject that rock, and He falls on us in judgment we will be ground to powder. Daniel, in a vision, saw Jesus Christ as a great rock, not cut with human hands, destroying all the ungodly nations of the world (Daniel 2:34-35). The saddest "prayer meeting" in the Bible is found in Revelation 6. The unrepentant on earth during the tribulation are crying out to the rocks to hide them, instead of crying out to *the* Rock of Ages to save them (Revelation 6:15-16).

Pray the word of God today!

Psalm 71:1-3 In thee, O LORD, do I put my trust: let me never be put to confusion. Deliver me in thy righteousness, and cause me to escape: incline thine ear unto me, and save me. Be thou my strong habitation, whereunto I may continually resort: thou hast given commandment to save me; for thou *art* my rock and my fortress.

Read Matthew 22:1-22

Matthew 22:21   They say unto him, Caesar's. Then saith he unto them, Render therefore unto Caesar the things which are Caesar's; and unto God the things that are God's.

The Pharisees and Herodians were normally great enemies. The Herodians were seen to be in league with the Roman government; the Pharisees were not.   They did have something in common, though. They hated Jesus. They thought they could get Him in trouble with a question.   Is it lawful to pay tribute (taxes) to Caesar, or not?   If he answered yes, those who sided with the Pharisees would turn against him. If He said, "no," then those who sided with the Herodians would accuse him of being anti-government.   This was the poll tax, less than 5 dollars a year, but a mark of submission to Roman rule.

Jesus took that denarius coin and showed it to them. He asked, "Who's image is inscribed on it?" They answered Caesar's. That is when Jesus uttered His very famous words, "Render to Caesar the things that are Caesar's and to God the things that are God's."   As Christians, we are actually living in two kingdoms. We are citizens of a heavenly kingdom first, but we are also living here. " Had the Jews rendered unto God His due, they would have never had to render *anything* to Caesar. In New Testament times, they would never have endured the occupying oppression of the Roman Empire if they had been obedient to their covenant with God." [55]

Living in these two kingdoms, we obey earthly rulers as an act of obedience to God (Romans 13:1-7, 1st Peter 2:13-17), but we also realize that if that earthly government should go against a higher law of God, we must obey God, rather than man (Acts 5:29).

Ask the Lord how you can be a good citizen of this nation, and His kingdom too!

---

[55] Enduring Word Commentary, David Guzik

Read Matthew 22:23-46

Matthew 22:36-40 Master, which *is* the great commandment in the law? Jesus said unto him, Thou shalt love the Lord thy God with all thy heart, and with all thy soul, and with all thy mind. This is the first and great commandment. And the second *is* like unto it, Thou shalt love thy neighbour as thyself. On these two commandments hang all the law and the prophets.

The Jewish rabbis enumerated over 600 different commandments in the Law. Which was the most important of those commands? Jesus answered that question for us, the two that have to do with love. As we read the Ten Commandments in Exodus 20, we find that the first four commandments have to do with loving God. If we love God, we will not have any other gods before Him. We will not take His Name in vain, etc. The last six commandments have to do with loving our neighbor. We honor our parents, our closest and first neighbors, because we love God and them. We love our mate, so we do not commit adultery. We would not bear false witness or steal from those whom we love.

The New Testament tells us that love fulfills the Law of God.[56] This is a love that we do not have in ourselves; it comes from the Holy Spirit within us. Romans 5:5 says that that love is "shed abroad" in our hearts by the Holy Ghost.

Let's pray that the Holy Spirit fills our hearts with the love of God!

---

[56] Romans 13:8-10, Galatians 5:14, James 2:8

Read Matthew 23:1-26

Matthew 23:11-12 11 But he that is greatest among you shall be your servant. 12 And whosoever shall exalt himself shall be abased; and he that shall humble himself shall be exalted.

These statements are paradoxes, statements that seem to contradict one another.   In the eyes of the world, it is a paradox that the way to greatness is through becoming a servant.   It is a paradox that exalting oneself will cause us to be humbled, and that humility leads to exaltation.   It is like saying that the way up is down.   This is not how things normally work in this world.

 We are living in a kingdom with a different operating system than the one in this world.   The culture of the kingdom of God is dramatically different.   As Christians, we submit ourselves to the King and His kingdom.   We understand that we live our lives under kingdom principles like this one, "Humble yourselves in the sight of the Lord, and He shall lift you up."[57]

This is why we pray today, "Thy Kingdom come, Thy will be done, on earth as it is in heaven!"[58]

---

[57] James 4:10
[58] Matthew 6:10

Read Matthew 24:27-24:14

Matthew 24:8 All these *are* the beginning of sorrows

In the preceding verses, Jesus gave us a list of things to expect in the time we are living in now, the time between His first and second comings. These things have been a part of our world and will continue to be until He comes. They include the deception of imposters claiming to be Jesus Christ, wars and rumors of wars, famines, epidemics, and earthquakes in various places. We are not to be overly troubled by these things, they are to be expected in these days.

Jesus said that they are the *beginning of sorrows*. Sorrows is from a Greek word that literally means labor pains. Just as labor pains become more intense and closer together as the birth approaches, these signs will likewise become more frequent and intense as the coming of Jesus draws nearer. These things remind us that Jesus is coming. Interestingly, we are never told to get ready for His return, always to *be* ready.

The very last prayer in the Word of God has to do with His return and is a fitting prayer for every child of God.

Revelation 22:20b, " Even so, come, Lord Jesus."

Read Matthew 24:15-51

Matthew 24:37   But as the days of Noe *were*, so shall also the coming of the Son of man be.

We are told that the days before the return of Jesus will be like the days before Noah's flood.   The world of that day was corrupt, wicked, and violent.   Perversion was also a part of that culture before the flood. Jesus tells us that life was going on as always, with not a thought to the "lateness of the hour," not a thought that judgment was coming.   That is what He speaks of with eating, drinking, marrying, and giving in marriage. These are normal things.

Before the flood, there was also a preacher of righteousness[59], one who was warning of coming judgment and pointing to the only means of salvation, the ark.   We fulfill that same role today.   We tell the world that judgment is coming, and only by coming into the ark (the Lord Jesus Christ) can we be saved.

Come into the ark, the sky grows dark,
There's a storm called, "God's Great Judgment Day"
From its fierce angry waves, in the ark you'll be safe,
Come into the Ark today.[60]

---

[59] 2 Peter 2:5

[60] "Come into the Ark," Gordon Jensen

Read Matthew 25:1-30

Matthew 25:13 Watch therefore, for ye know neither the day nor the hour wherein the Son of man cometh.

These words are Jesus' conclusion to the parable of the wise and foolish virgins. Middle Eastern brides waited in anticipation for the day that their bridegroom would come for them and the marriage would take place. They must be ready at all times, for He could come unexpectedly. Five of the brides, or virgins, were wisely prepared for the bridegroom's coming, while five were not.

The Lord Jesus Christ is *our* Heavenly Bridegroom. The church is His bride. One day He will return to earth for the Bride that He purchased with His own blood on the cross. We are told to be ready always, because we do not know the day, nor the hour of His return. But, we wait with great joy and anticipation for what the Bible calls our "Blessed Hope[61]." Jesus is coming for His bride!

I think of the words of an old hymn:

> Are you ready?
> Are you ready?
> Are you ready for the judgment day?
> Are you ready?
> Are you ready?
> For the judgment day?[62]

---

[61] Titus 2:13
[62] "There's a Great Day Coming," Will L. Thompson

Read Matthew 25:31-26:13

Matthew 25:40 And the King shall answer and say unto them, Verily I say unto you, Inasmuch as ye have done *it* unto one of the least of these my brethren, ye have done *it* unto me.

Jesus gave these words as He described the judgment of the nations. Sheep nations were sent to His right hand, goat nations to His left. The criteria for this judgment seems to have been what they did or did not do for those who were in need. Jesus made the statement in both a positive and a negative way. If you have done it unto them, you have done it unto me. If you have not done it unto them, you have not done it unto me.

We must be careful of how we treat God's people. Mistreating those who are a part of His earthly body can be disastrous. When Jesus spoke to Paul on the Road to Damascus, He said, "Saul, Saul, why persecutest thou *me*[63]." So far as we know, He had never met Jesus, but he had persecuted and tormented His church. Doing so, was the same as doing it unto the Lord Himself.

As we demonstrate love and care for others in the body, it is just as if we are doing it for the Lord. We might ask ourselves:

How can I love Jesus by loving and caring for those He places in my path today?

---

[63] Acts 9:4

Read Matthew 26:14-35

Matthew 26:29 But I say unto you, I will not drink henceforth of this fruit of the vine, until that day when I drink it new with you in my Father's kingdom.

The Lord's Supper reminds us of several things. We remember His death. We remember that we are part of His body. We remember to examine ourselves. We remember that Jesus is coming again.

This was the last Passover/Lord's Supper Jesus would eat with His disciples until He ate and drank with them in the Father's Kingdom. Perhaps that speaks of some great time of rejoicing in the Kingdom Age, the Millennium. Perhaps, it is a reference to the Marriage Supper of the Lamb in heaven, which I personally believe to be true[64]. Whatever the case, when we take the bread and cup, we remember that Jesus is returning, and that this will not be the last time we take it. The next time may be in the Father' house. By receiving the Lord's Supper when given the opportunity we show the Lord's death until He comes.

We see reminder around us every day…Jesus is coming again!

He's coming soon, He's coming soon,
With joy we welcome His returning,
It may be morn, it may be night or noon,
We know He's coming soon[65].

---

[64] Revelation 19:9
[65] He's Coming Soon, Thoro Harris.

Read Matthew 26:36-59

Matthew 26:39 And he went a little further, and fell on his face, and prayed, saying, O my Father, if it be possible, let this cup pass from me: nevertheless not as I will, but as thou *wilt*.

As Jesus agonized, and prayed, in the Garden of Gethsemane, He was anticipating what was ahead. He was going to suffer and die on the cross. This was a part of the baptism of suffering that He predicted would come His way. He is only hours away from the cross.

His praying was so agonizing that the Scriptures tell us that His sweat became like great drops of blood. His statement here truly shows us what it is to take up the cross.

Jesus totally resigned himself to the Father's will. If it is possible, if there is any other way, that is what I want, but if this is the plan of God for my life, thy will be done. We may have some of those Gethsemane prayers in our own lives, as we struggle between what we want and what we believe to be the will of God for our lives.

A good prayer to pray today is this, "Thy will be done!"

Read Matthew 26:57-75

Matthew 26:75 And Peter remembered the word of Jesus, which said unto him, Before the cock crow, thou shalt deny me thrice. And he went out, and wept bitterly.

Peter was one that boldly proclaimed that he would *never* forsake the Lord.[66] I think he honestly believed that He would stand faithful to the end, but He did not realize the depth of His own weakness. The night Jesus was betrayed, He denied knowing Him three times, one time sealing his words with a curse!

As Peter heard the early morning crow of that rooster, he must have been devastated. Luke adds that Jesus looked at him from the cross just as it happened.[67] It is no wonder that bitter tears began to flow from His eyes, and he must have wondered, "Can the Lord ever use *me* again?"

Repentance brings restoration. We know that Peter truly repented, for the Lord forgave and restored Him. We also know that he went on to become the first preacher at Pentecost[68] and ultimately gave His life for preaching the Gospel. We have all done things we regret. What an amazing blessing that the Savior will forgive when we ask. Let's rejoice in that truth today!

1 John 1:9 If we confess our sins, he is faithful and just to forgive us *our* sins, and to cleanse us from all unrighteousness.

---

[66] Matthew 26:33-35
[67] Luke 22:60-61
[68] Acts 2

Read Matthew 27:1-26

Matthew 27:3 Then Judas, which had betrayed him, when he saw that he was condemned, repented himself, and brought again the thirty pieces of silver to the chief priests and elders,

Peter denied the Lord, yet found forgiveness and restoration through repentance[69].   Judas betrayed the Lord, and, sadly, did *not* find repentance.   The King James Version says that he "repented himself." The word Matthew used means that he was remorseful, sorry about the consequences of his sin without any indication of a changed heart. True repentance leads to change.[70]

We find similar words spoken of Esau.   He found no place of repentance, though he sought it carefully with tears. [71]   God tells us in His Word that there are two kinds of sorrow, the world's sorrow and the godly sorrow that leads to repentance[72].   There is a big difference between being sorry that we have sinned against God and being sorry for the consequences of our sin.

May God give us all the kind of heart described in Psalm 51:17

The sacrifices of God *are* a broken spirit: a broken and a contrite heart,
O God, thou wilt not despise.

---

[70] Matthew 3:7-8
[71] Hebrews 12:27
[72] 2 Corinthians 7:9-10

Read Matthew 27:27-57

Matthew 27:50 Jesus, when he had cried again with a loud voice, yielded up the ghost.

The Bible says that Jesus "yielded up" or "gave up" the ghost. In reality, no one killed Him, He gave His life. He made it very clear, "No man takes it from Me, but I lay it down of Myself. I have power to lay it down, and I have power to take it up again."[73] There is no doubt that the cross was a voluntary giving of His life.

We can be so grateful today that He said yes to the cross. When did He first say, "Yes?" Psalm 40:7-8 puts these words in His mouth *prophetically*, "I delight to do Thy will." Revelation calls Him the Lamb slain from the foundation of the world.[74] The cross was never an afterthought, it was in the heart of God from the beginning.

Had he chosen to do so, He could have called for tens of thousands of angels who would have delivered Him,[75] yet He went to the cross for the joy that was set before Him.[76] Rejoice in the truth today, "When He died for you, He did so willingly!"

> They bound the hands of Jesus in the garden where he prayed,
> They led him through the street in shame,
> They spat upon the Saviour so pure and free from sin,
> They said crucify him he's to blame.
> He could have called ten thousand angels
> To destroy the world and set him free.
> He could have called ten thousand angels,
> But he died alone for you and me.[77]

---

[73] John 10:18
[74] Revelation 13:8
[75] Matthew 26:53
[76] Hebrews 12:1-2
[77] "Ten Thousand Angels," Ray Overholt

Read Matthew 27:57-28:20

Matthew 28:19-20 Go ye therefore, and teach all nations, baptizing them in the name of the Father, and of the Son, and of the Holy Ghost: Teaching them to observe all things whatsoever I have commanded you: and, lo, I am with you alway, *even* unto the end of the world. Amen.

This is Jesus' Great Commission, His marching orders to those of us who are in His Army. This is not just for those who are in full time ministry, this is a commission given to all Christians. He calls us all to be part of reaching the world with the Gospel.

We are to do more than just make converts. He says that we are teach all nations, all people. That literally means to make disciples, devoted followers of Jesus. We are training them, and teaching them, to do the same thing, to go out and make even more disciples. When we are doing this, He promises us His presence!

What is the mission field He has given you?

Lord lay some soul upon my heart, and love that soul through me, and may I bravely do my part to win that soul for Thee.[78]

---

[78] "Lord, Lay Some Soul Upon My Heart,"   B. B. McKinney

Read Mark 1:1-20

Mark 1:9-11 And it came to pass in those days, that Jesus came from Nazareth of Galilee, and was baptized of John in Jordan. And straightway coming up out of the water, he saw the heavens opened, and the Spirit like a dove descending upon him: And there came a voice from heaven, *saying*, Thou art my beloved Son, in whom I am well pleased.

This Scripture reminds us that the One True God is a Triune Being-Father, Son, and Holy Spirit. Though the specific *word* Trinity does not appear in the Bible, the concept described by that word, One God in Three Persons, is clearly seen from Genesis to Revelation. In Genesis, God said, "Let **US** make man in **OUR** image, after **OUR** likeness."[79] In Revelation, we find One who was sitting on the throne in Heaven (the Father), the Lamb (the Lord Jesus Christ),[80] *and* the Sevenfold[81] Spirit of God.[82]

At Jesus' Baptism, God the Son was standing in the water, God the Father spoke from heaven, and God, the Holy Spirit descended from heaven like a dove. When we are baptized in the Name of the Lord Jesus Christ (by His authority) we acknowledge that truth, by being baptized in the Name of the Father, the Son, and the Holy Ghost.[83]

The One True God is worthy of all praise today. Let us worship Father, Son, and Holy Ghost!

Holy, holy, holy! Lord God Almighty!
Early in the morning our song shall rise to thee;
Holy, holy, holy! merciful and mighty,
God in three persons, blessed Trinity![84]

---

[79] Genesis 1:26
[80] Revelation 5:6,13
[81] There is only one Holy Spirit, but in Scripture seven is the number of something perfect and complete.
[82] Revelation 1:4, 3:11, 4:5, 5:6
[83] Matthew 28:19
[84] Reginald Heber

Read Mark 1:21-45

Mark 1:22 And they were astonished at his doctrine: for he taught them as one that had authority, and not as the scribes.

We are not told **what** Jesus taught in the synagogue at Capernaum, but we are told **how** He taught. He taught with authority. They were not used to hearing that kind of teaching. Their teachers, the scribes, often just repeated what various rabbis said about a subject. They could rarely give a bold, "thus saith the Lord" from God's Word. Authority is the right and power to do something based on position. Jesus' position as the Son of God, the Author of the Word, gave Him the right to proclaim that Word with power.

Today, we are His representatives, His ambassadors, proclaiming His Word in the power of the Holy Ghost.[85] Peter speaks of this in 1 Peter 4:11, "If any man speaks, let him speak as the oracles of God." May the Lord give us the power to proclaim His Word with authority! Outside of the Word of God, we cannot speak with authority.

Acts 4:31 And when they had prayed, the place was shaken where they were assembled together; and they were all filled with the Holy Ghost, and they spake the word of God with boldness.

---

[85] 2nd Corinthians 5:20

Read Mark 2:1-22

Mark 2:5 When Jesus saw their faith, he said unto the sick of the palsy, Son, thy sins be forgiven thee.

Jesus was preaching the Word in Capernaum. The crowds were so large that it would have been impossible to get close to where He was preaching. The house was full, and people were packed tightly around the door listening to Jesus' words. Four men came to that meeting carrying a friend with a desperate need. The King James Version says that he was "sick of the palsy." That means that through birth, injury, or illness he was at least partially paralyzed. We know that he could not walk, because they had to carry him. If they could just get their friend to Jesus, he would be healed!

When they saw that getting to Jesus through the crowd was going to be impossible, they came up with an alternative plan. They took him up on the flat roof of the house, and removing roofing tiles lowered him down to where Jesus was preaching. Jesus does not speak of the man's faith here, but the faith of his friends. True and faithful friends will always direct us to Jesus, and true faith will always make Him its object. We see both here—true friends and true faith.

May we be true friends to those He places in our lives, ever ready to point the way to Jesus!

Read Mark 2:23-3:19

Mark 3:13-15 And he goeth up into a mountain, and calleth *unto him* whom he would: and they came unto him. And he ordained twelve, that they should be with him, and that he might send them forth to preach, and to have power to heal sicknesses, and to cast out devils:

The Gospel of Luke adds that Jesus spent an entire night in prayer before calling the twelve.[86] We are not told *why* He chose the ones that He did, only that it was His choice.   He called, and they came!

The word apostle means "one who has been sent out," and He did send them out to preach, to heal, and to cast out demons.   However, the most important thing was just being WITH Him.   That "being with Jesus" is what transformed their lives.   Years later, the authorities in Jerusalem would marvel at some of these men.   Even though, in the eyes of the world, they were "ignorant and unlearned," they had obviously been with Jesus[87] and they were never the same.

The most important appointment we have today is that of "being with Jesus."   That is where, and when, *our* lives are changed.

---

[86] Luke 6:12
[87] Acts 4:13

Read Mark 3:20-4:12

Mark 4:9 And he said unto them, He that hath ears to hear, let him hear.

Jesus spoke these words after giving the parable of the sower. Some have said it is better called the parable of the soils. The harvest is determined by the condition of the soil the seed is sown upon. Jesus explains that the seed is good seed. In fact, it is the best seed; it is the Word of God. The various soils represent different kinds of human hearts. Some hearts are like hard soil, not allowing the seed to germinate.   Some are like rocky soil, not allowing the roots to grow deeply.   Some hearts are like soil overgrown with weeds, weeds that choke out the Word of God.   Still others are like rich, prepared soil that brings forth an abundant harvest.

Because we have ears to hear His words, we can also cry out to Him to prepare our hearts to *receive* the Word. Receiving the Word into a heart prepared by the Holy Spirit will bring an abundant harvest of spiritual fruit.   Perhaps our daily prayer when taking this year-long walk through the New Testament should be, "Father, prepare my heart to receive Your Word!"

Word of God speak
Would you pour down like rain
Washing my eyes to see
Your majesty
To be still and know
That you're in this place
Please let me stay and rest
In your holiness
Word of God speak[88]

---

[88] "Word of God Speak," Mercy Me

Read Mark 4:13-34

Mark 4:23-24   If any man have ears to hear, let him hear. And he said unto them, Take heed what ye hear: with what measure ye mete, it shall be measured to you: and unto you that hear shall more be given.

The word "hear" appears seven times in the forty-one verses of Mark 4.   Seven times in the New Testament we are given *these* words, "He that hath an ear let him hear what the Spirit says unto the churches."[89]   We are told that faith comes from *hearing* the Word of God.[90]   James tells us that we are to be *swift* to hear and slow to speak.[91]

Then, we are told here in Mark 4 to be *careful* of what we listen to, "Take heed what you hear."   This is a noisy world, with many voices vying for our attention.   Paying attention to the wrong things can bring great confusion,[92]   but carefully listening to His voice, the truth of His Word, brings freedom and peace.[93]   Take heed what you hear today!

Open my eyes, Lord, we want to see Jesus,
To reach out and touch Him, and tell Him we love Him,
Open our ears, Lord, and help us to listen,
Open our eyes, Lord, we want to see Jesus.[94]

[89] Revelation 2:7, 11, 17, 29; 3:6, 13, 22.
[90] Romans 10:17
[91] James 1:19
[92] 1 Corinthians 14:33
[93] John 8:32, Isaiah 26:3
[94] "Open Our Eyes," Robert Cull

Read Mark 4:35-5:20

Mark 5:7 And cried with a loud voice, and said, What have I to do with thee, Jesus, *thou* Son of the most high God? I adjure thee by God, that thou torment me not.

The Gospel of Mark shows Jesus' authority again and again. Here we see His authority over the powers of darkness as he casts a legion[95] of demons out of a man. Matthew mentions that there were actually two of these men; Mark and Luke only mention the spokesman of the two. He was so tormented that people were afraid of him. They tried to restrain him for their safety and his own to no avail. But, the powers of darkness were no match for the power of God. Jesus set Him free.

I think it is interesting that the demon spirits speaking from the man, before his deliverance, recognized some important truths. First, they recognized that Jesus is the Son of God. That knowledge must have made them tremble with fear.[96] Second, they recognized that Jesus had the power to torment them. Matthew adds more of what they said, "Are you come to torment us *before* the time[97]?" Satan and his minions know that their time is short, and that they are appointed to eternal judgment. Hell is a place prepared for the devil and his angels,[98] and it will only take *one* of God's holy angels to lock Satan in the bottomless pit.[99] Jesus conquered Satan on the cross, and now he is a conquered foe.[100]

What a blessing to walk in that victory *today*.

We've got the power in the Name of Jesus,
We've got the power in the Name of the Lord,
Though Satan rages, we will not be defeated,
We've got the power, in the Name of the Lord.[101]

---

[95] A group of thousands.
[96] James 2:19
[97] Matthew 8:29
[98] Matthew 25:41
[99] Revelation 20:1-3
[100] Colossians 2:14-15
[101] "We've Got the Power," Laverne Tripp

Read Mark 5:21-43

Mark 5:28 For she said, If I may touch but his clothes, I shall be whole.

Jesus healed many folks who were sick, but He did not always do it the same way. Healing came through His touch[102], an act of obedience[103], and on one occasion from mud.[104] Most of the time He was present, but He did not have to be. He could simply speak the word.[105] Most of His healings were immediate, but at least one was gradual.[106]

The woman with the issue of blood is still another kind of healing. She had been afflicted with a bleeding condition for many years. Because of this, she would have been considered ceremonially unclean, separated from the rest of society. Jesus did not touch her, she reached out and touched Him. It was a deliberate touch. He could tell her touch from that of the others in the crowd, because it was deliberate and charged with faith. Jesus said, "Your faith has made you whole!"

Sometimes we need to persevere, make our way through the crowd, and have a determined faith that will not give up, just as she did. Determine to touch Heaven, to touch Him, when you pray today!

---

[102] Matthew 8:14-15
[103] Luke 17:14
[104] John 9:6
[105] Matthew 8:8
[106] Mark 8:22-26

Read Mark 6:1-20

Mark 6:1 And he went out from thence, and came into his own country; and his disciples follow him.

Jesus was back in His hometown of Nazareth. Those who had known Him as He grew up in Joseph's carpenter shop were amazed. They could not imagine how such powerful words and deeds could come from one they simply called "the Carpenter." As a prophet, he did not find honor in His own hometown,[107] and He did not perform many mighty miracles there, because of their unbelief.[108] The people that had known His family for years were offended by Him. Even his siblings, the natural children of Joseph and Mary, did not believe until *after* the resurrection.[109]

This is a fulfillment of the words spoken in John 1, "He was in the world, and the world was made by Him, and the world knew Him not. He came unto His own, and His own received Him not. But as many as received Him, to them gave He power to become the Sons of God, even to them that believe on His Name."[110] There will always be those who reject Him, but we want to be one of those who receive and follow Him wherever He leads.

"Take up thy cross and follow Me," I hear the blessed Savior call, How can I make a lesser sacrifice when Jesus paid it all?[111]

---

[107] Luke 6:4
[108] Mark 6:5, Matthew 13:58
[109] John 7:5
[110] John 1:10-11
[111] "Take up Thy Cross and Follow Me," Alfred Ackley

Read Mark 6:21-44

Mark 6:34 And Jesus, when he came out, saw much people, and was moved with compassion toward them, because they were as sheep not having a shepherd: and he began to teach them many things.

The disciples have just returned from a preaching tour that took them to many towns and villages in Galilee. Jesus sent them out two by two to preach, teach, heal the sick, and cast out demons. The power of God was.[112] evident in these meetings and many were healed and delivered. It was fruitful ministry, but also very tiring. They scarcely had time to stop long enough to eat a meal. Jesus called them to come with him to a desert place where they could rest apart from the people and the rigors of ministry

They slipped away by ship, hoping to find some much-needed rest across the Sea of Galilee. The crowds of needy people, realizing where they were going, ran along the shore and actually got there *before* Jesus and the twelve. So much for rest and relaxation, they were met by at least 5,000 men not counting women and children.

How easy it would be to become impatient with those who followed them. After all, they needed to "get away" like anyone else. The disciples must have been a little "put out" by the crowds that followed them. Jesus, however, was always so patient with the needs of others, even when it interrupted His schedule. He was moved with compassion toward them, saw them as sheep not having a shepherd, and taught them. Before the day was over He even fed them all! May we realize today that though we do need rest, our schedule is His schedule. Our time belongs to Him.

Oh, to be His hand extended,
Reach out to the oppressed,
Let me touch Him, let me touch Jesus,
So, that others may know and be blessed.[113]

---

[112] Mark 6:30-31
[113] "His Hand Extended," Author Unknown, Lillenas Publishing Company, Kansas City, Missouri.

Read Mark 6:45-7:13

Mark 6:47-48 And when even was come, the ship was in the midst of the sea, and he alone on the land. And he saw them toiling in rowing; for the wind was contrary unto them: and about the fourth watch of the night he cometh unto them, walking upon the sea, and would have passed by them.

This took place immediately after an amazing miracle. Jesus fed five thousand men, not counting the women and children with just a few loaves and fish. In doing so, He revealed Himself as the Mighty Creator. Multiplication of loaves and fish was nothing for the One who spoke the worlds into existence.

After that amazing miracle, He sent the disciples back across the Sea of Galilee by themselves, while He remained to spend time in prayer. Jesus was not with them now, and it seemed as if everything was going wrong. No matter how hard they rowed they were getting nowhere, because the wind was against them. They were exhausted to start with. They had crossed over in the first place hoping to get some much-needed rest, but that did not happen.[114] It must have seemed even worse, because it seemed Jesus was not with them.

Though they could not see Him, He could see them, even in the dark of night. What a blessing to know that we are never outside of His watchful eye. Though He sometimes seems far away, He has promised never to leave us or forsake us.[115]

Proverbs 5:21 For the ways of man *are* before the eyes of the LORD, and he pondereth all his goings.

---

[114] Mark 6:31-34
[115] Hebrews 13:5

Read Mark 7:14-37

Mark 7:21-23 For from within, out of the heart of men, proceed evil thoughts, adulteries, fornications, murders, Thefts, covetousness, wickedness, deceit, lasciviousness, an evil eye, blasphemy, pride, foolishness: All these evil things come from within, and defile the man.

Many things were considered spiritually unclean under the Old Covenant. This even included certain foods that were not "kosher." Jesus made it clear that it was not eating unclean foods, or touching unclean things, that made one unclean.[116] An unclean life came from an unclean heart.

We are told that the human heart, outside of His salvation, is deceitful above *all* things and desperately wicked.[117] Jesus said that the evil things that can come from our mouths have their origin in our hearts.[118] One of the miracles of His salvation is to give us a new heart.[119]

Today, my prayer is like that of David when reminded of the wickedness of his own heart.

Psalm 51:7-13 Purge me with hyssop, and I shall be clean: wash me, and I shall be whiter than snow. Make me to hear joy and gladness; *that* the bones *which* thou hast broken may rejoice. Hide thy face from my sins, and blot out all mine iniquities. Create in me a clean heart, O God; and renew a right spirit within me. Cast me not away from thy presence; and take not thy holy spirit from me. Restore unto me the joy of thy salvation; and uphold me *with thy* free spirit. *Then* will I teach transgressors thy ways; and sinners shall be converted unto thee.

---

[116] Mark 7:18-19, Acts 10:9-15, 1 Timothy 4:4-5.
[117] Jeremiah 17:9
[118] Matthew 12:34
[119] Ezekiel 26:26

Read Mark 8:1-21

Mark 8:15 And he charged them, saying, Take heed, beware of the leaven of the Pharisees, and *of* the leaven of Herod.

Leaven often represents sin and false doctrine in the Word of God. Not having commercial yeast as we do, they used a form of sourdough, a small bit of the previous batch of bread dough was retained after every baking. Even though it was a small amount, when mixed in with the next batch, it was enough to grow and permeate the dough, causing it to rise. The idea is that it only takes a small amount of leaven to permeate something. In the Gospel of Luke, Jesus tells us that the leaven of the Pharisees was the sin of hypocrisy, spiritual play acting.[120] The leaven of Herod, on the other hand, was more of a political thing, but still sin.

When speaking of a particularly vile sin that was allowed in the church at Corinth, Paul warned them that just as a little leaven could leaven the whole lump of dough, their acceptance of sin was like a dangerous leaven infiltrating the church.[121] It has been said of the leaven of sin that it will always take us further than we wanted to go, it will keep us longer than we wanted to stay, and it will cost us more than we wanted to pay. My prayer today is this, "Father, remove all leaven from my heart."

Search me, O God,
And know my heart today;
Try me, O Savior,
Know my thoughts, I pray.
See if there be
Some wicked way in me;
Cleanse me from every sin
And set me free.[122]

---

[120] Luke 12:1
[121] 1 Corinthians 5:6
[122] "Search Me," J. Edwin Orr.

Read Mark 8:22-38

Mark 8:34 And when he had called the people *unto him* with his disciples also, he said unto them, Whosoever will come after me, let him deny himself, and take up his cross, and follow me.

The call to all of Jesus' disciples then and now has been this, "Follow Me." A disciple of Jesus will follow Him to the waters of baptism, they will follow Him to the outpouring of the Holy Spirit, and they will follow Him to the cross. We cannot add to what He did there, for it was a perfect finished work.[123] Still, He calls us to take up our cross and follow.

For us, taking up our cross may mean praying as Jesus did in the Garden of Gethsemane. He prayed, "Father if it be possible, let this cup pass from me: nevertheless not as I will, but as Thou will."[124] We pray, "Thy will be done on earth as it is in heaven," knowing that we can trust the will of our Father. Thy will be done, Father!

> Have Thine own way, Lord, Have Thine own way,
> Thou art the Potter, I am the clay,
> Mold me and make me, after Thy will,
> While I am waiting yielded and still.

---

[123] John 19:30
[124] Matthew 26:39

Read Mark 9:1-29

Mark 9:4 And there appeared unto them Elias with Moses: and they were talking with Jesus.

Someone once asked me, "Will we know one another in heaven?" I believe that the answer is clearly, "YES!" for several reasons, one of which is found here in Mark 9.

Jesus told His disciples that some of them who were standing there that day would not die until they had seen God's kingdom come with power.[125] None of those disciples are still living here on earth, and we have yet to see the return of Christ and the coming of His kingdom. However, six days later, three of them would be blessed with a *preview* of heavenly glory!

Peter, James, and John were on a mountain with Jesus and saw him transfigured before them. The Greek word translated "transfigured" is metamorphoo, a change into a completely different form. We get our word metamorphosis from the same root. Jesus' appearance was dramatically changed. They caught a glimpse of His heavenly glory. That is not all they saw. They also saw two great saints of God, Moses and Elijah, gone from this world for many years, but still very much alive, and very easily identified. Our loved ones who have died in Christ are still very much alive in the presence of God, and when we see them again, we will know them.

All this makes the promise of 1 Thessalonians 4 that much more comforting and wonderful!

1 Thessalonians 4:17-18 Then we which are alive *and* remain shall be caught up **together with them i**n the clouds, to meet the Lord in the air: and so shall we ever be with the Lord. Wherefore comfort one another with these words.

---

[125] Mark 9:1

Read Mark 9:30-50

Mark 9:41 For whosoever shall give you a cup of water to drink in my name, because ye belong to Christ, verily I say unto you, he shall not lose his reward.

Did you ever feel that what you can do for the Lord and His kingdom is so very small? We have probably all felt that way at some time in our lives. Though we are saved by grace alone[126], the New Testament does speak of various rewards and crowns for faithful service in His kingdom.[127] Even small acts of service, done in His Name do not go unnoticed. It may be something as seemingly insignificant as a cup of water, but it will not go unrewarded. Whatever we do, we do it heartily as unto the Lord,[128] desiring to be His faithful stewards.[129]

I think of the words of an old Ira Stanphill song, "If just a cup of water, I place within your hands, then just a cup of water is all that I demand....be faithful weary pilgrim, the morning I can see, take up your cross and follow close to Me."[130]

Colossians 3:17 And whatsoever ye do in word or deed, *do* all in the name of the Lord Jesus, giving thanks to God and the Father by him.

---

[126] Ephesians 2:8-10
[127] 1 Corinthians 9:25, 1 Peter 5:4, 2nd Timothy 4:8, James 1:12, Revelation 2:10, Revelation 3:11
[128] Matthew 25:40, Colossians 3:23
[129] 1 Corinthians 4:2
[130] "Follow Me," Ira Stanphill

Read Mark 10:1-25

Mark 10:14-15 But when Jesus saw *it*, he was much displeased, and said unto them, Suffer the little children to come unto me, and forbid them not: for of such is the kingdom of God. Verily I say unto you, Whosoever shall not receive the kingdom of God as a little child, he shall not enter therein.

We once heard of a young child that had been taken from this life very tragically and some were wondering, "Do children automatically go to heaven when they die?" There is surely what some have called an "age of accountability" when a child is old enough to understand their need of a Savior and be responsible before God, but what about the time *before* that? I believe the Scriptures give us some wonderful insight into that question.

David and Bathsheba lost the first child they had together. Despite that great loss, David was able to take comfort in knowing that he would see his child again. He said, "I shall go to him, but he shall not return to me."[131] Jesus says here in Mark 10 that the kingdom of heaven is inhabited by those who become *as little children*. May God give us that kind of simple childlike faith.

> Jesus loves me this I know,
> For the Bible tells me so,
> Little ones to Him belong,
> They are weak, but He is strong,
> Yes, Jesus loves me,
> Yes, Jesus loves me.
> Yes, Jesus loves me,
> The Bible tells me so[132].

---

[131] 2nd Samuel 12:23
[132] "Jesus Loves Me," Anna Bartlett Warner

Read Mark 10:26-45

Mark 10:43-45 But so shall it not be among you: but whosoever will be great among you, shall be your minister: And whosoever of you will be the chiefest, shall be servant of all. For even the Son of man came not to be ministered unto, but to minister, and to give his life a ransom for many.

What is ministry? The original Greek word translated here as minister is diakonos, a word that was sometimes used for a servant, especially one who waited on tables, ministering to the needs of others. Leadership in the unsaved world is much different, Jesus describes it as someone exercising authority over another[133]. Spiritual leadership is not like that at all. Those who would be great leaders in the kingdom of God must have servant hearts.

Jesus gives us an example to follow in this. He came to minister, to serve, and ultimately to give His life. He demonstrated this with all that He did. Do you remember how He washed the disciples' feet[134] a task normally reserved for the lowliest of slaves? That night He gave us a picture of spiritual leadership and ministry. He came as a Servant and He calls us to serve.

Make me like You, Lord, please make me like You,
You are a Servant, Please make me one too,
Lord, I am willing, do what You must do, to make me like You, Lord,
Please, make me like You.[135]

---

[133] Mark 10:42-43
[134] John 13:14
[135] "Make Me Like You," Carol and Jimmy Owens.

Read Mark 10:46-11:11

Mark 11:2-3 And saith unto them, Go your way into , village over against you: and as soon as ye be entered into it, ye shall find a colt tied, whereon never man sat; loose him, and bring *him*. And if any man say unto you, Why do ye this? say ye that the Lord hath need of him; and straightway he will send him hither.

There were differences of opinion among the Jews as to how their Messiah would come and announce Himself. Some of them looked at Scriptures like Daniel 7:13 and said that the Messiah would come gloriously with the clouds of heaven. Others looked at Zechariah 9:9 and determined that the Messiah would come with great humility riding on a donkey's colt. Still others tried to reconcile this a different way saying that the, "Messiah would come humbly to an *unworthy* Israel, but mightily to a *worthy* Israel. Since Israel considered itself worthy, they only looked for a triumphant, conquering Messiah."[136]

Today, we know that He came humbly riding on a colt the first time, knowing that He would give His life. We also know that He *will* come again! When He returns, it will not be humbly riding on a colt, but gloriously in the clouds of heaven riding a white horse.[137] We are looking for the return of our Great King and Messiah, Jesus Christ!

Hebrews 9:28 So Christ was once offered to bear the sins of many; and unto them that look for him shall he appear the second time without sin unto salvation.

---

[136] <u>Enduring Word Commentary</u>, Mark, David Guzik.
[137] Revelation 1:7, Revelation 19:11ff

Read Mark 11:12-33

Mark 11:24 Therefore I say unto you, What things soever ye desire, when ye pray, believe that ye receive *them*, and ye shall have *them*.

We can only truly believe for those things that are according to His Word and His Will.   Romans 10:17 says that faith comes by hearing and hearing by the Word of God.   The promises in the Bible build our faith.   For example, we can believe God for wisdom, because we know, from His Word, that He has promised it to us.[138]   The promise of His Word helps build our faith so that we can pray and believe Him for wisdom. The Apostle John says that, "if we ask any thing according to his will [according to His Word], he heareth us: And if we know that he hear us, whatsoever we ask, we know that we have the petitions that we desired of him. "[139]   Through the precious promises of the Word we can be partakers of His divine nature and escape the corruption that is in this world through lust.[140]

We can come boldly to our Father's throne and ask for those things that He has promised in His Word, knowing that we are praying according to His will.[141]

---

[138] James 1:5-6
[139] 1 John 5:14-15
[140] 2 Peter 1:4
[141] Matthew 7:7-11, Matthew 21:22, John 14:13-14, John 15:7, John 15:16, John 16:24, John 16:26, James 4:2-3.

Read Mark 12:1-27

Mark 12:26-27 And as touching the dead, that they rise: have ye not read in the book of Moses, how in the bush God spake unto him, saying, I *am* the God of Abraham, and the God of Isaac, and the God of Jacob? He is not the God of the dead, but the God of the living: ye therefore do greatly err.

The men who came to Jesus with a question were Sadducees, a group that, among other things, did not believe in the resurrection of the dead, because they did not believe it was taught in the Torah, the first five books of the Bible.   Finding the truth does not seem to have been their objective. They came with an agenda, asking a "clever" question they thought would make Jesus look silly.

Under Old Testament Law, if a man died without an heir, his next of kin was to marry his widow.   The first child they had would then become recipient of the late man's estate.   This process was called levirate marriage.   Their question, asked tongue in cheek, went something like this, "What if a woman outlives seven husbands?   Which one will she be married to in the resurrection?"   They believed that they had Jesus over a proverbial barrel with their question. That shows how little they knew about Him!

The One who is all Wisdom answered their question clearly from the Word of God.   Marriage is the most precious of all earthly relationships. However, heavenly relationships will be on an even higher plane. There will be no marriage, or giving in marriage in the resurrection; apparently, the Lord has something even better for us.   The truth of the resurrection *is* clearly taught in the Torah.   When God spoke to Moses from the burning bush in Exodus 3, He said, "I am the God of your father, the God of Abraham, the God of Isaac, and the God of Jacob," and as Jesus added, "God is *not* the God of the dead, but the living." I am glad that He is my God now, and He will continue to be my God in the eons of eternity!

Revelation 21:7 He that overcometh shall inherit all things; and I will be his God, and he shall be my son.

Read Mark 12:28-44

Mark 12:28 And one of the scribes came, and having heard them reasoning together, and perceiving that he had answered them well, asked him, Which is the first commandment of all?

Recognizing Jesus' wise answer to the question raised by the Sadducees earlier in the chapter, a scribe, an expert in the Law of God, came to Him with still another question. Which of God's commandments is the most important?

Jesus made it clear that all of God's Law can be distilled into two commandments, both having to do with love. If we love God with all our heart, soul, mind, and strength, we will also want to honor Him, His Name, and His Holiness.[142] If we truly love our neighbor as ourselves, we will not want to harm him in any way.[143]

In the New Covenant, we walk in the Law of Love. God's Word says that love is the fulfilling of the Law.[144] Jesus' half-brother, James, calls the Law of Love the Royal Law.[145] This is greater than natural human love, a supernatural love "shed abroad" in our hearts by the Holy Spirit.[146]

1 John 4:16 And we have known and believed the love that God hath to us. God is love; and he that dwelleth in love dwelleth in God, and God in him.

---

[142] Exodus 6:1-11
[143] Exodus 6:12-17
[144] Romans 13:8-10,
[145] James 2:8
[146] Romans 5:5

Read Mark 13:1-31

Mark 13:2 And Jesus answering said unto him, Seest thou these great buildings? there shall not be left one stone upon another, that shall not be thrown down.

They were looking at the Third Temple in Jerusalem, commonly called Herod's Temple. God gave King Solomon the privilege of building the first temple in Jerusalem. It was destroyed by the Babylonians when the Jews went into exile. Miraculously, they returned to the land, and God allowed them to rebuild the temple in the days of Ezra and Zerubbabel. Finally, King Herod, began rebuilding and enlarging the temple. That "new and improved temple" was the one Jesus and the disciples were looking at that day.

It was a beautiful building. The ancient Jewish historian Josephus says that the outside of the temple was covered with gold plates, gold so polished it was blinding in the sunlight. Where there was no gold visible, the marble walls were such a pure white that it looked like snow on the temple. Yet, Jesus said that the temple would be destroyed so thoroughly that not one stone would be left on another. This would happen in AD 70 when the Romans took Jerusalem and destroyed God's temple. Herod's Temple had only been complete seven years before it was destroyed.[147]

Today, living in the New Covenant, we do not visit an earthly temple. We do not have to go *somewhere* special to meet God, though that may have been true in the Old Covenant. His Word says that our body is now the temple of the Holy Spirit,[148] and that He is with us always.[149]

Ephesians 2:20-22 And are built upon the foundation of the apostles and prophets, Jesus Christ himself being the chief corner *stone*; In whom all the building fitly framed together groweth unto an holy temple in the Lord: In whom ye also are builded together for an habitation of God through the Spirit.

---

[147] The Book of Revelation does reveal that there will be one final temple on that site.
[148] 1 Corinthians 6:19-20
[149] John 14:16

Read Mark 13:32-14:21

Mark 13:35-37 Watch ye therefore: for ye know not when the master of the house cometh, at even, or at midnight, or at the cockcrowing, or in the morning: Lest coming suddenly he find you sleeping. And what I say unto you I say unto all, Watch.

We are told many times in the New Testament to watch, or to be watchful. That is, most often, a translation of a Greek word (gregoreo) which means to be spiritually awake and alert. The same word is translated vigilant in 1 Peter 5:8, "Be sober, be vigilant; because your adversary the devil, as a roaring lion, walketh about, seeking whom he may devour." When Jesus found His disciples sleeping, instead of praying, He told them to "watch and pray lest they enter into temptation."[150] We are told that we must not sleep (spiritually) like others, but that we must watch and be sober.[151]

Most of the time, watchfulness has to do with our attitude toward the Lord's return. We are to be spiritually awake, because His coming is imminent. We are not told to "get ready" for His coming, but to "BE ready." He could come at any moment, and we don't want to be sleeping when He comes.

Romans 13:11 And that, knowing the time, that now *it is* high time to awake out of sleep: for now *is* our salvation nearer than when we believed.

---

[150] Matthew 26:41
[151] 1 Thessalonians 5:6

Read Mark 14:22-42

Mark 14:25 Verily I say unto you, I will drink no more of the fruit of the vine, until that day that I drink it new in the kingdom of God.

The unleavened bread and cup of the Lord's Supper will forever have great significance for the followers of Jesus Christ.   The Passover meal spoke of Israel's deliverance while slaves in Egypt.   The Lord's Supper speaks of our deliverance from an even greater bondage, the bondage of sin.   Jesus Christ, our Passover Lamb, died for us![152]   The bread speaks of His body that was broken, the cup speaks of the blood that He shed.[153]

The Lord's Supper also looks forward to His return.   Jesus told the disciples that He would not drink the fruit of the vine with them **_until_** He drank it new with them in the Father's kingdom.   Some believe this may be a reference to some glorious event in the Millennium or to the marriage supper of the lamb in heaven.[154]   Whatever the case, each time we come to the Lord's Table here on earth, we are looking forward to that which is to come.   What a blessing it will be to sit at the table with Jesus and rejoice in His goodness on that day!

 1 Corinthians 11:26 For as often as ye eat this bread, and drink this cup, ye do shew the Lord's death **till he come.**

---

[152] 1 Corinthians 5:7
[153] 1 Corinthians 11:24-25
[154] Revelation 19:7-9

Read Mark 14:66-15:21

Mark 14:72 And the second time the cock crew. And Peter called to mind the word that Jesus said unto him, Before the cock crow twice, thou shalt deny me thrice. And when he thought thereon, he wept.

Peter's denial was part of a satanic plot, but the Lord was praying for blessings, in spite of it. The Lord is Omniscient—All Knowing. He knew that Peter was going to fail, and He knew that He was going to repent. He also knew that Peter would be uniquely gifting in encouraging others after that. We can only imagine what a comfort Peter was to those who, like him, had failed.[155] You see, the Lord is not only all knowing, He is Omnipotent—all powerful. He alone has the power to take what Satan has meant for evil and bring good from it.

This reminds us that *our* failures need not be fatal. If we will turn to Him in repentance, we can find restoration and comfort just as Peter did!

2 Corinthians 1:3-4 Blessed *be* God, even the Father of our Lord Jesus Christ, the Father of mercies, and the God of all comfort; Who comforteth us in all our tribulation, that we may be able to comfort them which are in any trouble, by the comfort wherewith we ourselves are comforted of God.

---

[155] Luke 22:31-33

Read Mark 15:22-47

Mark 15:34 And at the ninth hour Jesus cried with a loud voice, saying, Eloi, Eloi, lama sabachthani? which is, being interpreted, My God, my God, why hast thou forsaken me?

The darkness described in the previous verse was certainly a supernatural occurrence, not an eclipse.[156]   It was a dark time in more ways than one.   Jesus was bearing the tremendous weight of our sin. He was not sinful[157], but God's Word says He was "made to be sin *for* us,"[158] and that the Father laid on Him the iniquity of us all.[159]   Jesus faced judgment for sin, a judgment that we, as sinful humans, rightly deserved.

God says that the just penalty, the wages, of sin is death.[160]   That means physical death,[161] and spiritual death, which is separation from God.[162]   In a sense, Jesus faced both of those things on the cross. Because of *His* grace and mercy, my sins are forgiven, and I will never know what it is to be separated from God![163] That is cause for eternal rejoicing!

He paid a debt He did not owe, I owed a debt I could not pay, I needed someone to wash my sins away, and now I sing a brand-new song, "Amazing Grace," Christ Jesus paid the debt that I could never pay.[164]

---

[156] The Jews used a lunar calendar. Passover was always observed when the moon was full. There is never an eclipse of the sun when the moon is full.
[157] Hebrews 4:15
[158] 2 Corinthians 5:21
[159] Isaiah 53:6
[160] Romans 6:23
[161] Hebrews 9:27
[162] Revelation 20:14
[163] Hebrews 13:15
[164] "He Paid a Debt," Ellis J. Crum.

Read Mark 16

Mark 16:19 So then after the Lord had spoken unto them, he was received up into heaven, and sat on the right hand of God.

It is important to note that Jesus is now seated at the right hand of the Father,[165] indicating that the 'work of the cross' is done. He offered a perfect sacrifice for our sins, His own life, once for all.[166] When that sacrifice was complete, He could say, "it is finished."[167] That was not a cry of defeat, but a shout of victory!

No priest before Him could ever say, "it is finished," for it never was. Worship in the tabernacle and temple meant offering the same sacrifices over and over. There was no time, or place, for those priests to sit. In fact, there were not even any chairs in the temple. Jesus, having finished what He came to do, sat down at the Father's right hand. Praise the Lord for a "finished" salvation. There is nothing we can add to what Jesus has done.

Hebrews 12:2 Looking unto Jesus the author and finisher of *our* faith; who for the joy that was set before him endured the cross, despising the shame, and is set down at the right hand of the throne of God.

---

[165] Hebrews 1:3, Hebrews 10:12
[166] Hebrews 10:10
[167] John 19:30

Read Luke 1:1-25

Luke 1:15 For he shall be great in the sight of the Lord, and shall drink neither wine nor strong drink; and he shall be filled with the Holy Ghost, even from his mother's womb.

Zachariah and his wife Elisabeth were childless and well up in years. They had prayed many years for a son, but that prayer had not yet been answered.   Here in Luke 1, Gabriel appears to Zachariah and tells him that his long-standing prayer request is about to be answered. He and Elisabeth are going to have a son. They are to name him John, which means "God is Gracious." He would be a gift of God's grace, and his life would be far from ordinary.   He would be a bold prophet of God very much like Elijah of old.

The most remarkable thing about John was that he would be filled with the Holy Spirit even in his mother's womb.   The Scriptures are clear; God's plan for our lives begins *before* we are born.   He told the young prophet Jeremiah that He knew him and set him apart as a prophet *before* he was in his mother's womb.[168]   Paul had that same realization about his own life and ministry.   He said that he was separated (set apart unto God) in his mother's womb.[169]   Even more amazing is the fact that God knew us before the world began.[170]   I rejoice that He has a plan for my life.

Let's rejoice in that truth along with the Psalmist David today!

Psalm 139:13-14   13 For thou hast possessed my reins: thou hast covered me in my mother's womb. 14 I will praise thee; for I am fearfully *and* wonderfully made: marvelous *are* thy works; and *that* my soul knoweth right well.

---

[168] Jeremiah 1:4-5
[169] Galatians 1:5
[170] Ephesians 1:4

Read Luke 1:26-56

Luke 1:38 And Mary said, Behold the handmaid of the Lord; be it unto me according to thy word. And the angel departed from her.

Gabriel, the same angel that appeared to Zacharias earlier in Luke 1 now appears to Jesus' mother, Mary. Once again, he is announcing a miraculous birth. Even though she is a virgin, Mary is going to become the mother of Jesus, the One who is the Son of God, the Messiah, the King of an everlasting kingdom! Jesus, the Word, was going to become a man in Mary's womb, a miracle we call the incarnation.[171]

The incarnation would be a miracle of the Holy Spirit. The Holy Spirit would overshadow Mary. That word can mean to cover as with a cloud. It is the same word we find in Matthew 17:5, describing the glory cloud that overshadowed Jesus when He was transfigured.[172] This is probably the same cloud that overshadowed the tabernacle in the Old Testament.[173] Could it even be the cloud into which Jesus ascended[174] or the cloud we see at His return?[175]

Mary's yieldedness to the Holy Spirit is a wonderful example for all of us. She said, "yes," to the plan of God for her life saying, "be it unto me according to Thy word." Let's determine to follow her example and say "yes" to Him today.

I'll say, Yes, Lord, Yes, to Your will and to Your way, I'll say, Yes, Lord, Yes, I will trust You and obey, when Your Spirit speaks to me, with my whole heart I'll agree, and my answer will be Yes, Lord, Yes.

---

[171] John 1:14
[172] Matthew 17:5
[173] Exodus 40:34
[174] Acts 1:9
[175] Revelation 1:7

78

Read Luke 1:57-80

Luke 1:67 And his father Zacharias was filled with the Holy Ghost, and prophesied.

The ministry of the Holy Spirit is very evident in both of Luke's writings—the Gospel of Luke and Acts.   First, it was prophesied that John would be filled with the Holy Ghost in his mother's womb,[176] then Gabriel told Mary that the miracle of the incarnation[177] would involve the *overshadowing* of the Holy Spirit[178] Later Mary went to visit her cousin Elisabeth and when she spoke to her Elisabeth was filled with the Holy Ghost[179]   When John was born, his father Zacharias, was filled with the Holy Spirit and prophesied, glorifying God.[180]   When Jesus was baptized, the Spirit came down in the form of a dove[181] and He began His earthly ministry in the power of the Holy Spirit.[182] Yes, the ministry of the Holy Spirit was important then, but it is clear that His work is to be important in our lives today too.   The last command in the Gospel of Luke and the first command in the Acts pertains to that truth.

Luke 24:49 And, behold, I send the promise of my Father upon you: but tarry ye in the city of Jerusalem, until ye be endued with power from on high.

Acts 1:4-5 And, being assembled together with *them*, commanded them that they should not depart from Jerusalem, but wait for the promise of the Father, which, *saith he*, ye have heard of me. For John truly baptized with water; but ye shall be baptized with the Holy Ghost not many days hence.

> Spirit of the Living God fall fresh on me,
> Spirit of the Living God fall fresh on me,
> Break me, Melt Me, Mold me, Make me,
> Spirit of the Living God, fall fresh on me.[183]

---

[176] Luke 1:15, 17
[177] God becoming a man. The Word becoming flesh (John 1:14).
[178] Luke 1:35
[179] Luke 1:41
[180] Luke 1:67
[181] Luke 3:22
[182] Luke 4:14
[183] "Fall Fresh on Me," Daniel Iverson

Read Luke 2:1-21

Luke 2:10-14 And the angel said unto them, Fear not: for, behold, I bring you good tidings of great joy, which shall be to all people. For unto you is born this day in the city of David a Saviour, which is Christ the Lord. And this *shall be* a sign unto you; Ye shall find the babe wrapped in swaddling clothes, lying in a manger. And suddenly there was with the angel a multitude of the heavenly host praising God, and saying, Glory to God in the highest, and on earth peace, good will toward men.

Rejoicing in the birth of Jesus is not just a once a year thing. Let's join the angels every day in shouting, "Glory to God in the highest! The Savior has come!" That one herald angel was soon joined with a multitude of the heavenly host. Perhaps all the holy angels appeared that night, because, after all, this was the most important announcement those heavenly messengers had ever made. If they did all appear there could have been more than 100,000,000 angels. Revelation 5:11 speaks of the number of angels around the throne of God as ten thousand times ten thousand and thousands of thousands!

Why was this spectacular announcement made to such a humble group as the shepherds? Why were they among the very first to see Jesus in Bethlehem? Probably, because they still looked for the coming of the Messiah, while others had lost that hope. They lived with anticipation and childlike faith. This could be the day the Messiah comes to Israel! I hope we have that same kind of hopeful anticipation regarding His Second Coming. He is, after all, returning for those who look for Him!

Hebrews 9:28 So Christ was once offered to bear the sins of many; and **unto them that look for him** shall he appear the second time without sin unto salvation.

Read Luke 2:22-38

Luke 2:36-38 And there was one Anna, a prophetess, the daughter of Phanuel, of the tribe of Aser: she was of a great age, and had lived with an husband seven years from her virginity; And she *was* a widow of about fourscore and four years, which departed not from the temple, but served *God* with fastings and prayers night and day. And she coming in that instant gave thanks likewise unto the Lord, and spake of him to all them that looked for redemption in Jerusalem.

Here is another instance of someone looking for—anticipating—the coming of Jesus.   This godly woman had longed for the coming of her Messiah for many years.   How many years had she waited?   We don't know, but by this time she was a very old woman.   She had been married for only seven years when her husband died and now she had been a widow for eighty-four years, making her over a hundred years old.   When Joseph and Mary brought Jesus to the temple that day, she was not surprised by His arrival, because she had been looking for Him.

We do not know the day, nor the hour, of His return, but like Anna, we are looking for Him.   Those who are watching will not be unprepared when He comes.   We anticipate, we watch, we wait, looking forward to the return of our Lord.   We are never told to get ready, but always "Be Ready!"

Luke 12:40 Be ye therefore ready also: for the Son of man cometh at an hour when ye think not.

Read Luke 2:39-3:8

Luke 3:4 As it is written in the book of the words of Esaias the prophet, saying, The voice of one crying in the wilderness, Prepare ye the way of the Lord, make his paths straight.

John the Baptist was the forerunner, the one who prepared the way for the coming of Jesus.   Preparation for His coming came through repentance, turning away from the crooked path of sin and beginning to walk on a road Jesus would later call "strait and narrow."[184]   Those who repented signified that by being baptized—immersed in water.

John called people to prepare for the first coming of the Lord Jesus Christ.   We call people to prepare for His return.   Repentance toward God is still the road to that preparation.   His Word says that He is calling all men everywhere to repent.[185]   Repentance begins with godly sorrow[186] and involves an "about face," turning *from* sin and turning *to* the Lord Jesus Christ.   If we confess our sins, He is faithful and just to forgive us our sins and cleanse us from all unrighteousness.[187]

Acts 20:21 Testifying both to the Jews, and also to the Greeks [Gentiles], repentance toward God, and faith toward our Lord Jesus Christ.

---

[184] Matthew 7:13-14
[185] Acts 17:30
[186] 2nd Corinthians 7:10
[187] 1 John 1:9

Read Luke 3:10-38

Luke 3:23 And Jesus himself began to be about thirty years of age, being (as was supposed) the son of Joseph, which was *the son* of Heli,

This begins sixteen verses of names, tracing Jesus' earthly ancestry all the way back to Adam. The genealogies and lists of names in Scripture are not the first place most of us turn to when reading the Bible, but they are still an important part of God's revelation, with much to teach us. For example, in his genealogy Matthew, who wrote to Jews, made it clear that Jesus was a fellow Jew and the rightful heir to King David's throne.[188] He was both a son of Abraham and a son of David. For that reason, Matthew begins with Abraham and follows the generations to the Lord Jesus Christ.

The Gospel of Luke, on the other hand, was not written for a Jewish audience, but for Gentiles, specifically a man named Theophilus.[189] Luke himself was a Gentile medical doctor who had come to faith in Christ. By tracing Jesus' earthly ancestry back to Adam, Luke reminds us that Jesus is not just the Savior of the Jews, those who descend from Abraham, but He came to die for all the descendants of Adam. Though sinless, Jesus is a descendant of Adam like all other human beings. God became a man, one of us!

A Bible translator to a distant tribe saved the genealogies for last, because he thought them the least important part of the gospels. But when he finally finished them last of all, the tribesmen were astounded! They told the translator, "You mean to tell us that this Jesus was a *real* person, with *real* ancestors? We had no idea!"[190]

I rejoice today that He came to save the fallen sons and daughters of Adam, because that includes me!

---

[188] Matthew 1:1
[189] Luke 1:3
[190] Enduring Word Commentary, "Gospel of Luke," David Guzik.

Read Luke 4:1-21

Luke 4:14 And Jesus returned in the power of the Spirit into Galilee: and there went out a fame of him through all the region round about.

Luke's writings, the Gospel of Luke and Acts, have an emphasis on the work of the Holy Spirit in Jesus' life and later in the life of His church. Luke 4 gives us several examples of that emphasis.

First, Luke 4:1 tells us that Jesus was full of the Holy Ghost. Just before this the Spirit had descended on Him in the form of a dove when He was baptized in water. The first work of the Spirit we see in His life is that of leading Him into the wilderness where He was tempted by the devil for forty days. Empowered by the Spirit and the Spirit-inspired Word of God, He overcame Satan. We can overcome him the same way!

Second, after His wilderness temptation, Luke 4:14 tells us that He went back to Galilee and began His public ministry. This was a time of great miracles and popularity for Jesus. Luke's words in Acts 10:38 are very descriptive of this time, "God anointed Jesus of Nazareth with the Holy Ghost and with power: who went about doing good, and healing all that were oppressed of the devil; for God was with Him." He always ministered in the power of the Holy Spirit.

Third, Jesus revealed that He was the Messiah, the Anointed One (Luke 4:18). He read verses from Isaiah[191], verses about One anointed by the Holy Spirit and said, "This day is this scripture fulfilled in your ears." He declared Himself the Messiah—the Christ,[192] the One proclaiming the Salvation of the Lord! In fact, He *is* that salvation!

Praise Him that the same Holy Spirit will work and move in *your* life!

---

[191] Isaiah 61:1-3
[192] The New Testament title Christ and the Old Testament Messiah both speak of One anointed by the Spirit.

Read Luke 4.22-44

Luke 4:32 And they were astonished at his doctrine: for his word was with power.

Jesus was rejected in Nazareth, the place where He was raised. People from His hometown synagogue, people that had probably been a part of His life since childhood, were about to kill Him, because He spoke the truth.

It is interesting to notice what happened next. He went to Capernaum and taught in the synagogue there. A demon possessed man was in attendance that day and the demon spirits within him cried out, "Let us alone; what have we to do with thee, thou Jesus of Nazareth? Are thou come to destroy us? I know thee who thou art; the Holy One of God." Jesus silenced him. He was not about to let evil spirits proclaim His identity. It is interesting that even the powers of darkness knew things that the members of the synagogue in Nazareth, very religious people, did not know, or refused to believe. As to what demon spirits believe, James says, they believe that there is one God and tremble at that knowledge[193], something that many human beings do not believe. It is not enough, though, to know that He exists, He must be our Lord and Master.

Luke 4:36 And they were all amazed, and spake among themselves, saying, What a word *is* this! for with authority and power he commandeth the unclean spirits, and they come out.

---

[193] James 2:19

Read Luke 5:1-16

Luke 5:13   And he put forth *his* hand, and touched him, saying, I will: be thou clean. And immediately the leprosy departed from him.

The dreaded disease of leprosy was especially feared and despised in New Testament times.   One who was a leper was consigned to a life of separation from the rest of society.   A leper was unclean and could not fellowship with others, even his own family.   A leper must keep his mouth covered and cry out "unclean, unclean" wherever he goes lest someone inadvertently come near him, or worse yet, touch him.[194] One rabbi boasted of throwing stones at lepers to keep them away.

Jesus' response to this leper was different than anything he had experienced before. This man knew that Jesus *could* heal him, but was not sure He would want to. After all, he was a leper, a person thought to be under the curse of God, a person *no one* cared about.   Jesus proved that He was both willing *and* able.   The first loving human touch that leper had experienced since becoming a leper was the touch of Jesus. Jesus could have spoken the word from afar and healed Him, but He chose to touch Him. What a wonderful act of compassion and mercy!   When Jesus touched Him, He was no longer unclean; his life was forever changed.   That's what the Lord did when He saved you and me. He reached out and touched our unworthy lives, making us clean and pure. Let us give thanks for His touch today!

He touched me, Oh, He touched me,
And Oh, the joy that floods my soul,
Something happened and now I know,
He touched me, and made me whole.[195]

---

[194] Leviticus 13:45-46
[195] "He Touched Me," Bill Gaither

Read Luke 5.17-39

Luke 5:24 But that ye may know that the Son of man hath power upon earth to forgive sins, (he said unto the sick of the palsy,) I say unto thee, Arise, and take up thy couch, and go into thine house.

The crowds were so enormous at this point in Jesus' ministry that the friends of a paralyzed man went to great lengths to get him to Jesus. They lowered him through the roof down to where Jesus was teaching! Jesus' priority, and rightly so, was the man's spiritual condition. He first forgave his sins. The spiritual need should always be first priority.

Jesus' words were taken as blasphemy by some in the crowd. They begin to reason, or think to themselves, "only God can forgive sins." Jesus knew their thoughts, one more proof of His deity. He is Omniscient[196]. By healing the man He proved that He was Omnipotent[197] and as God did have the power to forgive sins. You may have heard someone say, "Jesus never claimed to be God." Of course, that is not true. He does so many times. Right here in Luke 5 He is claiming the power to forgive sins, something that is the prerogative of God alone. He is truly Immanuel, God with us!

> Immanuel, Immanuel,
> His Name is called Immanuel,
> God with us, revealed in us,
> His Name is called Immanuel.

---

[196] All Knowing.
[197] All Powerful

Read Luke 6:1-19

Luke 6:12 And it came to pass in those days, that he went out into a mountain to pray, and continued all night in prayer to God.

Jesus was a man of prayer. He spent all night praying over the twelve He chose and designated as His apostles, and those chosen men saw the importance of prayer in His life. One day, after He had been praying, they asked, "Lord, teach us to pray."[198] There is no record of their asking, "Teach us to preach and teach," or "Teach us to work miracles," but only, "Teach us to Pray." The priority and power of prayer was obvious in Jesus' life.

He had to make time to pray, just as we must make time to pray. We must allocate time for what is important to us[199]. After He fed the 5,000, Jesus sent the people, and even His apostles, away, so that He could go up on a mountain to pray alone.[200] As important as people and their needs were to Jesus, prayer was a priority. On another occasion, after what must have been very tiring ministry, ministry that went on into the night, Jesus got up the next morning before everyone else, so He could go to a solitary place and pray.[201] God-given rest is important, but meeting with the Father was a priority. No wonder His apostles saw how important prayer was to their Master.

How do we do this in our very busy lives? We would do well to ask as His disciples did then, "Lord, teach **us** to pray!" It won't "look the same" for all of us, but He will help us find a way to "make it work!"

---

[198] Luke 11:1
[199] A "time" helps us prioritize prayer, but it is more than just that set time. It is an attitude. We can breathe out words of prayer and praise throughout the day. Thus, we are told to pray without ceasing (1 Thessalonians 5:17).
[200] Matthew 14:23
[201] Mark 1:32-35

Read Luke 6:20-42

Luke 6:20   And he lifted up his eyes on his disciples, and said, Blessed *be ye* poor: for yours is the kingdom of God.

Jesus' teaching in Luke 6:20-49 is similar to what He taught in the Sermon on the Mount in Matthew 5-7.   Jesus was an itinerant preacher and probably preached some of the same things everywhere He went, just as traveling preachers do today.   The sermon He preached in Luke 6 does have material we don't find in Matthew 5, though.   Matthew gives us the blessings, or Beatitudes, for those with certain heart attitudes, while Jesus' sermon in Luke 6 adds corresponding curses, or woes, for those who do *not* have those attitudes.

The poor in spirit are blessed[202], while those who rely on their own riches are cursed[203].   Those who hunger and thirst after righteousness are blessed[204], but those who are self-righteous are cursed.[205]   Those who mourn over their sin will be blessed[206], but those who do not, and continue in that sin, will be cursed.[207]   There is a blessing for those who are hated and persecuted for righteousness' sake[208], but a curse for those who are loved by, and in love with, the world.[209]

This reminds us of the words we find in the Book of Deuteronomy.

Deuteronomy 30:19   I call heaven and earth to record this day against you, *that* I have set before you life and death, blessing and cursing: therefore **choose life**, that both thou and thy seed may live:

I choose life and blessing today....I choose Him!

---

[202] Matthew 5:3, Luke 6:20
[203] Luke 6:24, Revelation 3:17
[204] Matthew 5:6, Luke 6:21
[205] Luke 6:25
[206] Matthew 5:4, Luke 6:21
[207] Luke 6:25
[208] Matthew 5:10-12, Luke 6:22-23
[209] Luke 6:26, James 4:4

Read Luke 6.43-7.17

Luke 6:38   Give, and it shall be given unto you; good measure, pressed down, and shaken together, and running over, shall men give into your bosom. For with the same measure that ye mete withal it shall be measured to you again.

This verse is often quoted in regarded to God's blessing on those who give financially.   Of course, we have all found that to be true[210]. However, the context of Luke 6:38 reveals a different kind of giving. Here are some examples of that kind of giving in the context of this Scripture. We must give mercy to others, just as our Father has shown mercy to us, [211] and we must not give judgment and condemnation to others.   Doing so may bring a harvest of judgment and condemnation on us![212]

With the Holy Spirit's help, let us give mercy, grace, and forgiveness and then expect God's blessings good measure, pressed down, shaken together, and running over!

2 Corinthians 9:6 But this *I say*, He which soweth sparingly shall reap also sparingly; and he which soweth bountifully shall reap also bountifully.

---

[210] Malachi 3:10
[211] Luke 6:36
[212] Luke 6:37

Read Luke 7.18-48

Luke 7:47 Wherefore I say unto thee, Her sins, which are many, are forgiven; for she loved much: but to whom little is forgiven, *the same* loveth little.

While Jesus was eating in the home of a prominent Pharisee a sinful woman came in to the house and anointed His feet.   Some have suggested this was Mary Magdalene, but there is no real Bible evidence to prove this[213].   She was apparently a notorious sinner, perhaps even a former prostitute, and she was literally weeping so much at Jesus' feet that she could wash His feet with her tears and dry them with her hair.   She kissed his feet, and anointed them with expensive ointment.

Jesus' acceptance of this display of love made His host, Simon the Pharisee, doubt that He was truly a prophet from God. After all, Simon thought, a true prophet of God would know what kind of a woman she was and would not have allowed this public display. Jesus, being omniscient, knew exactly what Simon was thinking and answered accordingly.   He spoke of two men who owed a debt. One of them owed ten times as much as the other, the equivalent of 500 days' wages. The one to whom they owed the money chose to forgive both their debts.   Jesus' question for Simon went something like this, "Which one would love that former creditor most?"   Of course, it would be the one who had been forgiven most. The woman's display of gratitude was a result of sins forgiven.   We can never praise Him enough for forgiving our sins and saving our souls!

Thank You Lord for saving my soul.
Thank You Lord for making me whole.
Thank You Lord for giving to me,
Thy great salvation so rich and free.[214]

---

[213] In John 12:3 another woman anoints Jesus' feet, Mary of Bethany, but that is a separate incident.
[214] "Thank You Lord for Saving My Soul," Seth and Bessie Sykes

Read Luke 7.44-8.18

Luke 8:1-3 And it came to pass afterward, that he went throughout every city and village, preaching and shewing the glad tidings of the kingdom of God: and the twelve *were* with him, And certain women, which had been healed of evil spirits and infirmities, Mary called Magdalene, out of whom went seven devils, And Joanna the wife of Chuza Herod's steward, and Susanna, and many others, which ministered unto him of their substance.

Earlier in this chapter, we read of an unnamed woman who expressed her gratitude to Jesus by washing His feet with her tears, drying them with her hair, and anointing them with costly ointment. Through her act, Jesus taught that those who have been forgiven much also love much.   Later, as Jesus and the twelve traveled from village to village preaching the Gospel, a group of women who had been forgiven much used their resources to support the work of God. Through their generosity, Jesus and the apostles could preach and teach unhindered by undue financial concerns. Jesus brought deliverance and healing to these women and they were forever grateful!

There are many motives for giving to the work of the Lord.   One may give through habit, guilt, or even coercion. However, one of the best motives is gratitude for what the Lord has done in our lives. That was the motive of these women.

Lord, Thou lov'st the cheerful giver,
Who with open heart and hand
Blesses freely, as a river
That refreshes all the land.
Grant us then the grace of giving
With a spirit large and free,
That our life and all our living
We may consecrate to Thee.[215]

---

[215] "Lord, Thou Lov'st The Cheerful Giver," Robert Murray

Read Luke 8:19-39

Luke 8:19-21 Then came to him *his* mother and his brethren, and could not come at him for the press. And it was told him *by certain* which said, Thy mother and thy brethren stand without, desiring to see thee. And he answered and said unto them, My mother and my brethren are these which hear the word of God, and do it.

Jesus' mother Mary was undoubtedly one of the godliest women who ever lived. However, she is *not* due the prayer and praise that is offered to her in some circles. Jesus teaches here in Luke 8 that those who hear and obey the Word of God are his family too. On another occasion, someone shouted out to Jesus, "Blessed is the womb that bare thee, and the paps which thou hast sucked!" Jesus answered nearly the same way he did in Luke 8, "Blessed [rather] are they that hear the word of God and keep it."

Yes, His mother Mary was blessed, because she heard the Word of God and did it. She was obedient to the Lord's will for her life. We can be blessed in the same way, hearing His Word and doing it. May the Lord help us and give us grace!

When we walk with the Lord in the light of His Word,
What a glory He sheds on our way,
When we do His good will,
He abides with us still, and with all who will trust and obey.
Trust and obey, for there's no other way,
To be happy in Jesus than to trust and obey![216]

---

[216] "Trust and Obey," John H. Sammis

Read Luke 8.40-9-9

Luke 8:45 And Jesus said, Who touched me? When all denied, Peter and they that were with him said, Master, the multitude throng thee and press *thee*, and sayest thou, Who touched me?

This speaks of a woman with what the Bible calls an issue of blood. She was bleeding beyond her regular monthly time and had been doing so for twelve long years. This would have left her very anemic and weak. A woman in her condition was also considered unclean, as was anyone, or anything that touched her. This made her condition almost as devastating as leprosy[217]. She had used up all her resources looking for a doctor that could help her, but she had gotten no better. Mark adds that she had *suffered* many things from their attempts at medical treatment, but only grew worse[218]. Some old medical texts actually prescribed bleeding a person with a disorder like hers, believing the patient must have too much blood! She must have nearly given up all hope of having real life ever again.

When she heard of Jesus, though, something began to rise in her soul---faith and hope. She must have reasoned, "Jesus would not want to touch *me*, because I am unclean, but if I can just get through that crowd and touch *Him*, I know that I can be healed." So, she worked her way through the crowd, perhaps nearly at ground level because of her weakened condition, and amazingly was able to get close enough to touch the hem of Jesus' garment. The entire crowd was pressing around Him, but He could tell the difference between their touch and her touch. The deliberate touch of faith brought the woman in contact with His healing power. She left His presence healed, and walking in peace, something that she had known little of for twelve long years!

We can still touch Him, calling out to Him in prayer, and He is still the Healer of sick bodies and the Giver of peace.

---

[217] Leviticus 15:25
[218] Mark 5:26

Read Luke 9:10-27

Luke 9:10 And the apostles, when they were returned, told him all that they had done. And he took them, and went aside privately into a desert place belonging to the city called Bethsaida.

At the beginning of Luke 9 Jesus sent the disciples out on a preaching mission. They returned excited, but weary from the demands of ministry. Mark adds that they had been so busy they hadn't even taken time to eat, so Jesus took them to a desert place near Bethsaida, so they could rest.[219]

However, they found no rest there, because the crowds who followed Jesus saw where they were going and followed them. Jesus did not send the crowds away, but received them. He gave them the Word and He healed those who needed healing. This went on until, as Luke says, "the day began to wear away." That is not all that was "wearing away." The disciples, weary and hungry when they started, had gone still another day without stopping to eat or rest. That is probably why they finally asked Jesus to send the people away, so they could go back to town, find some food, and a place to stay. After all, they said, this is a desert, and there is no way to find a bite to eat here.

Of course, you know the rest of the story! Jesus multiplied their very limited supplies so that 5,000 men, not including the women and children were miraculously fed. There were even leftovers, twelve baskets full, enough to supply the need of the still hungry and weary apostles! He is a God of abundance, enough and even more than enough, if we will only trust Him!

He's more than enough, more than enough,
He is El Shaddai[220], the God of plenty,
The all-sufficient One, God Almighty, He is more than Enough.[221]

---

[219] Mark 6:31
[220] A Hebrew title for God, often translated as "God Almighty."
[221] "He's More than Enough," David Ingles.

Read Luke 9.28-48

Luke 9:28-29 And it came to pass about an eight days after these sayings, he took Peter and John and James, and went up into a mountain to pray. And as he prayed, the fashion of his countenance was altered, and his raiment *was* white *and* glistering.

Jesus made an amazing statement to His disciples in the previous chapter. He said, "There be some standing here, which shall not taste of death, till they see the kingdom of God." That promise was soon to be fulfilled in the lives of three of them that were with Him that day.

He took Peter, James, and John with Him up on a mountain to pray. As He prayed, His appearance began to change dramatically. Luke says, "The fashion of His countenance was altered." Matthew adds that His face literally shone like the sun and His clothes became as "white as light."[222] Jesus allowed them a glimpse, a preview, of His heavenly glory, a glory that was 'veiled in flesh' while He was here on earth. John saw that glory at least one more time before he left this world. When given the Revelation, he saw Jesus with a countenance "as the sun shines its strength,"[223] and as the light of the New Heaven and New Earth, a place that will no longer need the sun.[224]

As glorious as that experience was for them. They did not yet see Him in His *full* glory, that would come later. He is, after all, the Creator of the sun and all the myriad other stars out there in the His universe. The glory of the Creator far exceeds the sum of all His creation! Paul says He dwells in a light that "no man can approach unto."[225] That is what makes John's words about our future state so amazing.

1 John 3:1-3 Beloved, now are we the sons of God, and it doth not yet appear what we shall be: but we know that, when he shall appear, **we shall be like him; for we shall see him as he is.** And every man that hath this hope in him purifieth himself, even as he is pure.

---

[222] Matthew 17:2
[223] Revelation 1:16
[224] Revelation 21:23
[225] 1 Timothy 6:16

Read Luke 9.49-10.12

Luke 10:2 Therefore said he unto them, The harvest truly *is* great, but the labourers *are* few: pray ye therefore the Lord of the harvest, that he would send forth labourers into his harvest.

The Lord gave this word in the context of sending out thirty-five preaching teams, seventy men to go from village to village and preach. They were to go into every city and place where the Lord Himself would soon come, preparing the way for His visit. There were still many souls that needed to hear the truth, and the great need then, as now, was for workers. These men became a part of the answer to their own prayer. *Praying* for laborers, we are also willing to *be* laborers.

Though the seventy were a special group, the need for laborers is still great, and the need is now. On another occasion, Jesus said, "Say not ye, there are yet four months, and then cometh harvest? Behold, I say unto you, Lift up your eyes, and look on the fields; for they are white already to harvest."[226]   The crop fields of Israel were not yet ready to reap. They were still growing, and harvest was still months away. Yet, there was no such delay with God's harvest of souls. The fields of ripening spiritual grain were all around them, ready to hear, and receive, the truth of the Gospel. There is an urgency at harvest time. It is not His will that any of the precious grain be lost![227]

Like the seventy and others that Jesus commissioned, we have been "sent out." Pentecost, the outpouring of the Holy Spirit, means receiving His power to bring in the harvest before the final *storm* and His return.[228]

---

[226] John 4:35
[227] 2 Peter 3:9
[228] Acts 1:8, Acts 2:17

Read Luke 10.13-37

Luke 10:20 Notwithstanding in this rejoice not, that the spirits are subject unto you; but rather rejoice, because your names are written in heaven.

The thirty-five preaching teams Jesus sent out came back to report to Him. They must have shared many exciting stories and were full of joy, because of the great things that they had seen and experienced on their missionary venture. He had sent them out to preach and heal the sick, which they did. They also discovered something else on that trip. Demon spirits were subject to them in the Name of Jesus!

How did Jesus respond to their joyful discovery? First, He rejoiced with them that Satan has been cast down from his formerly exalted position. Jesus, of course, saw it happen! Some have also suggested that He was warning *them* against pride, the very sin that brought about Satan's fall. He also made it clear that His people need not fear Satan and his minions. He compares these spiritual entities to some of earths most venomous creatures---serpents and scorpions. The serpents and scorpions of the spiritual realm are no match for one coming in the Name of Jesus. They are under His feet and our feet! Have no fear!

As wonderful as spiritual power and authority is, it is not our greatest reason to rejoice. The greatest miracle of all is the salvation of our souls. Outside of that salvation, we would all be facing the same dark eternity as those "serpents and scorpions" of the demonic realm. We rejoice, because we are "Free Indeed" in Jesus[229]! I think of the words of a chorus we sometimes sing:

I'm so glad that the Lord saved me! I'm so glad that the Lord saved me!
If it had not been for Jesus, tell me, "Where would I be?"
I'm so glad that the Lord saved me!
He saved me! He saved me!
I'm so glad that the Lord saved me!
If it had not been for Jesus, tell me "Where would I be?"
I'm so glad that the Lord saved me![230]

---

[229] John 8:36
[230] "I'm So Glad that the Lord Saved Me," Carman Licciardello

Read Luke 10:38-11:23

Luke 11:13 If ye then, being evil, know how to give good gifts unto your children: how much more shall *your* heavenly Father give the Holy Spirit to them that ask him?

This Scripture is part of the teaching Jesus gave after the disciples asked, "Lord, teach us to pray."[231]   We are given wonderful promises about asking in this portion of Scripture. As parents, we know the great love we have for our children. In light of that, it is amazing to consider the love of our Heavenly Father, a love that is exponentially greater than ours. His love here is expressed by His generosity, His willingness to give to His children who ask.

If we ask in prayer, it will be given unto us. If we seek, we will find. If we knock in prayer, the door will be opened to us.   These three verbs are in a continuous tense, which means we keep on asking, keep on seeking, and keep on knocking[232]. Pray without ceasing.[233]

We need never worry about our Father giving us the wrong thing, something that is not good for us when we ask. For example, good earthly parents would never give a stone when asked for bread, how much less our infinitely loving Heavenly Father[234].   One of His greatest gifts, is the gift of the Holy Spirit, which He promises to those who will but ask![235]   If you are His child, it is your great privilege today to ask Him for what He has promised!

Heavenly Father, at this moment I come to You. I thank You that Jesus saved me, and I pray, Lord Jesus, baptize me now in the Holy Spirit. I receive the baptism in the Holy Spirit right now by faith in Your Word. May the anointing, the glory, and the power of God come upon me and into my life right now. May I be empowered for service from this day forward. Thank You, Lord Jesus, for baptizing me in Your Holy Spirit. Amen.[236]

---

[231] Luke 11:1
[232] Luke 11:9-10
[233] 1 Thessalonians 5:17
[234] Luke 11:11
[235] Luke 24:49, Acts 1:4, Acts 2:33, Acts 2:38
[236] www.cbn.com

Read 11:24-44

Luke 11:29   And when the people were gathered thick together, he began to say, This is an evil generation: they seek a sign; and there shall no sign be given it, but the sign of Jonas the prophet.

Jesus spoke these words to those who had already ignored the many amazing signs and wonders seen in His ministry. They would see one final sign, a sign He calls the sign of the prophet Jonas (Jonah). Jesus compares His own death and resurrection to Jonah's time in the great fish.   Just as Jonah spent three days and three nights in the belly of a fish before what must have seemed like a resurrection, Jesus would spend three days in the grave and then be resurrected.[237]

Among the ungodly Gentiles of Nineveh, the response to Jonah's "resurrection" and preaching had been city-wide repentance.   Unlike the notorious sinners in Nineveh who repented, many of the religious Jews who listened to Jesus that day had not repented at His preaching and would not repent at the great sign of His coming resurrection.

Then He speaks of the visit of the Queen of Sheba.   Though a Gentile, she traveled from a far country just to hear the wisdom of King Solomon.[238]   Jesus' listeners that day had a "Greater than Solomon" in their midst, but they would not listen to His words.   Repentant Gentiles would receive God's blessings rather than the sin-calloused religious who heard Him, but did not respond with repentance and faith.

The great miracle of His resurrection, a miracle proved by many infallible proofs,[239]   is a sign that calls us all—Jew or Gentile, Religious or non-religious—to repentance and faith.

Acts 20:21   Testifying both to the Jews, and also to the Greeks, repentance toward God, and faith toward our Lord Jesus Christ.

---

[237] Matthew 12:40
[238] 1 Kings 10
[239] Acts 1:3

Read Luke 11:45-12:12

Luke 12:6-7 6 Are not five sparrows sold for two farthings, and not one of them is forgotten before God? 7 But even the very hairs of your head are all numbered. Fear not therefore: ye are of more value than many sparrows.

The Word of God reveals that God is far above His creation, but He has also chosen to be an active part of it.   Theologians use the big words transcendence (God is far above) and immanence (God is near) to describe those two facets of His nature.

When David saw the glory of God's creation, He was amazed. It made him feel so small and insignificant that he asked, "What is man that Thou art mindful of him?"[240]   God's created universe, just the part that we are aware of, is far greater than our mortal minds can comprehend.   Some have estimated that there are more stars in the universe than there are grains of sand on planet earth!   Some of those stars are so far away that it takes their light, traveling at 186,000 miles per second, years to reach us.   In light of the vastness of creation, Earth is less than a speck of dust, and we humans were created from the *dust* of that speck!.[241]   If the creation is that great, how much greater is the Creator!

One might ask, "does a Creator that great care about this planet and its 'creatures of dust'?" Amazingly He does. He loves us so much that He became one of us in the Person of Jesus Christ.[242]   He gave His life for us, and someday we will be like Him![243] Our opening verses remind of His great care for His creation.   A tiny bird does not fall from its nest without the Creator knowing about it.   He knows everything about us, down to the tiniest details.   We are worth far more than sparrows. Our value to Him is seen in what He was willing to pay to redeem us—His own lifeblood[244]

Why should I feel discouraged, why should the shadows come,
Why should my heart be lonely, and long for heav'n and home,
When Jesus is my portion? My constant Friend is He:
His eye is on the sparrow, and I know He watches me;
His eye is on the sparrow, and I know He watches me[245]

---

[240] Psalm 8:1-3
[241] Genesis 2:7, Psalm 103:14
[242] John 1:1-3, 14
[243] 1 John 3:1-3
[244] 1 Peter 1:18-19
[245] "His Eye is on the Sparrow," Civilla D. Martin

Read Luke 12:13-40

Luke 12:35-36 Let your loins be girded about, and *your* lights burning; And ye yourselves like unto men that wait for their lord, when he will return from the wedding; that when he cometh and knocketh, they may open unto him immediately.

This figure of speech is a common one in the New Testament. It is much like Jesus' parable of the wise and foolish virgins.[246] When the Master returned, some were ready, and some were not. We could summarize this teaching in two words, "BE READY." It is not so much about GETTING ready as it is about BEING ready. There is a difference.

The Lord could return to earth at any time of the day or night. That is why He calls us to readiness. His coming is compared in Scripture to that of a thief in the night. If one was expecting a robber to visit his home at a certain time, he would be prepared, but that kind of visit is never announced. Thieves take people by surprise. In a similar fashion, many will be taken by surprise when the Lord returns. Sadly, many will not be prepared.

Elsewhere we are told that He is returning for those who are looking for Him.[247] He is not coming as a thief for those of us who are prepared. We are expecting Him any time now!

1 Thessalonians 5:4 But ye, brethren, are not in darkness, that that day should overtake you as a thief.

---

[246] Matthew 25:1-13
[247] Hebrews 9:28

Read Luke 12:41-59

Luke 12:47-48 47 And that servant, which knew his lord's will, and prepared not *himself*, neither did according to his will, shall be beaten with many *stripes*. 48 But he that knew not, and did commit things worthy of stripes, shall be beaten with few *stripes*. For unto whomsoever much is given, of him shall be much required: and to whom men have committed much, of him they will ask the more.

We have all probably heard the expression, "to whom much is given, much will be required," an expression taken from here in Luke 12. Jesus' words are addressed to all of us. We are to be like the wise stewards He speaks of in this passage of Scripture.[248] A steward is one who is responsible for what belongs to another, especially in that person's absence. We are responsible for what our Master has placed in our hands, and upon His return, we will give an accounting.[249]

We must not be like the other stewards Jesus speaks of here. They lived wanton, evil lives. They apparently believed that their master was not going to return any time soon. In that way, they are like the scoffers Peter describes, those who do as they please while asking, "Where is the promise of His coming[250]?"

Our prayer is that on the day we stand before Him we will hear these words, "Well done, *thou* good and faithful servant: thou hast been faithful over a few things, I will make thee ruler over many things: enter thou into the joy of thy lord."[251]

---

[248] Luke 12:41
[249] 2 Corinthians 5:10
[250] 2 Peter 3: #-4
[251] Matthew 25:21

Read Luke 13:1-21

Luke 13:6-9 He spake also this parable; A certain *man* had a fig tree planted in his vineyard; and he came and sought fruit thereon, and found none. Then said he unto the dresser of his vineyard, Behold, these three years I come seeking fruit on this fig tree, and find none: cut it down; why cumbereth it the ground? And he answering said unto him, Lord, let it alone this year also, till I shall dig about it, and dung *it*: And if it bear fruit, *well*: and if not, *then* after that thou shalt cut it down.

It is believed that the fig tree in this parable represents Israel. The Lord had ministered in their midst for three years, looking for spiritual fruit, but had found very little. If there was no repentance, their nation would be cut down.[252] This is a little like the parable of the vineyard in Isaiah 5:1-7, where the Lord planted His vineyard (Israel) in a very fruitful place and did everything He could to help them produce, yet when He came looking for the harvest, He only found sour wild grapes. Despite all He had done, there was no spiritual fruit of repentance and righteousness.

Though this speaks of the nation of Israel, there is an application for all of us. In John 15:1-5 Jesus says that He is the vine and we are the branches. If a branch does not bear fruit, it is taken off. It if does bear *some* fruit it may be pruned to help it become more productive. A branch can only bear fruit when it is connected to the vine. We can only bear spiritual fruit when we are in relationship with the Lord Jesus Christ. Fruit flows from that relationship, and our Father is glorified when the fruit of the Spirit is growing in our lives.[253]

John 15:5 I am the vine, ye *are* the branches: He that abideth in me, and I in him, the same bringeth forth much fruit: **for without me ye can do nothing.**

---

[252] Israel did cease to be a nation a few years later in AD 70 and would not be restored until about 1948.
[253] John 15:8, Galatians 5:22-23

Read Luke 13.22-14.6

Luke 13:24 Strive to enter in at the strait gate: for many, I say unto you, will seek to enter in, and shall not be able.

This begins Jesus' response to a question that was asked in verse 23, "Will only a few be saved?" Jesus directs His response back to the questioner's own spiritual condition. *You* must strive to enter in at the strait gate yourself. The gate to heaven is not a broad gate, but a narrow one. Not everyone will go through that gate. One of the most dangerous doctrines of this present day is Universalism, the belief that all roads and all gates lead to heaven. Christians are sometimes viewed as judgmental for suggesting that the way to heaven may be limited. What a dangerous deception it is to suggest that there is more than one way to be saved. But, ultimately, it is not what I *say*, but what Jesus *says* that is important. He makes it very clear how many ways there are.

John 14:5-6 Thomas saith unto him, Lord, we know not whither thou goest; and how can we know the way?[254] Jesus saith unto him, I am **the** way, **the** truth, and **the** life: no man cometh unto the Father, but by me.

---

[254] Jesus had been telling them that He was going to prepare a place for them. Thomas wanted to know the way to heaven. In verse 6 Jesus makes the way to that place very clear.

Read Luke 14:7-24

Luke 14:15 And when one of them that sat at meat with him heard these things, he said unto him, Blessed *is* he that shall eat bread in the kingdom of God.

Jesus was eating a meal at the home of a prominent Pharisee when someone uttered the above words, words that echo those found in Revelation 19:9, "Blessed are they which are called unto the marriage supper of the Lamb." The parable that follows is a response to his words.

Jesus speaks of a man who had prepared a great supper and invited many people to come and enjoy it with Him. Despite the wonderful invitation, everyone made up excuses for not being able to attend. Their excuses ran all the way from, "I can't come, because I just bought some property," to, "I can't come, because I just got married." When those originally invited did not come, the doors were opened to all. He said, "Go out into the highways and hedges and compel them to come in that my house may be full."

One might build a case for saying that this parable speaks of the rejection of Jesus' message by the Jews (those who were originally invited) and the subsequent opening of the door to Gentiles (the poor, the maimed, the halt, and the blind). Regardless, there is a clear application for all of us. We have been invited to enjoy the Lord's glorious salvation. How will we respond to that invitation? The words of an old Gospel song make it clear what our response must be.

> I've received an invitation from the glorious King of kings,
> I am going to be there!
> To be present at the banquet when the Lord his ransomed brings,
> I am going to be there!
> I've received an invitation, glory, glory to his name!
> To the great marriage supper of the Lamb;
> And the Lord command has given for the summons to prepare,
> I am going to be there![255]

---

[255] "I've Received an Invitation," C. H. Morris.

Read Luke 14.25-15.10

Luke 15:10 Likewise, I say unto you, there is joy in the presence of the angels of God over one sinner that repenteth.

The salvation of a soul brings great joy to the courts of heaven, and it should bring great joy among God's people here on earth. In Luke 15 Jesus speaks of three lost things that were later found: a lost sheep, a lost coin, and a lost son. All three speak of why the Lord came to earth, "To seek and to save that which was lost."[256]

The man with 100 sheep lost only one of them. He still had 99% of his flock, but he did not find rest until he had rescued the 1%. What church would not rejoice to see 99% of their community come to Christ. That would be an amazing revival, but not a time to quit reaching the lost. The Lord is not willing that any should perish, nor should we be.[257] The salvation of even one soul should be cause for **great** celebration on earth and in heaven!

---

[256] Luke 19:10
[257] 2 Peter 3:9

Read Luke 15:11-32

Luke 15:17   And when he came to himself, he said, How many hired servants of my fathers have bread enough and to spare, and I perish with hunger!

A wayward child can be a parents' greatest grief.   The wayward son Jesus speaks of here had a sense of entitlement.   He took his inheritance and squandered it on sin of every kind, and it cost him dearly.   As it has often been said, "Sin will take you farther than you want to go, keep you longer than you want to stay, and cost you more than you want to pay."   That was certainly the case for this wayward boy.   He found himself friendless, penniless, and hungry, so hungry he would have gladly eaten what the pigs were eating.   Satan's blinders never allow us to see where sin is taking us, only the pleasure of the moment[258]!

The Bible says that he finally "came to himself."   He had an awakening.   Blinders were being removed from his eyes.   The Holy Spirit was dealing with him, and God, in His grace was giving him opportunity to repent.   His father, back home, must have been on his knees!   If you have a wayward child, stay on your knees, don't give up on them.   Pray that they will "come to themselves" that the Lord will open those eyes blinded by the "god of this world."[259]   Don't give up!

Galatians 6:9   And let us not be weary in well doing: for in due season we shall reap, if we faint not.

---

[258] **Hebrews 11:25**   Choosing rather to suffer affliction with the people of God, than to enjoy the pleasures of sin **for a season**;

[259] **2 Corinthians 4:4**   In whom the god of this world hath blinded the minds of them which believe not, lest the light of the glorious gospel of Christ, who is the image of God, should shine unto them.

Read Luke 16.1-18

Luke 16:11 If therefore ye have not been faithful in the unrighteous mammon, who will commit to your trust the true *riches*?

Jesus prefaces this with a parable about a dishonest steward, one in charge of another person's affairs. He had been squandering what belonged to his master and was about to be "found out." He knows that he will likely lose his job. The jobs that a steward fired for dishonesty might get were limited. The thought of digging ditches the rest of his life frightened him. He had an idea for securing his future. He began to write off debts that others owed to his master. Perhaps those former debtors would be there for *him* when he was without a job. What is the point of this parable? Jesus is certainly not condoning dishonesty. But, it is as someone once said, "If we pursued the Kingdom of God with the same vigor and zeal that the children of this world pursue profits and pleasure, we would live in an entirely different world."[260]

We are His stewards today. We must not be dishonest or covetous. We must use what God has entrusted to us wisely, with eternity in mind. How can we best use the material blessings entrusted to us? Our use of money, called unrighteous mammon here, speaks volumes about the state of our hearts. If we are not faithful stewards of material things, how can God entrust us with true riches?

Matthew 6:19-21 Lay not up for yourselves treasures upon earth, where moth and rust doth corrupt, and where thieves break through and steal: but lay up for yourselves treasures in heaven, where neither moth nor rust doth corrupt, and where thieves do not break through nor steal: For where your treasure is, there will your heart be also.

---

[260] Enduring Word Commentary, David Guzik

Read Luke 16.19-17.10

Luke 16:22 And it came to pass, that the beggar died, and was carried by the angels into Abraham's bosom: the rich man also died, and was buried;

Before the death and resurrection of Jesus Christ the righteous dead went to a place called Abraham's bosom, while the ungodly went to hell. The godly are now in heaven with the Lord, while the ungodly remain in hell. Jesus describes the life, death, and eternity of two very different men. One of them is now in heaven with the Lord, while the other is still in hell awaiting his final judgment.

Jesus description of these two eternities gives us insight into the horrors of hell. Hell is a conscious place. After death, his body was buried, but the rich man was tormented by flames. After death his body was buried, but he still knew what it was to have thirst. After death his body was buried, yet he had concern for his lost brothers back on earth. Sadly, it was too late for him to witness to them. At this very moment, he is still enduring all of those things awaiting the Great White Throne Judgment, at which time he will be consigned to the Lake of Fire, a destiny the Bible calls the Second Death.[261] As some used to say there is still a heaven to gain and a hell to shun!

In light of this horrifying description, I am so grateful for what He has promised those who are in Christ, those who are overcomers through His blood. We need not fear the second death!

Revelation 2:11 He that hath an ear, let him hear what the Spirit saith unto the churches; He that overcometh shall not be hurt of the second death.

---

[261] Revelation 20:14

Read Luke 17.11-37

Luke 17:20-21 20 And when he was demanded of the Pharisees, when the kingdom of God should come, he answered them and said, The kingdom of God cometh not with observation: 21 Neither shall they say, Lo here! or, lo there! for, behold, the kingdom of God is within you.

The Pharisees were looking for the coming of God's kingdom on earth, a kingdom promised throughout the Word of God. Jesus made it clear that the kingdom of God was not *just* a future hope; it was a present reality. The Pharisees could not see that present reality. When Jesus told them, "the kingdom of God is within you," it literally meant, "the kingdom of God is in your midst." The King of kings was standing before them, yet their hearts were too hard to receive Him.

When we pray as Jesus commanded us to pray, we are praying for both the future and present realities of His kingdom. We look forward to His return and rule on the earth, and we recognize that He is in our midst now and we must yield to Him as King.

Matthew 6:10 Thy kingdom come. Thy will be done in earth, as *it is* in heaven.

Read Luke 18:1-17

Luke 18:14 I tell you, this man went down to his house justified *rather* than the other: for every one that exalteth himself shall be abased; and he that humbleth himself shall be exalted.

Jesus speaks of two men going to the temple to pray, one of them is a well-respected religious man, a Pharisee, the other is a despised publican, a crooked tax collector. The Bible says that the Pharisee prayed "with **himself**." His prayers did not reach beyond his own ears. They were a boastful list of the things that he had, and had not done, comparing himself favorably with others. On the other hand, the publican prayed a simple prayer from a humble and repentant heart, "God be merciful to me, a sinner." Of the two prayers, his reached the throne of God.

We can never be justified by our own good works[262]. Any spiritual accomplishment we can boast[263] about is described by Isaiah as filthy rags[264]. Every good and perfect gift, including the gift of salvation and forgiveness, comes from above[265]. That is, we cannot take credit for it. Until, like the Publican, we recognize that we are sinners, in need of His mercy, we can never be saved. The prayer of David in Psalm 51 is a good place to start.

Psalm 51:1-4 Have mercy upon me, O God, according to thy lovingkindness: according unto the multitude of thy tender mercies blot out my transgressions. Wash me thoroughly from mine iniquity, and cleanse me from my sin. For I acknowledge my transgressions: and my sin *is* ever before me. Against thee, thee only, have I sinned, and done *this* evil in thy sight: that thou mightest be justified when thou speakest, *and* be clear when thou judgest.

---

[262] Luke 16:15,
[263] Ephesians 2:8-9
[264] Isaiah 64:6
[265] James 1:17

Read Luke 18:18-43

Luke 18:18 And a certain ruler asked him, saying, Good Master, **what shall I do** to inherit eternal life?

The young man in this Scripture believed that he could be saved by keeping the Law of God. Is that possible? Matthew 19 adds some more of the conversation Jesus had with him. He asks, "**What good thing shall I do** that I may have eternal life?" Jesus begins to enumerate the commandments of God, commandments which the young man believes he has kept all his life. Has he, or has any man, truly kept them all his life? Jesus made it clear that he was certainly not keeping the tenth, "Thou shalt not covet." His command, "Sell what you have and give to the poor, and come follow me," diagnosed the young man's true spiritual condition, because at that statement, he walked away sorrowfully,[266] valuing his great possessions more than obedience to the Savior.

This goes along with what Jesus taught in the Sermon on the Mount[267]. We may say that we have not committed adultery, but have we looked with lust in our hearts? We may say that we have never murdered, but do we have ungodly anger in our hearts? James says that if we have offended in one point of the Law, we have become guilty of all.[268] Jesus could make a request of any of us, a request that would diagnose our true spiritual condition, just as He did this man's.

We are either coming to God based on what we have done or what Christ has done for us. No one will ever be justified by the works of the Law.[269] The words of this old hymn say it very well.

Not the labor of my hands
Can fulfill Thy law's demands;
Could my zeal no respite know,
Could my tears forever flow,
All for sin could not atone;
Thou must save, and Thou alone.
Nothing in my hand I bring,
Simply to the cross I cling;
Naked, come to Thee for dress;
Helpless look to Thee for grace;
Foul, I to the fountain fly;
Wash me, Savior, or I die.[270]

[266] Matthew 19
[267] Matthew 5-7
[268] James 2:10
[269] Romans 3:20, Romans 3:28, Galatians 2:16, Galatians 3:11, Galatians 3:24, Galatians 5:4
[270] "Rock of Ages," Augustus M. Toplady

Read Luke 19:1-27

Luke 19:9-10 And Jesus said unto him, This day is salvation come to this house, forsomuch as he also is a son of Abraham. For the Son of man is come to seek and to save that which was lost.

Zacchaeus was a publican, one of the most despised members of society. Publicans were tax collectors, collecting revenue for the Roman government. Not only did they work for the despised oppressors, the Romans, they were often very dishonest. They grew rich, because they collected extra for themselves. Because of this, the word 'publican' became a synonym for 'vilest of sinners.' Zacchaeus was not just a publican, he was the *chief* of those vile sinners.

His desire to see Jesus was obviously more than just idle curiosity. Because of what happened next, we know that the Lord saw spiritual hunger in Zacchaeus' heart. The Lord called him by name and invited Himself to his house. As Jesus and Zacchaeus spent time together, a great miracle happened! Zacchaeus' spiritual hunger and thirst led to true repentance and salvation, evidenced by the restitution that he was willing to make. The Law required that when stolen money was returned, twenty percent was to be added to it[271]. Zacchaeus' restitution went far beyond this. Someone once said, "If God has your wallet, He has the rest of you too."

Zacchaeus was not saved, because his good works at the end outweighed his evil works before. He was saved through faith and repentance, a repentance evidenced by his willingness to make restitution. Good works do not save us, but they will be the evidence of true salvation.

Ephesians 2:8-10 For by grace are ye saved through faith; and that not of yourselves: *it is* the gift of God: Not of works, lest any man should boast. For we are his workmanship, created in Christ Jesus ***unto good works,*** which God hath before ordained that we should walk in them.

---

[271] Numbers 5:7

Read Luke 19.28-48

Luke 19:41 And when he was come near, he beheld the city, and wept over it,

Jesus was not weeping silently here.   The Greek word Luke uses indicates that He was sobbing, weeping aloud, even wailing.[272]   What He saw caused Him great pain and sorrow.   He had just been greeted by great crowds as He entered Jerusalem on Palm Sunday. But, for the most part, He was being rejected by His own people, just as prophesied, "He is despised and rejected of men; a man of sorrows, and acquainted with grief: and we hid as it were our faces from him; he was despised, and we esteemed him not."[273]

He wept at the results of their rejection.   A few short years later in AD 70 the Romans would do to Jerusalem exactly what Jesus prophesied. The ancient Jewish historian, Josephus[274], describes the destruction. The Romans surrounded the city, cutting off all supply routes.   Without supplies, men women and children began to die of starvation.   At first, they buried the bodies, but soon there were too many and they started tossing them over the city walls. Even Titus, the Roman emperor, was disgusted when he saw such horrible death and carnage. The city was destroyed, including God's temple.   The destruction was so complete that literally, "not one stone was left on another."[275]   Their rejection cost them dearly.

His weeping reminds us that, just as the Word declares, God is not willing that any should perish, nor does He rejoice in the death of the wicked.[276] Although rejection brings judgment and great sorrow to the heart of God, repentance brings salvation and great joy. If you have not yet received Him, turn from your sin and turn to Him now, before the time of judgment comes. Heaven will rejoice!

Luke 15:7 I say unto you, that likewise joy shall be in heaven over one sinner that repenteth, more than over ninety and nine just persons, which need no repentance.

---

[272] κλαίω (klah'-yo). Strong's Talking Greek & Hebrew Dictionary.
[273] Isaiah 53:3
[274] *Wars of the Jews*, 5.12.1-3, Flavius Josephus.
[275] Mark 13:2
[276] Ezekiel 33:11, 2 Peter 3:9

Read Luke 20.1-19

Luke 20:15-16 15 So they cast him out of the vineyard, and killed *him*. What therefore shall the lord of the vineyard do unto them? 16 He shall come and destroy these husbandmen, and shall give the vineyard to others. And when they heard *it*, they said, God forbid.

This is the conclusion of another of Jesus' parables, a parable that speaks of the Jews' rejection of Him and the dire consequences that would follow. Isaiah uses some of the same imagery in the parable of the vineyard in Isaiah 5:1-7. The Lord planted His vineyard (Israel) in a very fruitful place (the land of Israel). He did everything He could for His vineyard, including building a fence around it for protection. Sadly, when He came looking for fruit, He found none.

In Jesus' parable, the Lord placed husbandmen (caretakers) in charge of His vineyard. These husbandmen probably represent the religious leaders of Israel. He sent prophets to check on His vineyard and those who were watching it, but the religious leaders rejected and abused them. Finally, He sent His own son, and the caretakers of the vineyard rejected and killed the son too, just as they would soon turn Jesus over to be crucified. Rejection brings judgment. Soon, those ungodly religious leaders would no longer have charge of God's people. That ministry would be turned over to others[277].

This parable teaches that judgment and destruction will come to those who reject the Son. We also know that to receive the Son is to receive life. What have *you* done with the Son?

1 John 5:12 **He** that hath the Son hath life; *and* he that hath not the Son of God hath not life.

---

[277] This is a reference to the church the Lord said He would build, not Jew or Gentile, but something new. Matthew 16:18, Galatians 3:28.

Read Luke 20.20-47

Luke 20:47, "Which devour widows' houses, and for a shew make long prayers: the same shall receive greater damnation."

Is all sin the same?   It *is* the same in that it separates us from a holy God[278].   It *is* the same in that we are all guilty sinners in need of a Savior[279].   However, it **is not** the same as to the degree of punishment one may receive in the hereafter.   The New Testament bears out that certain sins *are* worse than others in that regard.   Hypocrisy must be one of those sins.   In Luke 20:47, Jesus speaks of those who will receive **greater** damnation, because of the nature of their sin.

We find this principle elsewhere in the New Testament.   In Matthew 11:21-22 Jesus spoke of the cities of Chorazin and Bethsaida where He had done many mighty works.   He said that those cities would face a greater punishment on judgment day than some other cities who had not been so blessed.   Peter says in 2nd Peter 2:20-21 that it would be better to have never known the way than to have known and then turn away from it.   James 3:1 indicates that those who teach the Word may be held to a higher standard of judgment than others.   The principle behind these Scriptures must be the one we find in Luke 12:48, "To whom much is given, of him much shall be required."   In spite of this, we must *never* try to lessen our own sin, or compare it with that of others.   Sin should always be taken seriously, and confessed to God.   Confession brings cleansing, regardless of the sin.

1 John 1:8-10, "If we say that we have no sin, we deceive ourselves, and the truth is not in us. If we confess our sins, he is faithful and just to forgive us *our* sins, and to cleanse us from all unrighteousness. If we say that we have not sinned, we make him a liar, and his word is not in us."

---

[278] Isaiah 59:1-2
[279] Romans 3:10-12

Read Luke 21:1-33

Luke 21:1-4 And he looked up, and saw the rich men casting their gifts into the treasury. 2 And he saw also a certain poor widow casting in thither two mites. 3 And he said, Of a truth I say unto you, that this poor widow hath cast in more than they all: 4 For all these have of their abundance cast in unto the offerings of God: but she of her penury hath cast in all the living that she had.

The treasury was in the court of the women in the temple[280]. There were thirteen trumpet-shaped receptacles in that court, into which offerings were placed. Some of the thirteen were marked and designated for required offerings, others for voluntary offerings. It may have been a play on words, because of the shape of these receptacles, that Jesus spoke of hypocrites who "sounded a trumpet" when they gave so that others would applaud them for their giving.[281] This may have been the attitude of the rich men that Jesus speaks of here in Luke 21. Onlookers may have commended them for their generous gifts, but the One who really matters saw how *little* they actually gave.

On the other hand, the widow's gift must have seemed trivial by comparison. Those two mites, tiny copper coins, amounted to about 1% of a days' wages, and it was all she had. The sound of her dropping those tiny coins was probably not heard by anyone nearby, but the One who really matters knew how sacrificial her gift really was. Someone once said, "The value of a gift is determined by what it *cost* the giver; this is what made the widow's gift so valuable."[282]

2 Corinthians 9:6-7 6 But this *I say*, He which soweth sparingly shall reap also sparingly; and he which soweth bountifully shall reap also bountifully. 7 Every man according as he purposeth in his heart, *so let him give*; not grudgingly, or of necessity: for God loveth a cheerful giver.

---

[280]This was not an area for women only, but the area beyond which women could not go.
[281] Matthew 6:1-2
[282] Enduring Word Commentary, David Guzik.

Read Luke 21:34-22:23

Luke 22:16 For I say unto you, I will not any more eat thereof, until it be fulfilled in the kingdom of God.

Luke 22:18 For I say unto you, I will not drink of the fruit of the vine, until the kingdom of God shall come.

Jesus fulfilled all that the Passover Lamb represented by His suffering, death, and resurrection. The untold thousands of Passover lambs killed in the centuries before this were only shadows, shadows of the One *True* Passover Lamb, the Lord Jesus Christ![283] His death would fulfill all that was under the Law, bringing those who believe into the provisions of the New Covenant!

Keeping the Passover, according to the strict observance of the Law would become impossible after AD 70 when the temple was destroyed,[284] but the early Christians continued to observe the meal that Jesus instituted in that Upper Room, the breaking of bread, remembering His death.[285] This was a part of their worship on the Lord's Day, the first day of the week.[286] We are commanded to do likewise, until He comes.[287] Jesus is with us spiritually each time we come together in His Name,[288] but we will, in some marvelous new way, literally eat and drink with Him once again in the Father's Kingdom at the Marriage Supper of the Lamb. I am looking forward to that day!

Revelation 19:7-9 7 Let us be glad and rejoice, and give honour to him: for the marriage of the Lamb is come, and his wife hath made herself ready. 8 And to her was granted that she should be arrayed in fine linen, clean and white: for the fine linen is the righteousness of saints. 9 And he saith unto me, Write, Blessed *are* they which are called unto the marriage supper of the Lamb. And he saith unto me, These are the true sayings of God.

---

[283] Colossians 2:16-17, Hebrews 10:1, 1 Corinthians 5:7
[284] Deuteronomy 16:5-6
[285] Acts 2:42, Acts 2:46
[286] Acts 20:7
[287] 1 Corinthians 11:26
[288] Matthew 18:20

Read Luke 22.24-53

Luke 22:31-32 31 And the Lord said, Simon, Simon, behold, Satan hath desired *to have* you, that he may sift *you* as wheat: 32 But I have prayed for thee, that thy faith fail not: and when thou art converted, strengthen thy brethren.

The Lord knew that Peter was being 'set up' by Satan. He also knew that he would give in to that temptation, denying His Lord and sealing that denial with a curse.   Our Lord is omniscient (all knowing).   He knows what we are going to face tomorrow, and every tomorrow that will follow. Knowing what we will need in the days ahead, He is already interceding for us, as He was for Peter.   Jesus is praying that in all we face we will have unfailing overcoming faith![289]

Our Great Intercessor also knew that Peter would repent and find restoration.   He knew that what Satan meant for evil in Peter's life was going to be turned into something good.[290]   Peter was able to strengthen others facing battles of various kinds, because of what the Lord brought *him* through.   This is just what we are promised in in 2 Corinthians 1.

2 Corinthians 1:3-4 3 Blessed *be* God, even the Father of our Lord Jesus Christ, the Father of mercies, and the God of all comfort; 4 Who comforteth us in all our tribulation, that we may be able to comfort them which are in any trouble, by the comfort wherewith we ourselves are comforted of God.

---

[289] Hebrews 7:25
[290] Genesis 50:20, Romans 8:28

Read Luke 22:54-23:12

Luke 22:69 Hereafter shall the Son of man sit on the right hand of the power of God.

Jesus endured horrible cruelty at the hands of His accusers, even *before* He went to the cross. Some of what He endured must have been so vile that Luke does not speak of it specifically. He simply says that they spoke *many* blasphemous things against Him. His accusers asked, "Are you the Christ?" His answer speaks volumes about the condition of their hearts. He simply says, "If I tell you, you will not believe." In fact, He had already told them, but they rejected His words. Then they asked, "Are you the Son of God?" It is not as clear in English as it is in the original, but He answers very strongly that He is. That statement alone was enough for them to sentence Him. They were rejecting their Creator, their Messiah, the Son of God.

Jesus stood before **them** that day, but there is coming a day when the tables will be turned. They will stand before **Him** on the day of judgment. All who do not turn to Him as Savior now, will face Him as Judge then at the Great White Throne Judgment.[291] They will see Him in His power and glory. They will recognize who He is, and regret what they have done (or not done). They may even bow before Him, but it will be too late. Let us bow before Him *now*, confessing that He is Lord!

Romans 14:11 For it is written, *As* I live, saith the Lord, every knee shall bow to me, and every tongue shall confess to God.

---

[291] Revelation 20:11-15

Read Luke 23.13-43

Luke 23:30 Then shall they begin to say to the mountains, Fall on us; and to the hills, **Cover us.**

     As Jesus was led away to be crucified, great numbers of people, including some faithful women were weeping and wailing over what they were seeing. Don't weep for me, He said, weep for those who reject me.   Jesus was very much in control of what was happening. His life was not being taken from Him.   He was giving His life, no one really had the power to take it from Him.[292]   The greatest tragedy is that of not receiving Him.

     Jesus tells of the fate of those who reject Him.   Some of this may look forward to AD 70 when Jerusalem was destroyed, but it also seems to look beyond this to the Great Tribulation.   Jesus' words remind us of a time spoke of in Revelation 6, a time when those who reject Him will be in fear, because of His wrath being poured out on the earth.   Sadly, it does not seem that they repent, but vainly try to hide from Him. How wonderful to live in the day when salvation is available to all! Now is the time to come to Him for mercy and grace!

Revelation 6:15-17 15 And the kings of the earth, and the great men, and the rich men, and the chief captains, and the mighty men, and every bondman, and every free man, hid themselves in the dens and in the rocks of the mountains; 16 And said to the mountains and rocks, Fall on us, and **hide us** from the face of him that sitteth on the throne, and from the wrath of the Lamb: 17 For the great day of his wrath is come; and who shall be able to stand?

---

[292] John 10:17-18

Read Luke 23.44-24.18

Luke 23:45 And the sun was darkened, and the veil of the temple was rent in the midst.

The veil of the temple separated everyone from the Holy of Holies, the location of the Ark of the Covenant. In those days, the Ark represented the manifest presence of God on the earth. Only the High Priest could venture behind that veil, and then only at a specified time, with careful preparation. Entering that place carelessly would mean certain death!

The veil was heavy. Early Jewish sources indicate that it may have been as thick as a man's hand. It took more than a mere earthquake to rip it in two. It took a supernatural act of God, and demonstrated some glorious things that Jesus accomplished on the cross. First, He made a way for sinful human beings to gain access to the Father. Hebrews says that we can now come boldly to the throne of grace.[293] Second, the day of temples, special places one must visit to encounter God, is over. Now, the Lord says, our bodies are the temple of the Holy Ghost.[294] We can have access to the Father through the Lord Jesus Christ!

Romans 5:1-2 1 Therefore being justified by faith, we have peace with God through our Lord Jesus Christ: 2 By whom also we have access by faith into this grace wherein we stand, and rejoice in hope of the glory of God.

---

[293] Hebrews 4:16
[294] 1 Corinthians 6:19-20

Read Luke 24:19-53

Luke 24:49 And, behold, I send the promise of my Father upon you: but tarry ye in the city of Jerusalem, until ye be endued with power from on high.

Luke records Jesus' final words to His disciples before He ascended back to heaven. They were to tarry in Jerusalem. Some say the word tarry means to "wait with anticipation." That is what they did. After Jesus ascended to heaven, they met for prayer and continued in prayer for ten days until the Day of Pentecost. Those ten days were filled with expectation. They were not told how long to tarry, only to tarry until they were endued with power from on high. In Acts 1, Luke adds more detail about what Jesus told them to expect. The power would come through the experience of the Baptism in the Holy Spirit.[295] Through that experience, the Holy Spirit would provide the power they needed to reach the whole world for Jesus.[296] All who obediently tarried were filled with the Holy Spirit, spoke in other tongues, and received power to be His witnesses.[297]

We still need His power, if we are to accomplish what He has called us to do. I am glad that the Baptism in the Holy Spirit is still available to those who ask.

Luke 11:13 If ye then, being evil, know how to give good gifts unto your children: how much more shall *your* heavenly Father give the Holy Spirit to them that ask him?

---

[295] Acts 1:5
[296] Acts 1:8
[297] Acts 2:1-4

124

Read John 1:1-28

John 1:1-4 1 In the beginning was the Word, and the Word was with God, and the Word was God. 2 The same was in the beginning with God. 3 All things were made by him; and without him was not anything made that was made. 4 In him was life; and the life was the light of men.

God has provided us with four Gospels. Each of them tells us the story of Jesus from a different perspective. Matthew, written to a Jewish audience, begins with a genealogy tracing Jesus' earthly ancestry back to both David and Abraham. Mark, written to a Roman audience, is a book of action, telling more about what Jesus did than what He said. It is fast-paced and begins with His baptism. Luke begins with the most familiar version of the story of Jesus' birth, tracing His ancestry back to Adam, because He is the Savior of *all* mankind. John's story of Jesus begins long before the other three—in eternity past.

Jesus, the Word, heaven's greatest communication is eternal. He was present in the beginning when all else was created.[298] He was not only *with* God, He is God. That is the mystery of the Trinity. We worship only one God, yet He is revealed as Father, Son, and Holy Spirit. To deny that Jesus is God come in human flesh is one of the marks of a false cult.

Jesus, the Word, is Creator. All things were made by Him. The book of Colossians reminds us what that word "all" includes. It includes everything that is visible *and* everything that is invisible. It includes everything that is in heaven *and* everything that is on the earth. It includes everything in the material world *and* everything in the unseen spiritual world. Not only did He create everything, He sustains or holds it together.[299] All things were created by Him, and *for* Him.

[298] **Genesis 1:1** In the beginning God created the heaven and the earth.
[299] **Colossians 1:16-17** 16 For by him were all things created, that are in heaven, and that are in earth, visible and invisible, whether *they be* thrones, or dominions, or principalities, or powers: all things were created by him, and for him: 17 And he is before all things, and by him all things consist [literally holds them together].

Jesus, the Word, is light and life.   God is light and in Him is no darkness at all.[300]   He is said to dwell in light so glorious that no one can approach it.[301]   This will necessitate our bodies being glorified so that we can live in His presence some day.   Outside of that, it would be easier to stand eight inches from the sun itself than to stand in the Presence of the Son of God in all His glory, for His glory far outshines the sun and every other light in the universe combined.   His glorious light will be the light of our eternal home,[302] and His light brings life!

Jesus, the Word, became flesh and dwelt (literally made His tabernacle) among us. The Old Testament tabernacle was God dwelling among His people, while they were in the wilderness. Jesus is the ultimate fulfillment of that.   God came down and lived among us. He became a human being, living on earth, ultimately dying on our behalf.   What a wonderful Savior!   The words of some of the old hymns include some of this same great theology.   This familiar carol is a fine example of that "Jesus Theology!"

Christ, by highest heaven adored
Christ, the everlasting Lord;
Late in time behold Him come
Offspring of a virgin's womb.
Veiled in flesh the Godhead see;
Hail th' Incarnate Deity,
Pleased as man with man to dwell;
Jesus, our Emmanuel.
Hark the heralds angels sing, "Glory to the newborn king."
Hail, the heav'n-born Prince of Peace!
Hail, the Son of Righteousness!
Light and life to all He brings,
Ris'n with healing in His wings.
Mild He lays His glory by,
Born that man no more may die,
Born to raise the sons of earth, born to give them second birth.
Hark the heralds angels sing, "Glory to the newborn King.[303]

---

[300] **1 John 1:5** **This** then is the message which we have heard of him, and declare unto you, that God is light, and in him is no darkness at all.

[301] **1 Timothy 6:15-16** 15 Which in his times he shall shew, *who is* the blessed and only Potentate, the King of kings, and Lord of lords; 16 Who only hath immortality, dwelling in the light which no man can approach unto; whom no man hath seen, nor can see: to whom *be* honour and power everlasting. Amen.

[302] **Revelation 21:23** **And** the city had no need of the sun, neither of the moon, to shine in it: for the glory of God did lighten it, and the Lamb *is* the light thereof.

[303] "Hark the Heralds Angels Sing," Charles Wesley and George Whitefield.

Read John 1:29-51

John 1:29-30 29 The next day John seeth Jesus coming unto him, and saith, Behold the Lamb of God, which taketh away the sin of the world. 30 This is he of whom I said, after me cometh a man which is preferred before me: for he was before me.

John the Baptist was Jesus' cousin, a man sent by God to prepare the way for the coming of the Messiah.[304]   He was the last of the Old Testament prophets (dying before the cross and resurrection of Jesus), and though no miracles are attributed to him, Jesus called him the greatest of the prophets.[305]

There is so much in John's life that should be emulated in our own. Anointed by the Holy Spirit, He directed attention to Jesus all his earthly life and ministry[306].   He said of Jesus, "He must increase, I must decrease.[307]"   He directed attention to Jesus as the Lamb of God, the One who would take away the sin of the world, the message a fallen world still needs to hear!

By the power of the Holy Spirit may we decrease, so that Jesus can increase in our lives.   May our lives and witness ever and always point to Jesus, the Lamb of God!

Acts 1:8 But ye shall receive power, after that the Holy Ghost is come upon you: and ye shall be witnesses unto me both in Jerusalem, and in all Judaea, and in Samaria, and unto the uttermost part of the earth.

---

[304] **John 1:23 He** said, I *am* the voice of one crying in the wilderness, make straight the way of the Lord, as said the prophet Esaias.

[305] **Luke 7:28 For** I say unto you, among those that are born of women there is not a greater prophet than John the Baptist: but he that is least in the kingdom of God is greater than he.

[306] **John 16:13-14** 13 Howbeit when he, the Spirit of truth, is come, he will guide you into all truth: for he shall not speak of himself; but whatsoever he shall hear, *that* shall he speak: and he will shew you things to come. 14 He shall glorify me: for he shall receive of mine, and shall shew *it* unto you.

[307] **John 3:30 He** must increase, but I *must* decrease.

Read John 2

John 2:11 This beginning of miracles did Jesus in Cana of Galilee, and manifested forth his glory; and his disciples believed on him.

There are myths and apocryphal books about Jesus performing miracles as a little child. However, John makes it quite clear that Jesus' first miracle was turning water into wine. There is sometimes controversy about the nature of this wine. Was it fermented wine, or unfermented? The New Testament word can be used both ways. However, it seems highly unlikely that Jesus would violate the Word of God that makes it so very clear that we are not to even look upon intoxicating beverages[308]. It is tragic today that so many invite the demonic influence of alcohol into their homes at their weddings, while Jesus does not seem to be invited!

It is notable that Jesus and His disciples were invited to this wedding celebration, a celebration that might last several days, and they came and participated in the festivities! When godly people marry today, they should always make sure that Jesus is invited to the wedding and to the marriage that follows. In a very real sense, the vows are made before Him, the unseen Guest. He is the Creator of marriage and it is one of His greatest gifts. His plan is that the marriage covenant be an earthly picture of the relationship between the Lord and His Church, and His presence is the glory of a Christian home. Yes, Biblical marriage *is* under attack in our world today, but godly marriage is cause for great celebration!

Have you invited Jesus into your marriage? His presence makes all the difference in the world!

Lord, we invite You into our marriages, our homes, and our families. We want to live our lives knowing that You are our unseen Guest. We pray that your glory would be manifest in our homes, and that we would ever and always glorify Your Great Name by the way we live our lives. In Jesus' Name. Amen

---

[308] **Proverbs 20:1 Wine** *is* a mocker, strong drink *is* raging: and whosoever is deceived thereby is not wise.
Proverbs 23:29-35 29 Who hath woe? who hath sorrow? who hath contentions? who hath babbling? who hath wounds without cause? who hath redness of eyes? 30 They that tarry long at the wine; they that go to seek mixed wine. 31 Look not thou upon the wine when it is red, when it giveth his colour in the cup, *when* it moveth itself aright. 32 At the last it biteth like a serpent, and stingeth like an adder. 33 Thine eyes shall behold strange women, and thine heart shall utter perverse things. 34 Yea, thou shalt be as he that lieth down in the midst of the sea, or as he that lieth upon the top of a mast. 35 They have stricken me, *shalt thou say, and* I was not sick; they have beaten me, *and* I felt *it* not: when shall I awake? I will seek it yet again.

Read John 3:1-21

John 3:16-17 16 For God so loved the world, that he gave his only begotten Son, that whosoever believeth in him should not perish, but have everlasting life. 17 For God sent not his Son into the world to condemn the world; but that the world through him might be saved

    John 3:16 is probably the best-known verse in the Bible. It is part of Jesus' dealings with a prominent religious leader named Nicodemus. Many Jews of that day believed they were assured a place in heaven, because they could trace their ancestry back to Abraham.   One rabbi even spoke of Abraham standing at the gates of hell to make sure that not one of his descendants went there accidentally. However, Jesus makes it clear to Nicodemus, and to us, that it is not our natural birth that prepares us for eternity, but our spiritual birth. He makes it VERY clear, "You MUST be born *again*!"

    Someone once said, "If you are only born once, you will die twice, but if you are born twice, you will only die once." That is a very true statement.   If all we have is our physical birth, our entrance into this world, our sin will, ultimately, take us to hell, something Revelation calls the Second Death[309].   But, if we are born again, by the Spirit of God, the second death will have no power over us[310].

---

[309] **Revelation 21:8**   But the fearful, and unbelieving, and the abominable, and murderers, and whoremongers, and sorcerers, and idolaters, and all liars, shall have their part in the lake which burneth with fire and brimstone: which is the second death.

[310] **Revelation 20:6**   Blessed and holy *is* he that hath part in the first resurrection: on such the second death hath no power, but they shall be priests of God and of Christ, and shall reign with him a thousand years.

How are we born again? Is simply believing in the existence of God enough. No, the Bible tells us that even demon spirits believe that much.[311] Jesus illustrates the kind of belief that does save us with an unusual story from the Old Testament. The Israelites sinned and judgment for their sin came in the form of dangerous snakes. Many people died from their venomous bites, but Moses was given an unusual solution. He was told to make a brass representation of one of those reptiles and put it atop a pole, so all could see it. It would be a reminder of their sin and its consequences--death. But, they were also promised, "if you will look, you will live."[312] Today, we don't look to a brazen serpent, we look to the cross. The cross reminds *us* of *our* sin and its consequences---death. The wages of sin is still death![313] His death was judgment for our sins, but if we will look to Him, we can live!

Isaiah 45:22 Look unto me, and be ye saved, all the ends of the earth: for I *am* God, and *there is* none else.

---

[311] **Revelation 20:6** Blessed and holy *is* he that hath part in the first resurrection: on such the second death hath no power, but they shall be priests of God and of Christ, and shall reign with him a thousand years.

[312] **Numbers 21:4-9** 4 And they journeyed from mount Hor by the way of the Red sea, to compass the land of Edom: and the soul of the people was much discouraged because of the way. 5 And the people spake against God, and against Moses, Wherefore have ye brought us up out of Egypt to die in the wilderness? for *there is* no bread, neither *is there any* water; and our soul loatheth this light bread. 6 And the LORD sent fiery serpents among the people, and they bit the people; and much people of Israel died. 7 Therefore the people came to Moses, and said, We have sinned, for we have spoken against the LORD, and against thee; pray unto the LORD, that he take away the serpents from us. And Moses prayed for the people. 8 And the LORD said unto Moses, Make thee a fiery serpent, and set it upon a pole: and it shall come to pass, that every one that is bitten, when he looketh upon it, shall live. 9 And Moses made a serpent of brass, and put it upon a pole, and it came to pass, that if a serpent had bitten any man, when he beheld the serpent of brass, he lived.

[313] **Romans 6:23** For the wages of sin *is* death; but the gift of God *is* eternal life through Jesus Christ our Lord.

Read John 3:22-36

John 3:30   He must increase, but I *must* decrease.

These words from the mouth of John the Baptist, summarize the way that he lived his life.   John was the forerunner, the one calling people to prepare for the coming of the Messiah.   John 1 says that he came to bear witness of the Light, the Lord Jesus Christ[314].   That is the same word we find in Acts 1:8 where it is said that *we* will bear witness in the power of the Holy Spirit[315].   The word in the original Greek language is 'martyria.'   You may notice that it bears a resemblance to the English word martyr, because they both come from the same root word.   A martyr is one who gives his or her life for a cause.   We may not all be called to die for our faith, but the Holy Spirit will give us power to bear witness faithfully until He calls us home.

The Holy Spirit will always seek to glorify the Lord Jesus Christ[316], so when we are operating in His power and anointing, we will have the same attitude that John had.   Jesus must increase, we must decrease.   A truly Spirit-filled Christian will bear witness of the Light of the World as long as they live.

Acts 1:8   But ye shall receive power, after that the Holy Ghost is come upon you: and ye shall be witnesses unto me both in Jerusalem, and in all Judaea, and in Samaria, and unto the uttermost part of the earth.

---

[314] **John 1:6-8** 6 There was a man sent from God, whose name *was* John. 7 The same came for a witness, to bear witness of the Light, that all *men* through him might believe. 8 He was not that Light, but *was sent* to bear witness of that Light.

[315] **Acts 1:8**   But ye shall receive power, after that the Holy Ghost is come upon you: and ye shall be witnesses unto me both in Jerusalem, and in all Judaea, and in Samaria, and unto the uttermost part of the earth.

[316] **John 16:13-14** 13 Howbeit when he, the Spirit of truth, is come, he will guide you into all truth: for he shall not speak of himself; but whatsoever he shall hear, *that* shall he speak: and he will shew you things to come. 14 He shall glorify me: for he shall receive of mine, and shall shew *it* unto you.

Read John 4:1-30

John 4:14   But whosoever drinketh of the water that I shall give him shall never thirst; but the water that I shall give him shall be in him a well of water springing up into everlasting life.

Jesus and the disciples were going back to Galilee from Judea.   They took the route that most devout Jews would not have taken, even if it were shorter, the road that took them through Samaria.   The Samaritans were despised by many of the Jews, for a number of reasons.   Their ancestors were Jews who had intermarried with the pagan people in the land, and they developed a religion which was contrary to that of the Jews.   They even had their own temple, rather than the temple in Jerusalem.   Samaria might have been considered the worst of "bad neighborhoods" and most Jews did not willingly spend time with those who were from there.   But, as it turns out, there was a clear reason to take that route.   There was a thirsty soul there, one ready to receive the Good News!

It was no accident that Jesus met a thirsty woman at Jacob's well that day, for this was a divine appointment.   She was there at an unusual time, the heat of the day, a time most women would have long since drawn their water, but it was God's perfect timing.   She had a checkered past, having been married five times, and was now living in sin with someone else[317]. Each time she must have thought to herself, "Maybe this relationship will fill the emptiness I feel." Of course, none of them did.   Only Jesus can satisfy the deep longing in the human heart.   Jesus told her of the Living Water, the wonderful salvation that He offered, and that she would never again have to look for happiness and fulfillment in all the wrong places.   Things could be eternally different for her!   She immediately began to tell others, and her testimony must have been effective, because years later when Philip went down to Samaria, he found them ready to receive the Gospel[318].   How powerful is the testimony of a changed life!

John 4:28-29 28 The woman then left her waterpot, and went her way into the city, and saith to the men, 29 Come, see a man, which told me all things that ever I did: is not this the Christ?

---

[317] There are some today who equate living together with marriage.   After all, they say, "marriage is just a piece of paper."   That is obviously not what Jesus believed.   She may have been living with a man, but Jesus made it clear, he was *not* her husband.

[318] Acts 8

Read John 4:31-54

John 4:35 Say not ye, There are yet four months, and *then* cometh harvest? behold, I say unto you, Lift up your eyes, and look on the fields; for they are white already to harvest.

Earlier in this chapter, Jesus shared amazing Gospel truths with a Samaritan woman at Jacob's well[319]. She believed and went back to town telling everyone about Jesus and what she had heard[320]. Following this, Jesus reminded His disciples of a popular saying of that day, "There are four months and then comes harvest." It was the equivalent of saying, "We won't worry about that until tomorrow. Harvest is still a long way off." But, they could not afford to wait when it came to the harvest of lost souls in Samaria. The time was *now*!

They found the people ready to receive the truth. The Holy Spirit had prepared their hearts and Samaria was truly now "white already to harvest!" Many Samaritans came to faith, because of the testimony of the woman who first shared Jesus with them. They were so ready!

Wanting to know more, they begged Jesus to stay longer, and over a period of two days, many others believed that Jesus was the Christ, the Messiah, the Savior of the world! Sometimes we are sowing seeds, sometimes we are watering, but the harvest is always His[321]. The need of that hour, and this one, is for laborers in God's whitened harvest fields.

Luke 10:2 Therefore said he unto them, The harvest truly *is* great, but the labourers *are* few: pray ye therefore the Lord of the harvest, that he would send forth labourers into **His Harvest.**

---

[319] Review yesterday's reading for some more insight on this.
[320] **John 4:28-29** 28 The woman then left her water pot, and went her way into the city, and saith to the men, 29 Come, see a man, which told me all things that ever I did: is not this the Christ?
[321] **1 Corinthians 3:6-7** 6 I have planted, Apollos watered; but God gave the increase. 7 So then neither is he that planteth anything, neither he that watereth; but God that giveth the increase.

Read John 5:1-23

John 5:8-9 8 Jesus saith unto him, Rise, take up thy bed, and walk. 9 And immediately the man was made whole, and took up his bed, and walked: and on the same day was the sabbath.

Many needy people were gathered on the five covered porches that surrounded the Pool of Bethesda. Bethesda means "house of mercy" a very fitting name, in light of what happened next. At certain times, the water in that spring-fed pool would move in a certain way. They believed that an unseen angel was troubling the water at those times and the first person in would receive their healing. It must have been sheer pandemonium as all of those folks tried their hardest to be the first one in when the waters were troubled. Can you imagine the disappointment most of them must have felt when they never quite made it and went home just as they came?

One man had been so disappointed for thirty-eight years. Jesus knew he had been waiting a long time, and asked, "Do you really want to be healed?" Of course, he wanted healing very much, but with his physical condition that had been impossible. He could never quite make it into the water first, but his disappointment turned to joy as Jesus healed him in a moment of time.

As wonderful as physical healing is, though, there is something far more important. Later when Jesus saw this man in the temple He said, "Sin no more, lest a worse thing come unto thee." This does not necessarily mean that his sickness was caused by personal sin. But, it does mean, though, that dying in one's sin, and spending eternity apart from God, is a far worse fate than merely being crippled for an earthly lifetime. The most important healing is *always* the healing of a sin-sick soul!

John 5:14 Afterward Jesus findeth him in the temple, and said unto him, Behold, thou art made whole: sin no more, lest a worse thing come unto thee.

Read John 5:24-47

John 5:25-26 25 Verily, verily, I say unto you, The hour is coming, and now is, when the dead shall hear the voice of the Son of God: and they that hear shall live. 26 For as the Father hath life in himself; so hath he given to the Son to have life in himself;

All life—physical *and* spiritual—is a gift from God. God breathed into the first man, Adam, and he became a living soul. [322] Every human being since has received their life from God. Because of this, Christians honor the sanctity of human life from "the womb to the tomb."

We also know that spiritual life comes from God. Outside of Him, we are dead in our trespasses and sin[323]. We are headed toward an eternity without God, a destiny the Bible calls the Second Death[324]. But, the moment we place our trust in Him, all that changes, we pass from death to life![325] Even our physical bodies will rise again on the Day of Resurrection, because of His life-giving command.

This is only possible, because He is Life. Unlike human beings who receive life as a gift, God has life inherent within Himself. He alone is the Life-Giver. Rejoice today in the life that is in the Son of God!

1 John 5:11-13 11 And this is the record, that God hath given to us eternal life, and this life **is in his Son**. 12 He that hath the Son hath life; *and* he that hath not the Son of God hath not life. 13 These things have I written unto you that believe on the name of the Son of God; that ye may **know** that ye have eternal life, and that ye may believe on the name of the Son of God.

---

[322] **Genesis 2:7** **And** the LORD God formed man *of* the dust of the ground, and breathed into his nostrils the breath of life; and man became a living soul.

[323] **Ephesians 2:1** And you *hath he quickened*, who were dead in trespasses and sins;

[324] **Revelation 21:8** But the fearful, and unbelieving, and the abominable, and murderers, and whoremongers, and sorcerers, and idolaters, and all liars, shall have their part in the lake which burneth with fire and brimstone: which is the second death.

[325] **John 5:24** **Verily**, verily, I say unto you, He that heareth my word, and believeth on him that sent me, hath everlasting life, and shall not come into condemnation; but is passed from death unto life.

Read John 6:1-21

John 6:9 There is a lad here, which hath five barley loaves, and two small fishes: but what are they among so many?

We often call this miracle, the feeding of the five thousand, but there were actually far more people than that. The original Greek language indicates that five thousand was just the number of men. We can assume there were also a great many women and children. There may have been as many as fifteen or twenty thousand hungry people there that day.

As the Creator of the universe, Jesus could have spoken a meal into existence. He could have rained down manna from heaven as He did for the Israelites, or satisfied their hunger with just a word. He did none of those things, but, instead allowed others to be a part of the miracle. First, a young man was willing to give up his simple lunch of five small barley loaves and two fish. Jesus blessed that lunch and began to break it, and as He did, the miracle of multiplication began to occur! His twelve disciples distributed the miraculous bounty provided by the Lord, and soon realized that there was plenty for everyone. There always is! There were even leftovers to take home, twelve baskets full, enough for each of the twelve to take some home.

What you have may seem meagre, not enough to meet the need. However, that kind of thinking does not take into consideration the power of the One we serve. It has been rightly said that "little is much when God is in it." He is still able to stretch and multiply what is submitted to Him.

Philippians 4:19 But my God shall supply all your need according to
his riches in glory by Christ Jesus.

Read John 6:22-40

John 6:32-33 Then Jesus said unto them, Verily, verily, I say unto you, Moses gave you not that bread from heaven; but my Father giveth you the true bread from heaven. 33 For the bread of God is he which cometh down from heaven, and giveth life unto the world.

Jesus had just fed thousands, miraculously, with only a few loaves of bread and some fish. As always, he used the miracle as a teaching point. Some in that crowd were asking Him for some kind of sign that they might believe---maybe a sign like their ancestors saw during the time of Moses.[326] One wonders why the miraculous multiplication of the bread and fish was not sign enough for them to believe. Jesus reminded them of how the Lord provided for their ancestors, sending down manna from heaven every day. Manna was a perfect, nourishing, and completely supernatural food. It appeared on the ground every morning, and there was enough for all.

But, as wonderful as the manna had been, and as wonderful as the feeding of the five thousand had been, they were only previews, pictures, of the real Bread from Heaven. Jesus makes it clear that *He* is the Bread of Life. That means that He is the One sent down from Heaven to provide all that we need. He is our everything, offering eternal life and eternal satisfaction. He told them, "I am the bread of life: he that comes to me shall never hunger; and he that believes on me shall never thirst."[327] He is all that I will need now and forever!

> He is my reason for living,
> Oh He is the king of all kings
> I long to be His possession,
> Oh, He is my everything![328]

---

[326] **John 6:30-31** 30 They said therefore unto him, What sign shewest thou then, that we may see, and believe thee? what dost thou work? 31 Our fathers did eat manna in the desert; as it is written, He gave them bread from heaven to eat.
[327] John 6:35
[328] "He is My Reason for Living," Dallas Frazier

Read John 6.41-71

John 6:51 I am the living bread which came down from heaven: if any man eat of this bread, he shall live forever: and the bread that I will give is my flesh, which I will give for the life of the world.

Bread is often called the staff of life, so it is fitting that Jesus calls Himself the Living Bread, the Bread that came down from Heaven. In fact, in Him we will find all that we need for life and eternity.[329] What does Jesus mean when He speaks of eating the bread and living forever? The satisfying bread of His salvation has been offered to us, but we must choose to do something about it. His salvation is a gift that we must receive[330]. We are reminded of that truth each time we take the Lord's Supper together, eating the bread and drinking the cup.

As Jesus spoke of His body and blood, looking forward to the cross, many of His followers were unable to receive His Words. They found them offensive. They just seemed too much for them. They said, "This is a hard saying; Who can hear it?[331]" And here we also find one of the saddest verses in the New Testament, "Because of His words, many of His disciples went away and did not walk with Him again!"[332] At that time, Jesus looked at Peter, one of the inner circle of disciples and asked, "Will you go away also?"[333] Peter's answer is a powerful statement of faith, "Lord, to whom shall we go? thou hast the words of eternal life. And we believe and are sure that thou art that Christ, the Son of the living God."

What about you? Have you heard His Words of Life? Do you believe that He is the Christ, the Son of the Living God? Have you received the One who is the Living Bread! There is life in no other!

John 1:12 But as many as received him, to them gave he power to become the sons of God, *even* to them that believe on his name:

---

[329] 2nd Peter 1:3
[330] John 1:12
[331] John 6:60
[332] John 6:66
[333] John 6:67

Read John 7:1-31

John 7:5 For neither did his brethren believe in him.

There are some very sad statements in this chapter. First, "Jesus would not walk in Jewry[334], because the Jews sought to kill him,"[335] and He said, "The world cannot hate you; but me it hateth, because I testify of it.[336]" I think the saddest words of all are these, "Neither did his brethren believe in him."

Jesus' brothers, actually half-brothers[337], those raised in the same carpenter's home in Nazareth with Him, the children of Joseph and Mary, did not yet believe. Jesus' words, spoken in His hometown, are very telling, "A prophet is not without honor, save in his own country, and in his own house."[338] Some of those among His circle of family and friends even thought he was out of His mind at times, because He was so involved in ministry that He did not even take time for meals.[339]

Did his family ever become believers? They certainly did! The miracle of His resurrection must have convinced them, because we find them present with the followers of Jesus in the Upper Room where Jesus' mother, his brothers, and a total of 120 others were baptized in the Holy Spirit.[340] Two of those former unbelieving brothers went on to write inspired Scripture---James and Jude. Do you have loved ones that still do not believe? Take heart, there is hope. Continue to pray for them. Pray that they have an encounter with the Living Lord! The words of Jesus' formerly unbelieving brother, Jude, are so very relevant at this point.

Jude 1:21 Keep yourselves in the love of God, looking for the mercy of our Lord Jesus Christ unto eternal life.

---

[334] The area around Jerusalem where many of the devout Jews lived.
[335] John 7:1
[336] John 7:7
[337] **Mark 6:3** Is not this the carpenter, the son of Mary, the brother of James, and Joses, and of Juda, and Simon? and are not his sisters here with us? And they were offended at him.
[338] Matthew 13:57
[339] **Mark 3:20-21** 20 And the multitude cometh together again, so that they could not so much as eat bread. 21 And when his friends heard *of it*, they went out to lay hold on him: for they said, He is beside himself.
[340] Acts 1:12-14, Acts 2:1-4

Read John 7:32-52

John 7:37-39 37 In the last day, that great *day* of the feast, Jesus stood and cried, saying, if any man thirst, let him come unto me, and drink. 38 He that believeth on me, as the scripture hath said, out of his belly shall flow rivers of living water. 39 (But this spake he of the Spirit, which they that believe on him should receive: for the Holy Ghost was not yet *given*; because that Jesus was not yet glorified.)

This was the final day of the eight-day Feast of Tabernacles, and Jerusalem was crowded with worshippers there for the feast. It was one of the greatest times of rejoicing and celebration on their religious calendar.   For the first seven days of the feast, the priests went to the Pool of Siloam and drew a pitcher of water, carrying it back to the temple with a procession of musicians, singers, and worshippers following behind. Once they reached the temple, the water would be poured out as an offering to the Lord.   The water represented the miraculous provision of water that God gave the Israelites when they were in the wilderness. However, on the eighth day, what John calls the "great day" of the feast, there was no water poured out.   Instead, they prayed for water, it was in this context, thousands of worshippers praying for water, that Jesus made His amazing statement about the *living* water. If you will remember, in John 4 Jesus spoke to a Samaritan woman about that water. He said it would be like a well, springing up into everlasting life[341].   Jesus was speaking to *her* about the presence of the Holy Spirit in our lives at salvation.   We can enjoy the benefits of that well of living water, for the Spirit dwells in every truly born-again believer. [342]   However, salvation is not the only work of the Holy Spirit.   We are also promised, and should earnestly seek to be baptized in the Spirit, an empowering for service[343].   I believe that is what Jesus is speaking of here in John 7.   When we are baptized in the Spirit, that same living water flows forth from our lives in ministry, joy, blessing, the gifts of the Spirit, and so much more!   Have you received the Holy Ghost since you believed?[344]   Have you been praying for water?   If not, why not ask Him right now for what He has promised you!

Luke 11:13 If ye then, being evil, know how to give good gifts unto your children: how much more shall *your* heavenly Father give the Holy Spirit to them that ask him?

---

[341] John 4:14
[342] Romans 8:9
[343] Acts 1:5
[344] Acts 19:1-7

Read John 7.53-8.24

John 8:7 So when they continued asking him, he lifted up himself, and said unto them, He that is without sin among you, let him first cast a stone at her.

At this point, the religious leaders of Jerusalem had a growing hatred and jealousy of Jesus. They often tried to trick Him into saying things that would snare Him, but of course they failed every time. That is what they were doing here. They brought a woman caught in the act of committing adultery. One may wonder what became of the man who was with her, but he is never mentioned! The penalty for committing adultery, under Old Testament Law, was death by stoning[345]. However, the Roman government in control at that time, did not give the Jews that right.   If Jesus had suggested stoning her as the Law of Moses demanded, He would have been in trouble with the Romans. Had He suggested letting her go, He would have been in trouble with the religious authorities. They would claim that He was disregarding the Law of Moses. How would He answer?

He answered with these words, "He that is without sin among you, let him cast the first stone."   Under the Law, a capital offense, such as murder or adultery, required the testimony of two or three witnesses [346]and those witnesses must be willing to cast the first stones, beginning the execution. Were the accusers willing to do that?   There is some indication that the original Greek actually reads, "He that is not guilty of this **same sin** let *him* cast the first stone."   Perhaps one she had been with was even among her accusers!   If not, they had all certainly committed adultery in their hearts.[347]   Full of shame and conviction, her accusers crept silently away.   Their sin was not in confronting sin, but in doing so hypocritically. The woman, on the other hand, must have had a repentant heart, for Jesus gives her these wonderful words of consolation, "Neither do I condemn thee, go and sin no more."   If *we* will come to Jesus with a repentant heart, He will speak those same sweet words to us today!

1 John 1:8-10 8 If we say that we have no sin, we deceive ourselves, and the truth is not in us. 9 If we confess our sins, he is faithful and just to forgive us *our* sins, and to cleanse us from all unrighteousness. 10 If we say that we have not sinned, we make him a liar, and his word is not in us.

---

[345] **Leviticus 20:10**
[346] **Numbers 35:30** ,Deuteronomy 19:15.
[347] **Matthew 5:27-28**

Read John 8:25-59

John 8:58-59   58 Jesus said unto them, Verily, verily, I say unto you, Before Abraham was, I am. 59 Then took they up stones to cast at him: but Jesus hid himself, and went out of the temple, going through the midst of them, and so passed by.

This is one of a number of times in the Gospel of John where Jesus makes the claim that He is God come in human flesh.   He said, "Before Abraham was, I am," and that was enough to throw the Jewish authorities into a rage. They were going to kill Him on the spot. The charge would have been blasphemy. We may not pick it up so easily in our English translations, but it was very clear to those who heard Him that day.   When He says, "Before Abraham was I AM," it is "ego eimi" in the original Greek of the New Testament. That means little to us, unless we are Greek speakers, but it is amazing to find out that it is the very same expression God used of Himself when speaking to Moses from the burning bush in Exodus 3:14!   When Moses asked the Lord about His name that day, the Lord said, "I AM THAT I AM[348]," which is the very same expression Jesus used of Himself here in John 8. It is no wonder that the very pious Jews took up stones to kill Him that day. He was claiming to be God!

Jesus uses that "ego eimi" phrase several times in the Gospel of John, each time making the same claim, "I am the Great I AM" of Exodus 3 come in human flesh!

1. I AM the Bread of Life (John 6:48).
2. I AM the Living Bread (John 6:51).
3. I AM the Light of the World (John 8:12).
4. I AM the Door of the Sheep (John 10:7).
5. I AM the Good Shepherd (John 10:14).
6. I AM the Resurrection and the Life (John 11:25).
7. I AM HE (John 13:19, John 18:5-8, Isaiah 41:4).
8. I AM the Way, the Truth, and the Life (John 14:6).
9. I AM the True Vine (John 15:1).
10.   I AM Alpha and Omega (Revelation 1:8[349]).

What a Mighty God is He![350]

---

[348] In the Septuagint, the ancient Greek translation of the Old Testament Scriptures, we find the very words that Jesus used in John 8, "Ego Eimi."   I AM.

[349] Although this is not in the Gospel of John, John was also the one inspired to write the Book of Revelation.

[350] Isaiah 9:6

Read John 9:1-12

John 9:2 And his disciples asked him, saying, Master, who did sin, this man, or his parents, that he was born blind?

Sickness and affliction like this man's blindness were not part of God's original plan for human beings.   Sickness, in general, is a result of mankind's fall into sin and the resulting curse.   In spite of that, Jesus makes it very clear here that not all sickness is a result of *personal* sin. It is not always something that *we* have done. The disciples, though, seem to have a mindset that is still prevalent in some circles today.   They believed the man was born blind because of someone's *personal* sin. It was something that either this man or his parents had done. Can a parents' sin impact the health of a baby? It certainly can. For example, think of a child born to a mother who drinks alcohol and is born with fetal alcohol syndrome. But, is parental sin *always* the reason? By no means!   For the man to have been born blind, because of his *own* personal sin would have *really* been a stretch.   Since he was born blind, he would have had to have sinned "in utero" that is while he was in his mother's womb!   Others might even say that he was blind, because he sinned in a previous life. Of course, that concept of "karma" and reincarnation is a pagan concept, and certainly has no part in a Christian's belief system.
What was Jesus' "take" on this? Who sinned?   Let His words speak for themselves, "Neither hath this man sinned, nor his parents."   What was the reason for His blindness then?   Jesus said it was that "the works of God should be made manifest in him."[351] Whatever the source of his blindness, the healing that ensued was going to bring glory to God.   While we strongly believe in divine healing, we would be remiss in saying that there aren't still some unexplainable mysteries. For example, why is one healed and another is not?   It is easy to attribute it to a "lack of faith," but that is simply not always the case.   The sovereignty, and timing, of God are beyond our ability to comprehend.   But until we know all the reasons why, we will continue to preach and believe that Jesus is both Savior and Healer.

Exodus 15:26 And said, If thou wilt diligently hearken to the voice of the LORD thy God, and wilt do that which is right in his sight, and wilt give ear to his commandments, and keep all his statutes, I will put none of these diseases upon thee, which I have brought upon the Egyptians: for I *am* the

---

[351] **John 9:3 Jesus** answered, Neither hath this man sinned, nor his parents: but that the works of God should be made manifest in him.

Read John 9.13-41

John 9:41 Jesus said unto them, If ye were blind, ye should have no sin: but now ye say, We see; therefore your sin remaineth.

There was a growing hatred of Jesus among the religious crowd in Jerusalem. It was instigated by Satan himself, but undoubtedly fueled by their jealousy of His popularity among the people. This, of course, would eventually culminate in His crucifixion. Earlier in this chapter, Jesus had healed a man that was born blind. Instead of rejoicing with him, those leaders made it a very controversial thing. After all, they said, "How could Jesus be of God, if He performed this miracle on the Sabbath?" Yet, others could not see how He could *not* be of God, after performing such an amazing miracle. Perhaps, they thought, it is a case of mistaken identity. Perhaps this is not the same man, or he really wasn't born blind. So, they began to investigate the validity of the miracle, and, of course, there was no doubt that it was genuine. He had truly been born blind, and now there was no doubt that he could see!

In spite of the facts, the religious leaders, refused to believe the truth, because they lived in the darkness of spiritual blindness. They claimed to be the enlightened ones, the ones who held the truth, yet they were actually blinder than the man that had once been blind. Someone once said, "No one is so blind as he who will not see[352]," and there are the words of the prophet Jeremiah, "Hear this, O foolish people, and without understanding; which have eyes and see not; which have ears, and hear not."[353] We are told in 2nd Corinthians 4:4, that there is one called the "god of this world," or Satan, who seeks to blind the minds, or spiritual understanding, of those who do not believe. Although, he can never extinguish the light of Christ or His truth, he can seek to blind eyes to it. That is the most tragic blindness of all.

If those religious leaders would have only admitted their spiritual blindness and turned to Jesus in repentance and faith, *their* eyes could have been opened, they could have seen the Light, and they could have been saved! Sadly, it does not appear that they did. What about you? Has He opened *your* eyes? Are *you* walking in His light?

Amazing Grace how sweet the sound that saved a wretch like me,
I once was lost, but now am found,
Was blind, but now, I see![354]

---

[352] Attributed to John Heywood, 1546.
[353] Jeremiah 5:21
[354] "Amazing Grace," John Newton

Read John 10:1-21

John 10:1 Verily, verily, I say unto you, He that entereth not by the door into the sheepfold, but climbeth up some other way, the same is a thief and a robber.

One of the most dangerous false doctrines is that of universalism. It is the idea that there is more than one way to heaven, or perhaps all roads will eventually lead there. As popular as that belief is today, it is a heresy that is responsible for many dying lost without Christ, and it is certainly never taught in God's Word.

In this chapter, Jesus calls Himself the Good Shepherd, and He compares His salvation to the sheepfold, the place where the sheep are kept. He tells us that the sheepfold has but one door. That door is Jesus Himself.[355] What about those who make the claim that there are other ways to heaven, other doors?   Jesus also makes that very clear. He says that those who try to find another way are thieves and robbers. Those who teach universalism are thieves, robbing the deceived of their very souls and eternity. A salvation that does not go through the Lord Jesus Christ is not salvation at all.

Perhaps one of Jesus' clearest statements about this is found in John 14:6 where He is telling the disciples about the way to heaven, the place that He calls the Father's House.   Hear His words and note the definite articles.

John 14:6 Jesus saith unto him, I am **THE** way, **THE** truth, and **THE** life: no man cometh unto the Father, but by me.

---

[355] **John 10:9** I am the door: by me if any man enter in, he shall be saved, and shall go in and out, and find pasture.

Read John 10:22-42

John 10:27 My sheep hear my voice, and I know them, and they follow me:

What does it mean to be one of Jesus' sheep? It means that we have come in through that one door, the Lord Jesus Christ, placing our full trust in Him as Lord and Savior. We recognize that He finished the work on the cross, and now offers us full salvation. What does He promise those who are His sheep? We see several promises about the Shepherd and His sheep here in John 10. Perhaps you can read and find more!

1. He gives abundant life to His sheep.
2. His sheep know Him
3. His sheep hear His voice.
4. He knows His sheep.
5. His sheep follow Him.
6. He gives His sheep eternal life.
7. His sheep will never perish.
8. His sheep are held in His hand,
9. No one can pluck His sheep out of His hand.

What a blessing to be one of the Good Shepherd's sheep!

Psalm 23:1-6 1 The LORD *is* my shepherd; I shall not want. 2 He maketh me to lie down in green pastures: he leadeth me beside the still waters. 3 He restoreth my soul: he leadeth me in the paths of righteousness for his name's sake. 4 Yea, though I walk through the valley of the shadow of death, I will fear no evil: for thou *art* with me; thy rod and thy staff they comfort me. 5 Thou preparest a table before me in the presence of mine enemies: thou anointest my head with oil; my cup runneth over. 6 Surely goodness and mercy shall follow me all the days of my life: and I will dwell in the house of the LORD forever.

Read John 11.1-31

John 11:11 These things said he: and after that he saith unto them, Our friend Lazarus sleepeth; but I go, that I may awake him out of sleep.

Sleeping is a common metaphor for the death of a believer. Lazarus had been very sick, and by the time Jesus arrived he had already died, but Jesus did not speak of his condition as death, but as sleep. His body was sleeping in the tomb, but you can be sure that his spirit was very much alive.

Some teach an unscriptural doctrine called soul sleep. It is the belief that *both* body **and** soul will sleep until the resurrection. The New Testament does not teach this.   For example, we know that Jesus told the repentant thief who was crucified with Him, "This day thou shalt be with me in Paradise[356]." We know that the apostle Paul fully believed that to absent from this body was not to be in an unconscious state, but meant being present with the Lord[357]. Even the account of the rich man and Lazarus, found in the Gospel of Luke, makes it clear that both the saved and the lost are very much aware after the death of the body[358].

Our Lord has promised never to leave us, or forsake us.   That means that living *or* dying, He is with us always!

1 Thessalonians 5:9-10 9 For God hath not appointed us to wrath, but to obtain salvation by our Lord Jesus Christ, 10 Who died for us, that, whether we wake or sleep, we should live together with him.

Philippians 1:21 For to me to live *is* Christ, and to die *is* gain.

---

[356] **Luke 23:43 And** Jesus said unto him, Verily I say unto thee, To day shalt thou be with me in paradise.
[357] **2 Corinthians 5:8 We** are confident, *I say*, and willing rather to be absent from the body, and to be present with the Lord.
[358] Luke 16:19-31. Note that this is a different Lazarus than the one raised here in John 11.

Read John 11:32-57

John 11:43 And when he thus had spoken, he cried with a loud voice, Lazarus, come forth.

Lazarus' body had been dead four days. They were reluctant to open his tomb, as Jesus asked, because his body was likely to be decomposing already. However, at Jesus' command, body and soul were reunited and Lazarus came back to life. Some have suggested that had Jesus simply said, "Come forth" instead of specifying Lazarus by name that all in that graveyard would have risen. Such is the power of His word. There is coming a day when all of those who are in the grave will hear His voice.[359]

The Word of God says that the Lord Himself will descend from heaven with a shout, with the voice of the archangel, and with the trump of God, and the dead in Christ shall rise first,[360] and that that coming resurrection is our Blessed Hope.[361] I hope to be listening for that call. It brings to mind an old spiritual that you may remember.

When He calls for me I will answer,
When He calls for me I will answer,
When He calls for me I will answer;
I'll be somewhere list'ning for my name.
I'll be somewhere list'ning,
I'll be somewhere list'ning,
I'll be somewhere list'ning for my name.
Oh, I'll be somewhere list'ning,
I'll be somewhere list'ning,
I'll be somewhere list'ning for my name[362].

---

[359] **John 5:28-29** 28 Marvel not at this: for the hour is coming, in the which all that are in the graves shall hear his voice, 29 And shall come forth; they that have done good, unto the resurrection of life; and they that have done evil, unto the resurrection of damnation.

[360] **1 Thessalonians 4:16-18** 16 For the Lord himself shall descend from heaven with a shout, with the voice of the archangel, and with the trump of God: and the dead in Christ shall rise first: 17 Then we which are alive *and* remain shall be caught up together with them in the clouds, to meet the Lord in the air: and so shall we ever be with the Lord. 18 Wherefore comfort one another with these words.

[361] **Titus 2:13** **Looking** for that blessed hope, and the glorious appearing of the great God and our Saviour Jesus Christ;

[362] "I'll be Somewhere Listening," Eduardo Lango.

Read John 12:1-19

John 12:12-13 On the next day much people that were come to the feast, when they heard that Jesus was coming to Jerusalem, Took branches of palm trees, and went forth to meet him, and cried, Hosanna: Blessed *is* the King of Israel that cometh in the name of the Lord.

The remainder of the Gospel of John will speak of Jesus' final week in Jerusalem. He had become very popular with many of the people. They were following Him in great numbers, because He had raised Lazarus from the dead,[363] and because they wanted to catch a glimpse of Lazarus. Lazarus had become somewhat of a celebrity himself because of his experience, so the people came not only to see Jesus, but to see the man alive after spending four days in the grave[364]! Yes, Jesus was popular with the people, except for one group, the religious leaders there in Jerusalem. They despised him. In fact, they were considering having Lazarus killed, because his testimony was encouraging too many people to follow Jesus.[365] It was in that kind of atmosphere that Jesus entered Jerusalem for the final time before His crucifixion. Thousands were already there for the Passover, and many of them, when they heard that Jesus was coming, greeted Him along the way with a reception fit for a king, waving palm branches, and shouting His praises. But, while one group was praising Him, another, sadly, was plotting His death. Even today, there are only two groups of people, those who have made Him King, and those who have rejected Him. What about you, have you received Him as King, Master, and Lord of *your* life? If not, do so without delay!

John 1:10-12 10 He was in the world, and the world was made by him, and the world knew him not. 11 He came unto his own, and his own received him not. 12 But as many as received him, to them gave he power to become the sons of God, *even* to them that believe on his name:

---

[363] See John 11.
[364] **John 12:9** **Much** people of the Jews therefore knew that he was there: and they came not for Jesus' sake only, but that they might see Lazarus also, whom he had raised from the dead.
John 12:17-19 17 The people therefore that was with him when he called Lazarus out of his grave, and raised him from the dead, bare record. 18 For this cause the people also met him, for that they heard that he had done this miracle. 19 The Pharisees therefore said among themselves, Perceive ye how ye prevail nothing? behold, the world is gone after him.
[365] **John 12:10-11** 10 But the chief priests consulted that they might put Lazarus also to death; 11 Because that by reason of him many of the Jews went away, and believed on Jesus.

Read John 12:20-43

John 12:28 Father, glorify thy name. Then came there a voice from heaven, *saying*, I have both glorified *it*, and will glorify *it* again.

Jesus' continual prayer during His earthly life and ministry was to glorify the Name of the Heavenly Father.   He prays that prayer here, just days before the crucifixion, and for the third time He hears an audible voice from heaven affirming His identity.

The first was at His baptism. Jesus was in the water, the Holy Spirit came down upon Him in the form of a dove, and the Father's voice spoke from Heaven with these words, "This is my beloved Son, in whom I am well pleased."[366] He is the Son of God!

The second was at the Transfiguration, where some of His heavenly glory was allowed to shine through.   Out of a cloud of glory, the Father's voice spoke once again, saying, "This is my beloved Son, in whom I am well pleased; hear ye Him."[367] He is the Son of God, and we dare not refuse what He says!

This third time, the Father's voice affirmed what Jesus had just prayed, "Glorify Thy Name," by saying, "I have both glorified it, and will glorify it again." Some thought that the voice was that of an angel, others thought it must have been thunder, but it was the Father's voice from heaven.   Jesus did not need that affirmation, but the disciples did.   He said, "The voice came not because of me, but for your sakes." He is the Son of God, we dare not refuse what He says, and like Him we must seek the Father's glory.

There is a Scriptural precedent that something must be confirmed in the mouth of two or three witnesses[368].   Here are three witnesses from heaven, affirming that Jesus is indeed the Christ, the Son of God, and that we must hear Him.   We must not refuse the One who speaks to us from heaven.   The writer of Hebrews says if those who rejected Moses' words (the one who spoke on the earth) did not escape God's judgment.   How much more will those who reject the voice of the One who speaks from heaven face that judgment.

Hebrews 12:25 See that ye refuse not him that speaketh. For if they escaped not who refused him that spake on earth, much more *shall not* we *escape*, if we turn away from him that *speaketh* from heaven:

---

[366] Matthew 3:17
[367] Matthew 17:5
[368] 2nd Corinthians 13:1

Read John 12:44-13:20

John 13:3-5 3 Jesus knowing that the Father had given all things into his hands, and that he was come from God, and went to God; 4 He riseth from supper, and laid aside his garments; and took a towel, and girded himself. 5 After that he poureth water into a basin, and began to wash the disciples' feet, and to wipe *them* with the towel wherewith he was girded.

Jesus, in coming to this earth, took upon Himself the form of a servant[369]. He laid aside His heavenly glory to live here as a man. The washing of feet was common practice, when one entered a home for a meal. People often went barefoot or in sandals and their feet would be soiled from the dusty streets. If a household had servants, it was the duty of the lowliest of them to wash the feet of the guests. This is what makes what Jesus did so remarkable.

Some have a literal foot washing service in conjunction with the Lord's Supper, and there is nothing wrong with that at all, but we must not forget that it is the symbolism that is *most* important. Jesus not only took the role of a servant, but He made it clear that we are also to take that same role among ourselves[370]. It is more than something we do occasionally as part of a church service; it is the walk, the daily lifestyle, of a follower of Jesus! This is what our Lord taught continually by both word and example

Mark 10:42-45 42 But Jesus called them *to him*, and saith unto them, Ye know that they which are accounted to rule over the Gentiles exercise lordship over them; and their great ones exercise authority upon them. 43 But so shall it not be among you: but whosoever will be great among you, shall be your minister: 44 And whosoever of you will be the chiefest, shall be servant of all. 45 For even the Son of man came not to be ministered unto, but to minister, and to give his life a ransom for many.

---

[369] **Philippians 2:6-8** 6 Who, being in the form of God, thought it not robbery to be equal with God: 7 But made himself of no reputation, and took upon him the form of a servant, and was made in the likeness of men: 8 And being found in fashion as a man, he humbled himself, and became obedient unto death, even the death of the cross.
[370] **John 13:13-14** 13 Ye call me Master and Lord: and ye say well; for *so* I am. 14 If I then, *your* Lord and Master, have washed your feet; ye also ought to wash one another's feet.

Read John 13:21-14:10

John 13:34 A new commandment I give unto you, That ye love one another; as I have loved you, that ye also love one another.

John has been called the Apostle of Love, because of the emphasis on love in his writings. His, for example, is the only one of the four Gospels that records Jesus' words in John 3:16, "For God so loved the world." He is the only one to tell us that "God is love,"[371] and He is the only one to record the words found here in John 13. We are to love others as He has loved us. When we do so, others will know that we are truly His disciples.

Love was not a new commandment in the sense that it had never been commanded by God before. At times Jesus quoted Leviticus 19:18, "Thou shalt love thy neighbor as thyself." But, it is a new commandment in the sense that Jesus gives new understanding of its implications. He calls it the greatest of the commandments.[372] Romans 13 tells us that love fulfills the Law of God.[373] This is not just ordinary human love, but supernatural love, agape love, love that we can only know through the power of the Holy Spirit.[374] We cannot love in this way, in our own strength and power. Humanly speaking, it is completely impossible, but by the power of the Spirit we can walk in His love, empowered to fulfill the Royal Law.

James 2:8 If ye fulfil the royal law according to the scripture, Thou shalt love thy neighbour as thyself, ye do well:

---

[371] **James 2:8 If** ye fulfil the royal law according to the scripture, Thou shalt love thy neighbour as thyself, ye do well:

[372] **Matthew 22:37-40** 37 Jesus said unto him, Thou shalt love the Lord thy God with all thy heart, and with all thy soul, and with all thy mind. 38 This is the first and great commandment. 39 And the second *is* like unto it, Thou shalt love thy neighbour as thyself. 40 On these two commandments hang all the law and the prophets.

[373] **Leviticus 19:18 Thou** shalt not avenge, nor bear any grudge against the children of thy people, but thou shalt love thy neighbour as thyself: I *am* the LORD.

[374] **Romans 5:5 And** hope maketh not ashamed; because the love of God is shed abroad in our hearts by the Holy Ghost which is given unto us.

152

Read John 14:11-31

John 14:12 Verily, verily, I say unto you, He that believeth on me, the works that I do shall he do also; and greater *works* than these shall he do; because I go unto my Father.

John 14-16 is Jesus' Upper Room Discourse, the teaching that He gave His disciples in the Upper Room the night He was betrayed. He tells them of a place that He is preparing for them (the Father's House). He tells them of a Person He is sending to help them (the Comforter), and He tells them of the Peace that He promises them along the way.

Here in John 14:12 He promises that those of us who believe in Him will do even greater works than what He did. How is that possible? To this date, no one has ever performed miracles greater in magnitude than those that Jesus performed. There must be something else to consider. This is all in the context of Jesus sending the Holy Spirit, the Comforter, to be with us. Jesus did all that He did in the power of the Spirit, but having taken on human flesh, He could only be in one place at a time. After Pentecost, His followers went out, and they continue to go out, empowered by the same Spirit. By their ministry, the ministry of Jesus has been multiplied many times over. Millions of His Spirit-filled followers preach the Gospel all over the world. At this moment, Jesus has His Holy Ghost powered representatives in nearly every corner of the world. Have you been filled with the Spirit? Are you one of His representatives in this world? Why not ask Him about it?

Mark 16:15 And he said unto them, go ye into all the world, and preach the gospel to every creature.

Read John 15:1-27

John 15:5 I am the vine, ye *are* the branches: He that abideth in me, and I in him, the same bringeth forth much fruit: for without me ye can do nothing.

The key to understanding Jesus' teaching here is probably found in these words, "Without me you can do nothing." We can only bear the kind of spiritual fruit that will please and glorify our Heavenly Father, when we are abiding. That means to remain or to continue in close relationship with our Lord Jesus Christ. We can no more bear spiritual fruit without that connection than a branch severed from a tree can continue to bear fruit, while disconnected from the source of *its* life. Jesus is the source of **our** life, and we do not bear spiritual fruit by trying, but by remaining connected to the Source. If we continue to abide in that relationship, we will not only be His disciples, but we will bear spiritual fruit that will glorify our Heavenly Father. Do not forget that fruit, by definition, grows and matures. My prayer is that all nine of the fruit of the Spirit will continue to grow and mature in our lives as we stay connected to Him, for without Him we can do nothing!

Galatians 5:22-23 22 But the fruit of the Spirit is love, joy, peace, longsuffering, gentleness, goodness, faith, 23 Meekness, temperance: against such there is no law.

Read John 16:1-28

John 16:7 Nevertheless, I tell you the truth; It is expedient for you that I go away: for if I go not away, the Comforter will not come unto you; but if I depart, I will send him unto you.

As hard as it must have been for them to accept, Jesus said that it was expedient for Him to go away, that is to ascend back to heaven. Expedient means beneficial, helpful, or advantageous. It would be expedient for them, because in returning to heaven, He would be able to send the Holy Spirit back to earth to be their Comforter. The word Comforter, when speaking of the Holy Spirit as it does here is a translation of the Greek word Paraklete, which literally means "one who is called alongside to help." The Comforter has been sent from Heaven to help us!

What kind of help does He offer? We see three things here in John 16, though there are MANY more! First, the Comforter, will bring the conviction of sin. He reveals our sin to us, so that we can repent and receive forgiveness (John 16:7-11). Second, the Comforter will guide us into all truth (John 16:13). He will direct us to the truth of the Word of God (John 17:17) and to Jesus, the One who is the Truth (John 14:6). Third, the Comforter will always seek to glorify the Lord Jesus Christ (John 16:14). That is one way we can always discern if something is truly from Him. The great Azusa Street revival marked the beginning of a new emphasis on the work of the Spirit in the lives of God's people. One hymn was sung at nearly every meeting in that years long revival[375], a song of joyful testimony, "The Comforter Has Come!"

Oh, spread the tidings 'round, wherever man is found,
Wherever human hearts and human woes abound;
Let every Christian tongue proclaim the joyful sound:
The Comforter has come!

The Comforter has come, the Comforter has come!
The Holy Ghost from Heav'n, the Father's promise giv'n;
Oh, spread the tidings 'round, wherever man is found—
The Comforter has come.[376]

---

[375] The Azusa Street revival in Los Angeles, California lasted from 1906-1909. Services were held three times a day, seven days a week for three years!
[376] "The Comforter Has Come," Francis Bottome

Read John 16:29-17:19

John 16:23   And in that day ye shall ask me nothing. Verily, verily, I say unto you, Whatsoever ye shall ask the Father in my name, he will give *it* you.

We are given many wonderful promises in the New Testament concerning asking and receiving.   What a wonderful blessing to serve One who hears *and* answers prayer!   But there are conditions to that promise.   We must pray in Jesus' Name.   This is far more than simply tacking the words the end of our prayers before the "Amen!"   For one thing, it means that we are in a right relationship with Him.   Second, it means that we are praying according to His authority, what His Word has promised us.   We cannot pray and expect to receive other than what He has promised in His Word.   When we pray according to the Word of God, we know that we are praying according to the Will of God, and when we pray according to the Will of God we can, in faith, expect an answer!

1 John 5:14-15   14 And this is the confidence that we have in him, that, if we ask any thing according to his will, he heareth us: 15 And if we know that he hear us, whatsoever we ask, we know that we have the petitions that we desired of him.

Read John 17.20-18.11

John 17:20-21 20 Neither pray I for these alone, but for them also which shall believe on me through their word; 21 That they all may be one; as thou, Father, *art* in me, and I in thee, that they also may be one in us: that the world may believe that thou hast sent me.

The "Our Father" though often called the "Lord's Prayer" is actually better called the disciple's prayer, for Jesus gave it in response to their request, "Teach us to pray.[377]"   However, Jesus Himself was a man of prayer, and John 17 gives us a beautiful glimpse into His life of prayer.

Did you realize that He not only prayed for His disciples that were with Him then, but He also prayed for you?   He says He prays not just for them alone, but for those who will believe through their word.   Of course, we know that it was the testimony of the apostles that gave us the New Testament Scriptures, through which all of us have received the Gospel.   We believe, because of their words, just as Jesus said it would be!

What was He praying for us? He prayed that we, His church, would be unified, that we would be one.   This is not the artificial unity of the modern ecumenical movement, which sometimes sacrifices the truth in order to achieve "unity."   This is the unity of the Spirit, the unity that unites all truly born-again believers into one body.   In reality, there is only one church, regardless of denominational affiliation, its members are those who have been redeemed by His blood, indwelt by His Spirit, and are now one body!

If you have been born again, I am so glad to say that we are one, we are family, we are a part of His church! If you are His, you are my brother, my sister. I truly rejoice to be part of the family of God!

---

[377] Luke 11:1ff

Read John 18:12-27

John 18:27   Peter then denied again: and immediately the cock crew.

Jesus had warned Peter that he would deny knowing Him that night. Of course, Peter, ever brash and outspoken, denied that it would ever happen.   Even if all of the others forsake you, he said, I will not.   Now, it has all become very *real*.   Even though he is some distance away, in the courtyard, the Gospel of Luke reminds us that he was close enough to see what was happening to Jesus at that very moment.   That means he could see as they slapped Jesus' face.   And, of course, he could see as Jesus turned, at that very moment, and looked at him.[378]   It is difficult to imagine the sorrow and pain he must have felt, realizing what he had done!

Thankfully, the Lord had given Peter great words of comfort before this ever happened though, words recorded in the Gospel of Luke.[379]   Jesus reminded Peter that what he would face was an attack of the enemy. Satan has desired to have you, Jesus said, that he might sift you like wheat. The enemy must have believed that Peter was all chaff, no wheat, and this test would prove it.   But, said Jesus, I have prayed for you and when (not if) you are converted, strengthen your brethren.   I have no doubt that when Peter did repent and received the comfort of the Lord's forgiveness that he was, all the days of his life, able to offer help and comfort to others who had failed as he had.[380]   This is all an example of what God's word tells us in 2 Corinthians 1.

2 Corinthians 1:3-4 3 Blessed *be* God, even the Father of our Lord Jesus Christ, the Father of mercies, and the God of all comfort; 4 Who comforteth us in all our tribulation, that we may be able to comfort them which are in any trouble, by the comfort wherewith we ourselves are comforted of God.

---

[378] **Luke 22:61**   And the Lord turned, and looked upon Peter. And Peter remembered the word of the Lord, how he had said unto him, Before the cock crow, thou shalt deny me thrice.

[380] **Luke 22:31-32** 31 And the Lord said, Simon, Simon, behold, Satan hath desired *to have* you, that he may sift *you* as wheat: 32 But I have prayed for thee, that thy faith fail not: and when thou art converted, strengthen thy brethren.

Read John 18:28-19:11

John 19:11   Jesus answered, Thou couldest have no power *at all* against me, except it were given thee from above: therefore he that delivered me unto thee hath the greater sin.

This is certainly true. They had no power over the Lord, except what had been allowed. After all, He was the Creator of the Universe come down to earth in human flesh. He could have destroyed the world with just a word, just as He created it.   When they arrested Him in the Garden of Gethsemane, He revealed that He could have called for twelve legions of angels to come to His aid.[381]   A legion was as many as 6,000 Roman soldiers, so that would mean 72,000 angels come to His rescue! However, He did not avail Himself of that help. Earlier in the Gospel of John He made it clear that no one was able to take His life from Him, but that He laid it down willingly.   He said, "I have power to lay it down, and I have power to take it again."[382]   The Lord's life was not taken, it was given! He gave HIMSELF for our sins. That makes all the difference in the world.

Galatians 1:2-5   2 And all the brethren which are with me, unto the churches of Galatia: 3 Grace *be* to you and peace from God the Father, and *from* our Lord Jesus Christ, 4 **Who gave himself for our sins,** that he might deliver us from this present evil world, according to the will of God and our Father: 5 To whom *be* glory for ever and ever. Amen.

---

[381] **Matthew 26:53**   Thinkest thou that I cannot now pray to my Father, and he shall presently give me more than twelve legions of angels?
[382] **Matthew 26:53**   Thinkest thou that I cannot now pray to my Father, and he shall presently give me more than twelve legions of angels?

<u>**Read John 19:12-30**</u>

John 19:30   When Jesus therefore had received the vinegar, he said, It is finished: and he bowed his head, and gave up the ghost.

     Jesus' words, "It is finished," were not words of defeat, but were actually a great shout of victory. "It is finished" is the English translation of but one word in the original Greek of John's Gospel. That word is "tetelestai" and it means "it stands completed." He had completed what He set out to do, giving His life for our sins.   It was only then, that He gave up the ghost. That expression is also important. It is not that He just died, but that He had completed His work, and now released His Spirit to the Father. This is still another proof that He gave His life, it was not taken from Him.

     The Bible calls Him our Great High Priest. Old Testament priests offered the same sacrifices over and over again.   You have probably read about those innumerable sacrifices in the Old Testament Scriptures.   However, Jesus gave His life as one final, and perfect, sacrifice, and unlike every other high priest before Him, he was able to sit down having completed His work. That is why the Book of Hebrews emphasizes that Jesus sat down. His work was complete.   We dare not add to, or take away from, a salvation that is perfect, complete and finished by Christ.   That is why we rejoice today that it truly is FINISHED!

Hebrews 10:11-12 11 And every priest standeth daily ministering and offering oftentimes the same sacrifices, which can never take away sins: 12 But this man, after he had offered one sacrifice for sins forever, sat down on the right hand of God;

Read John 19:31-20:10

John 19:34   But one of the soldiers with a spear pierced his side, and forthwith came there out blood and water.

The normal way to speed the death of a crucifixion victim was to break their legs.   Unable to push up on those broken limbs without excruciating pain, death was inevitable, apparently by suffocation. They did not do this to Jesus. For one thing, it had been prophesied that not one of His bones would be broken[383].   However, they did something else to make certain that He was dead.   They drove a spear into His side.   Cardiologists have surmised that they must have pierced the fluid filled pericardium around His heart. It was apparently a gaping wound, as Thomas would later speak of placing his hand into that wound.[384]

From Jesus' side flowed that which cleanses us.   Charles Spurgeon has an interesting thought on this, "As Adam fell asleep, and out of his side Eve was taken, so Jesus slept upon the cross the sleep of death, and from his side, where the spear was thrust, his Church was taken."   May we never forget that He shed His blood for us.   It was this Scripture that must have inspired William Cowper to write the words of this familiar old hymn.

There is a fountain filled with blood
Drawn from Emmanuel's veins;
And sinners plunged beneath that flood
Lose all their guilty stains.
Lose all their guilty stains,
Lose all their guilty stains;
And sinners plunged beneath that flood
Lose all their guilty stains.

---

[383] Psalm 34:20

[384] **John 20:24-25** 24 But Thomas, one of the twelve, called Didymus, was not with them when Jesus came. 25 The other disciples therefore said unto him, We have seen the Lord. But he said unto them, Except I shall see in his hands the print of the nails, and put my finger into the print of the nails, and thrust my hand into his side, I will not believe.

Read John 20:11-31

John 20:22   And when he had said this, he breathed on *them*, and saith unto them, Receive ye the Holy Ghost:

This was a Sunday evening, the day Jesus rose from the dead.   The disciples were still a bit fearful, still processing what they had seen and heard. Their fear must have turned to joy when Jesus appeared in the room!   First, He spoke peace to them.   Peace is something they had not experienced for several days.   Second, He showed them His hands and feet, proving that it was truly Him. Some have said that the only manmade thing we will see in heaven will be the scars in Jesus' hands and feet.   Third, He breathed on them and said, "Receive ye the Holy Ghost."

What actually happened in that upper room when Jesus breathed on them? In the Old Testament, one Hebrew word "ruach" can be translated as breath, wind, or spirit. The context reveals which is intended.   It is the same in New Testament Greek with the word "pneuma" which also means either breath, wind, or spirit. This is interesting when we think of Genesis 2:7 where God *breathed* on Adam, and he became a living soul, or Ezekiel 37 where God's wind blew on the dry bones bringing them to life.   When Jesus breathed on the disciples, they received spiritual life. They were born again, something that had been impossible before His death and resurrection.   They were now indwelt by the Holy Spirit in the sense that every saved person is today.   We should not assume, however, that this was the last experience they would have with the Holy Spirit. Jesus later told those same disciples to tarry in the city of Jerusalem until they were endued with power from on high[385].   Pentecost was still ahead!

Breathe on me, Breath of God,
Fill me with life anew,
That I may love what thou dost love,
And do what thou wouldst do.[386]

---

[385] Luke 24:49
[386] "Breathe on Me, Breath of God,"   Edwin Hatch

Read John 21

John 21:15 So when they had dined, Jesus saith to Simon Peter, Simon, *son* of Jonas, lovest thou me more than these? He saith unto him, Yea, Lord; thou knowest that I love thee. He saith unto him, Feed my lambs.

If you will remember, Peter had, just a few days earlier, denied even knowing the Lord. The Lord had revealed Himself personally to Peter on the day of His resurrection, but what happened here was Peter's public restoration. Three times Jesus asked Peter, "Do you love me?" Why did He repeat these words three times? Perhaps it was because Peter denied the Lord three times. Some have noted that Jesus uses the word agape (sacrificial love), while Peter answers with phileo (sometimes even translated friendship). It is not certain how much we can make of the use of these two Greek words, for some times they are used synonymously in the New Testament. However, one thing is very clear here. If Peter does love Jesus, that love is going to translate into ministry to others. He will be feeding the Lord's sheep, as an elder, a pastor of God's flock, the remainder of His days. By loving the people of God, He will be loving the Lord Himself. Perhaps he had this experience in mind, when he later wrote these words to others in ministry.

1 Peter 5:1-4 1 The elders which are among you I exhort, who am also an elder, and a witness of the sufferings of Christ, and also a partaker of the glory that shall be revealed: 2 Feed the flock of God which is among you, taking the oversight *thereof*, not by constraint, but willingly; not for filthy lucre, but of a ready mind; 3 Neither as being lords over *God's* heritage, but being ensamples to the flock. 4 And when the chief Shepherd shall appear, ye shall receive a crown of glory that fadeth not away.

Read Acts 1:1-26

Acts 1:8 But ye shall receive power, after that the Holy Ghost is come upon you: and ye shall be witnesses unto me both in Jerusalem, and in all Judaea, and in Samaria, and unto the uttermost part of the earth.

This verse is the outline for the entire book of Acts. The Gospel first went to Jerusalem and surrounding Judea, then to Samaria through the preaching of Philip, and finally to the uttermost parts of the earth.

This is also a verse that tells us the primary purpose of the outpouring of the Spirit in our lives. When the Spirit of God comes upon us we will receive power. Power is the Greek word dynamis, from which we get our English words dynamic, dynamo, and even dynamite. We are given this dynamite power to be His witnesses. Witnesses is the word "marturos" from which we get our English word "martyrs." More than just dying for the faith, a martyr is one who lives faithfully to the end. The Holy Spirit will empower us to do that very thing.

Let's pray that the Spirit of God helps us stay faithful, proclaiming the good news until He calls us home!

Read Acts 2:1-21

Acts 2:21   And it shall come to pass, *that* whosoever shall call on the name of the Lord shall be saved.

Are we living in the last days?   By the Scriptural definition, I believe that we certainly are!   Peter is preaching the first sermon after the amazing events of Pentecost.[387]   The people had questions about what they were witnessing.   Some even accused the Spirit-filled disciples of being drunk. They asked, "What does this mean?[388]   Peter took them to the Word of God for their answers, the prophecy of the prophet Joel. From Joel's prophecy, we see that the last days began with Pentecost[389] and will continue to the Day of the Lord a time of great judgments.[390]

What can we expect in the last days, the time between those two events (Pentecost and the Day of the Lord)?   We can expect that God will continue to pour out His Spirit on all flesh. In the Old Testament, the Spirit only came upon certain people at certain times. In the last days, He is being poured out on sons and daughters, young and old, servants and handmaidens.   There are no gender, age, or social barriers to this outpouring.   "All flesh" includes you and me!

We can also expect great spiritual opportunity in the last days. In the power of the Holy Spirit, we can proclaim the words of Acts 2:21, "Whosoever shall call on the Name of the Lord shall be saved!"   What about you, have you received what God has promised in these days?

---

[387] Acts 2:1-4
[388] Acts 2:12
[389] Acts 2:17
[390] Acts 2:19-20

Read Acts 2:22-47

Acts 2:38-39 Then Peter said unto them, Repent, and be baptized every one of you in the name of Jesus Christ for the remission of sins, and ye shall receive the gift of the Holy Ghost. For the promise is unto you, and to your children, and to all that are afar off, even as many as the Lord our God shall call.

As Peter preached, the Holy Spirit brought conviction to those who heard[391]. They asked, "What shall we do?" The answer to their question was clear. They must repent, turning from their sin. They must look to Jesus as Lord, being baptized by His authority.[392] Having done that, they could be filled with the Holy Spirit just as the 120 had been in the Upper Room.[393]

Once again, we see the promise of the Spirit being for "all flesh" just as we did at the beginning of Peter's message.[394] He said, the promise is unto you (the 3,000 who were saved that day), your children (the next generation), all that are afar off (others we see receiving this promise throughout the book of Acts), and as many as the Lord our God shall call (That means you and me!). *You* can be saved *and* filled with the Holy Spirit today!

---

[391] Acts 2:37
[392] Matthew 28:19
[393] Acts 2:1-4
[394] Acts 2:17

Read   Acts 3:1-26

Acts 3:6, "Then Peter said, Silver and gold have I none; but such as I have give I thee: In the name of Jesus Christ of Nazareth rise up and walk."

This account shows the gift of healing in operation, but also the Lord's perfect timing.   The lame man was about forty years old and had been crippled, unable to walk, from birth.[395]   Caring people brought him as far as the temple gate every day, so he could beg for enough money to survive. Some believe that the lame and blind were not even allowed in the temple itself.   Jesus did not follow that custom, however, healing many people *in* the temple.[396]

Jesus, the Great Healer, had undoubtedly been by that gate, and that very man on several occasions. Yet, the lame man did not receive his healing until the day Peter and John walked by on their way to a prayer meeting. There is more to healing than simply relieving human suffering, it serves to confirm the Word of God.[397]   Many people were at the temple at that time, because it was the hour of prayer. They all began to gather, seeing what God had done. Hearing the Word, many of them believed, and were saved. The previous count showed 3,000 believers, now it is up to 5,000.[398]   I rejoice in God's perfect timing!

He is still a miracle-working Savior!   May the Lord's perfectly-timed miracles bring glory to His Great Name.   This is what they prayed at the end of this great spiritual adventure.

Acts 4:29-30. "And now, Lord, behold their threatenings: and grant unto thy servants, that with all boldness they may speak thy word, By stretching forth thine hand to heal; and that signs and wonders may be done by the name of thy holy child Jesus."

---

[395] Acts 3:2, Acts 4:22
[396] Matthew 21:14
[397] Mark 16:20
[398] Acts 2:41, Acts 4:4

Read Acts 4:1-22

Acts 4:10-12, "Be it known unto you all, and to all the people of Israel, that by the name of Jesus Christ of Nazareth, whom ye crucified, whom God raised from the dead, *even* by him doth this man stand here before you whole. This is the stone which was set at nought of you builders, which is become the head of the corner. Neither is there salvation in any other: for there is none other name under heaven given among men, whereby we must be saved."

The apostles preached the Gospel after the healing of the lame man with amazing results.[399]   Now they have another wonderful opportunity; they can share the Gospel with the religious authorities. They did not perform the miracle in their own authority, but in the Name and Authority of the Lord Jesus Christ. Now they boldly proclaim Jesus Christ as the only way to salvation.

One of the most dangerous false teachings today is universalism in its various forms. Universalism is the belief that all roads, or at least most roads, will ultimately lead to heaven.   A friend attended a local funeral some years ago, in which the one officiating said, "There are seven broad ways that lead to heaven and surely our sister found one of those ways!"   There are not seven ways, or even two ways, there is only One Way—Jesus.   The apostles made it clear, there is only one Name that will bring salvation—the Name of Jesus! It does matter what you believe!   No other Name brings salvation.

This is what Jesus Himself taught. There are only two roads, the broad way that leads to destruction and the strait and narrow road that leads to everlasting life.[400]   He is *the* only way to heaven.[401]   Anyone who suggests there might be another way is described as a thief and a robber, robbing others of the truth that leads to eternal life.[402]   Rejoice in the Name that is Above All Names![403]

No other Name, but the Name of Jesus!
No other Name, but the Name of the Lord,
No other Name, but the Name of Jesus,
Is worthy of glory, and worthy of honor, and worthy of power and of praise.[404]

---

[399] Acts 4:4
[400] Matthew 7:13-14
[401] John 14:6
[402] John 10:1
[403] Philippians 2:9
[404] "No Other Name," Don Moen

Read Acts 4:23-5:11

Acts 5:3 But Peter said, Ananias, why hath Satan filled thine heart to lie to the Holy Ghost, and to keep back *part* of the price of the land?

The need was great among God's people. Many people, of their own free will, did what they could to help provide for their brothers and sisters. Some, like Barnabas, even chose to sell property to make those funds available to help.[405] This was apparently never mandated by the church, it was a voluntary action motivated by love in the church family.

Ananias and Sapphira, perhaps motivated by the attention others like Barnabas received for *their* giving, chose to sell some property also. Their sin was not in keeping back part of the money, but in lying about it.[406] Peter equates this with lying to the Holy Ghost, lying to God.[407] This Scripture proves the Holy Spirit, like the Father and the Son, is God. Lying to the Holy Ghost = Lying to God.

By our actions, we can vex the Holy Spirit,[408] resist Him,[409] quench His influence,[410] or grieve Him.[411] Seven times in Revelation alone we are told to hear what the Spirit is saying[412]. Father, give us ears to hear and a heart to obey!

Make Him welcome in your life today!

Holy Spirit, Thou art welcome in this place,
Holy Spirit, Thou art welcome in this place,
Omnipotent Father of Mercy and Grace,
Thou art welcome in this place[413].

---

[405] Acts 4:34-37
[406] Acts 5:4
[407] Acts 5:3-4
[408] Isaiah 63:9-10
[409] Acts 7:51
[410] 1 Thessalonians 5:19
[411] Ephesians 4:30
[412] Revelation 2:7, 11, 17, 29; 3:6, 13, 22.
[413] "Holy Spirit, Thou Art Welcome," Dottie Rambo

Read Acts 5:12-40

Acts 5:29 Then Peter and the *other* apostles answered and said, We ought to obey God rather than men.

The Lord was doing great miracles and the religious authorities were livid. They ordered the apostles put in prison, but that night the angel of the Lord released them! Rather than "laying low" for a while, they immediately resumed preaching and teaching in the temple, even though the leaders ordered them to cease. The boldness of the Holy Spirit was so very evident in their lives.

Good citizenship is commanded in the New Testament[414]. Christians should be the most law-abiding of citizens. However, if man's law should ever go against a higher law, God's Law, we have no alternative, but to resist.

There may come a day when you will be called upon to take a stand. On that day, know that the Holy Spirit will empower you, just as He did them!

Ephesians 6:10 Finally, my brethren, be strong in the Lord, and in the power of his might.

---

[414] Matthew 22:21, Romans 13:1-7, Titus 3:1, 1 Peter 2:13-17

Read Acts 5:41-6:15

Acts 5:41 And they departed from the presence of the council, rejoicing that they were counted worthy to suffer shame for his name.

The apostles had, once again, been brought before the authorities for preaching the Gospel. They were beaten and commanded not to preach or teach any more in the Name of Jesus.[415] Of course, this did not stop them. All of them, except John, eventually died martyr's deaths because they continued to preach the Gospel of the Lord Jesus Christ. They viewed it as a glorious honor, a cause for rejoicing, to suffer shame for His Name!

This would have been impossible before Pentecost. Now they had the power, as can we, to faithfully proclaim the truth no matter what[416]. Perhaps they also remembered the words of Jesus, "Blessed are ye, when *men* shall revile you, and persecute *you*, and shall say all manner of evil against you falsely, for my sake. Rejoice, and be exceeding glad: for great *is* your reward in heaven: for so persecuted they the prophets which were before you."[417]

Do you remember this old chorus? It's still my prayer today!

Keep me true, Lord Jesus, keep me true,
Keep me true, Lord Jesus, keep me true,
There's a race that I must run,
There are victories to be won,
Give me power, every hour, to be true.

[415] Acts 5:40
[416] Acts 1:8
[417] Matthew 5:11-12

Read Acts 7:1-22

Acts 7:22 And Moses was learned in all the wisdom of the Egyptians, and was mighty in words and in deeds.

In the middle of Steven's final sermon before they stoned him, we find an interesting verse about Moses. It says that he was *mighty* in both words and deeds. At first this may seem to conflict with what we read in Exodus about Moses. When God called him, he made various excuses, including claiming he was, "not eloquent and was slow of speech."[418]

It is interesting that Exodus 4:6 is what Moses said about himself, and Acts 7:22 is what God said about him. We find the same thing in the book of Judges. Gideon is fearful. He is hiding from his enemies, he recognizes his own weakness, yet God calls him a "Mighty Man of Valor."[419]

Remember, it is not what you say, or others say, it is what God says about you that really matters! What does His Word say about you? Search the Scriptures daily and find out!

John 8:31-32 Then said Jesus to those Jews which believed on him, If ye continue in my word, *then* are ye my disciples indeed; And ye shall know the truth, and the truth shall make you free.

---

[418] Exodus 4:10
[419] Judges 6:11-12

Read Acts 7:23-47

Acts 7:34 I have seen, I have seen the affliction of my people which is in Egypt, and I have heard their groaning, and am come down to deliver them. And now come, I will send thee into Egypt.

Steven is still preaching, a message that gives a panoramic view of Old Testament history. In Acts 7:34 he is quoting a part of Exodus 3:7, words the Lord gave Moses when he called him to lead the Israelites out of Egypt. The Israelites had been slaves of the Egyptians for many years. During those difficult years in Egypt, it may have seemed that God had forgotten them, but He had not.

He reminds them that He is a seeing God. I *have* seen the affliction of my people. Nothing escapes His notice. The eyes of the LORD are in every place, beholding the evil and the good (Proverbs 15:13). The eyes of the LORD run to and fro throughout the whole earth to show Himself strong in the behalf of those whose heart is perfect toward Him (2nd Chronicles 16:9). He also reminds them that He is a hearing God. The eyes of the LORD are upon the righteous, and His ears are open unto their cry (Psalm 34:15). The One who sees and hears will also deliver! He says, "I am come down to deliver them."

The enemy would have you to think that God does not see what is happening in your life and that He does not hear your cries for help. Nothing could be further from the truth. He not only sees and hears, He will deliver you in His perfect time!

Psalm 34:19 Many *are* the afflictions of the righteous: but the LORD delivereth him out of them all.

Read Acts 7:48-8:13

Acts 7:55-56 But he, being full of the Holy Ghost, looked up stedfastly into heaven, and saw the glory of God, and Jesus standing on the right hand of God, And said, Behold, I see the heavens opened, and the Son of man standing on the right hand of God.

Steven was one of the seven men chosen to oversee the feeding of the widows, he was a part of that group that would later become known as deacons, but he was also a mighty preacher of the Gospel, as was Philip, another of that number. Steven became the first member of the Lord's church to leave this world as a martyr. He is a wonderful example of one who lived right and died right.

One of the qualifications of those seven chosen men was that they be full of the Holy Ghost.[420]   The Holy Spirit gave Steven the power to live faithfully for God, and to die in that same victorious faith. It is said of him, at the very time of his death, that he was full of the Holy Ghost, and saw the Lord Himself giving him a "standing ovation" welcoming him home.

I want to be found faithful when He calls for me! What about you?

1 Corinthians 4:1-2 Let a man so account of us, as of the ministers of Christ, and stewards of the mysteries of God. Moreover it is required in stewards, that a man be found faithful.

---

[420] Acts 6:3

Read Acts 8:14-40

Acts 8:26 And the angel of the Lord spake unto Philip, saying, Arise, and go toward the south unto the way that goeth down from Jerusalem unto Gaza, which is desert.

Philip, like Steven, was one of the original seven chosen to help feed the widows in Jerusalem, and like Steven, he was also a powerful preacher of the Word. The death of Steven brought a time of great persecution for the young church, and everyone but the apostles was scattered.[421]

Everywhere they went, they preached the Gospel. Philip went to Samaria, where he preached, and saw a great revival with many saved and filled with the Holy Spirit. The revival spread into many Samaritan villages.[422]

In the midst of that great revival, God called the preacher away to one of the most isolated spots He could have sent him to, the desert road from Jerusalem to Gaza. On that road, he met a man, an Ethiopian, one with a hunger to know God. This was no chance meeting, it was what some would call a divine appointment, a meeting orchestrated by God. The Lord moved the evangelist from the city-wide revival to a deserted country road to see one soul come to Christ. He is not willing that any should perish.[423] He will always reveal Himself to those who seek Him, just as He did for this man.[424]

Isn't it wonderful to know that our steps are ordered by the Lord, just as Philip's were. Thank Him for that truth today!

Psalm 37:23 The steps of a *good* man are ordered by the LORD: and he delighteth in his way.

---

[421] Acts 8:1, 4
[422] Acts 8:25
[423] 2nd Peter 3:9
[424] Deuteronomy 4:29

Read Acts 9:1-25

Acts 9:15-16 But the Lord said unto him, Go thy way: for he is a chosen vessel unto me, to bear my name before the Gentiles, and kings, and the children of Israel: For I will shew him how great things he must suffer for my name's sake.

Acts 9 records an amazing transformation. Saul had been one of the greatest persecutors of Christians and was on his way to Damascus to do still more evil against the church. On the way, he had a life-changing experience, submitting his life to the Lordship of Jesus Christ.[425] He was told to go the house of a believer named Ananias where he would be healed, baptized, called into ministry, and would likely receive the Baptism in the Holy Ghost.

Understandably, Ananias was reluctant to minister to him at first. He did have quite an unsavory reputation. However, the Lord made it clear that Saul was a chosen vessel, and the Lord had a great plan for his life. That plan had been in the heart of God from the beginning.[426]

Saul, also known as Paul, would experience all the things prophesied in Acts 9:15-16. He would bring the Gospel to both Jews and Gentiles. He would even preach the Gospel to kings, likely even Caesar himself.[427] The most remarkable thing about this prophecy are the words, "I will show how great things he must *suffer* for my name's sake!" He did suffer many things in the work of the Lord,[428] but he knew that the sufferings of this present time are not worthy to be compared with the glory which shall be revealed in us.[429]

Whatever difficult times *we* face in the work of the Lord, it will be worth it all someday!

It will be worth it all, when we see Jesus,
It will be worth it all, when we see Christ,
One glimpse of His dear face, all sorrow will erase,
So bravely run the race, 'till we see Christ[430].

---

[425] Acts 9:6
[426] Galatians 1:15
[427] Acts 27:24
[428] 2nd Corinthians 11:23-29
[429] Romans 8:18
[430] "It Will be Worth it All When We See Jesus," Esther Kerr Rusthoi

Read Acts 9:26-43

Acts 9:31 Then had the churches rest throughout all Judaea and Galilee and Samaria, and were edified; and walking in the fear of the Lord, and in the comfort of the Holy Ghost, were multiplied.

This must have been such a sweet time of blessing in the church. They had come through such a horrible time of persecution, now their greatest persecutor, Saul, was one of them! The church was experiencing five wonderful things.

They had rest. This was not just the cessation of persecution, it was the rest Jesus promised the weary in Matthew 11:28. They were edified. This means that they were growing in the things of God, not just numerically, but spiritually. They were walking in the fear of God, which indicates God was also speaking to them, and they were growing in wisdom.[431] They were comforted by the Holy Ghost. Jesus had promised that the Holy Spirit would be the Comforter (paraklete), one who comes alongside of us to help us![432] The church was not just being added to, there was *multiplication!*

Let's pray these things for our church. Lord, may we enjoy Your sweet rest today. May we be edified, growing and maturing in the things of God. May we learn what it is to truly fear You. May we enjoy the sweet comfort of the Holy Spirit. May many souls be brought into Your kingdom!

---

[431] Psalm 25:14, Proverbs 9:10
[432] John 16:7

Read Acts 10:1-23

Acts 10:20 Arise therefore, and get thee down, and go with them, doubting nothing: for I have sent them.

Up to this time, nearly all who had come to faith in Christ had come from a Jewish background. That was about to change. God was simultaneously speaking to Peter, raised as a devout Jew, and Cornelius, a Gentile with a hunger to know God. As unlikely as it seemed in those days, God was going to bring a Jew and a Gentile together, so the Gentile, and his family, could find the Savior! This was a part of God's plan to pour out His Spirit on all flesh![433]

Previously, Peter would not have dreamed of visiting a Gentile home, any more than he would have dreamed of eating any unclean (non-Kosher) food. He believed that doing either would make *him* unclean. The Lord made it clear to him that he could now do both, saying, "Don't call what I have cleansed unclean!"[434] God was going to cleanse the Gentile Cornelius and his household through faith in Jesus Christ, just as He had cleansed Peter.

Aren't you glad that the Gospel is for *all*, Jew *and* Gentile! Rejoice today that you been made part of the family of God through faith in Jesus Christ! Rejoice that the Gospel is for all—that includes you and me! He is not willing that any (Jew or Gentile) should perish.[435]

2 Peter 3:9 The Lord is not slack concerning his promise, as some men count slackness; but is longsuffering to us-ward, not willing that any should perish, but that **all** should come to repentance.

---

[433] Acts 2:17
[434] Acts 10:15
[435] 2 Peter 3:9

Acts 10:24-48

Acts 10:44 While Peter yet spake these words, the Holy Ghost fell on all them which heard the word.

God promised to pour out His Spirit on *all* flesh.[436]   The Gospel and the outpouring of the Holy Spirit are available to all.   That promise is, ultimately, what brought Peter to Cornelius' house with the Gospel.

It was still unclear with some Jewish believers, whether people like Cornelius (Gentiles) could even be saved.   Something happened that day that removed all doubt.   Cornelius, and many others in his house, received the Gospel and believed in Jesus Christ.   Then, while Peter was still preaching to them, they were baptized in the Holy Spirit, just as others had been in Jerusalem at Pentecost[437] and in Samaria.[438]   Peter and those with him knew that it had happened, because of the evidence they saw and heard. Cornelius and his household were speaking in tongues.   The believing Jews with Peter knew that God would not give the gift of the Spirit to one who had not been truly born again.   What they were seeing, and hearing was proof that the Gentiles could come into the family of God!

Have you received His wonderful gift? The promise is for you too!

Acts 2:39 For the promise is unto you, and to your children, and to all that are afar off, *even* as many as the Lord our God shall call.

Galatians 3:14 That the blessing of Abraham might come on the Gentiles through Jesus Christ; that we might receive the promise of the Spirit through faith.

Luke 11:13 If ye then, being evil, know how to give good gifts unto your children: how much more shall *your* heavenly Father give the Holy Spirit to them that ask him?

---

[436] Joel 2:28, Acts 2:17
[437] Acts 2:1-4
[438] Acts 8:14-17

Read Acts 11:1-30

Acts 11:29 Then the disciples, every man according to his ability, determined to send relief unto the brethren which dwelt in Judaea:

A prophet named Agabus prophesied that a great famine was going to come. When the famine came the believers in Jerusalem were especially hard hit. That is when the church in Antioch decided to send a love offering to their suffering brothers and sisters in Jerusalem. This was not something the church mandated. No one twisted their arm. They all gave what they could, according to their ability. This is an example of the giving principles we find in 2 Corinthians 9:7. Giving is to be heart-felt. We give as we purpose in our hearts. It is to be voluntary. We do not give grudgingly. It is to be cheerful, for God loves a cheerful giver.

What we read in Acts 11:29 is an example of the care we are to have for one another in the Family of God. We are to rejoice with those who rejoice and weep with those who weep.[439] We are also told that there should be no division in the body, and that we must care for one another. When one of us suffers, we all suffer. When one of us is honoured, we all rejoice.[440]

It is a wonderful thing to be a part of God's family!

---

[439] Acts 12:15
[440] 1 Corinthians 12:25-26

Read Acts 12:1-25

Acts 12:1-2   Now about that time Herod the king stretched forth *his* hands to vex certain of the church. 2 And he killed James the brother of John with the sword.

Once again, the church was facing persecution. The first of the twelve apostles to be killed for his faith was James the brother of John.   He was killed by the sword, meaning he was probably beheaded. Eusebius, an ancient church historian, relates that the soldier who guarded him was so moved by James' testimony that he also professed faith in Christ and was beheaded along with James!   James faced death, victoriously, through the power of the Holy Spirit.

Herod being a typical politician and seeing that his actions pleased his base, arrested another of the apostles, Peter.   His plan was to make Peter face the same fate as James.   It is interesting to note that even though Peter knew that his death was probably imminent, he was sleeping in that prison cell rather than worrying!   This too reveals the work of the Holy Spirit in His life, bringing that wonderful fruit called peace.   Ultimately, he received a miraculous angelic deliverance, and went back to encourage those who had been praying for him.

Peter received an earthly deliverance, James a heavenly one.   It is wonderful to remember that whether we live, or die, we belong to the Lord.

Romans 14:8 For whether we live, we live unto the Lord; and whether we die, we die unto the Lord: whether we live therefore, or die, we are the Lord's.

Read Acts 13:1-22

Acts 13:2 As they ministered to the Lord, and fasted, the Holy Ghost said, separate me Barnabas and Saul for the work whereunto I have called them.

The church at Antioch had a heart for the lost. They were a sending church, sending out missionaries like Paul and Barnabas. Churches may ordain and send missionaries, but, ultimately, that is the work of the Holy Spirit.[441] He empowers the Lord's church to be witnesses in Jerusalem, Judea, Samaria, and unto the uttermost part of the earth.[442]

We see something about the calling and sending of missionaries Paul and Barnabas here in Acts 13. Their call, or at least a confirmation of it, came during a time of worship. The church was ministering to the Lord and fasting. Ministering to the Lord means they were worshipping. Fasting always includes prayer, so they were praying too. In that spiritual atmosphere, the Holy Spirit said, "Separate me Paul and Barnabas for the work whereunto I have called them." An atmosphere of worship, prayer, and fasting is still a good place to hear from God!

What about you? Are you open to hearing from God?

> Jesus use me, and Oh Lord don't refuse me,
> surely there's a work that I can do,
> And even though it's humble, help my will to crumble, though the cost be great, I'll work for You.[443]

---

[441] Acts 13:4
[442] Acts 1:8
[443] Jack Campbell

182

Read Acts 13:23-43

Acts 13:38-41 Be it known unto you therefore, men *and* brethren, that through this man is preached unto you the forgiveness of sins: And by him all that believe are justified from all things, from which ye could not be justified by the law of Moses. Beware therefore, lest that come upon you, which is spoken of in the prophets; 41 Behold, ye despisers, and wonder, and perish: for I work a work in your days, a work which ye shall in no wise believe, though a man declare it unto you

Paul, preaching at Antioch proclaims the Gospel of Jesus Christ. Jesus died, Jesus was buried, and Jesus rose again! Our eternity hangs on what we do with that good news. We see in these verses both a glorious promise and a fearful warning.

First, a glorious promise! If we will believe, and receive the Gospel, we can be both forgiven and justified. The debt of sin is removed, *and* the righteousness of Jesus is credited to our spiritual accounts. This was not possible under the Law, but can be ours today through faith.[444]

Second, a fearful warning! If we reject the Gospel, all the judgments promised in the Law will come upon us. He says, "Beware lest that come upon you which is spoken of in the prophets."[445] Those that will not wonder and be saved, shall wonder and perish.[446]

His promises and warnings are both to be taken seriously. I rejoice that He loves us enough to have given us both!

He paid a debt He did not owe, I owed a debt I could not pay, I needed someone to wash my sins away, and now I sing a brand-new song, amazing grace. Christ Jesus paid the debt that I could never pay[447].

---

[444] Romans 3:28, Romans 5:1, Galatians 2:16, Galatians 3:11, Galatians 3:24
[445] Habakkuk 1:5
[446] Matthew Henry
[447] "He Paid a Debt," Ellis J. Crum

Read Acts 14:8-15:2

Acts 14:22 Confirming the souls of the disciples, *and* exhorting them to continue in the faith, and that we must through much tribulation enter into the kingdom of God.

Paul brought a promise from God to a group of young Christians in Iconium, "They would face much tribulation on their way to heaven." They may not have wanted to hear that kind of promise, nor do we, but it will be true for all of us. We will all face our share of troubles. You can count on it.

In all of those coming tribulations, we are exhorted to "continue in the faith." Elsewhere we are told to hold fast to our profession of faith without wavering,[448] to endure to the end,[449] and to be faithful unto death.[450] We are told to endure hardships as good soldiers of Jesus Christ,[451] knowing that He will always be there to help and sustain us. Whatever we face on our way to glory, we can expect to see His grace and power all along the way.

Through many dangers, toils, and snares, I have already come, His grace has brought me safe thus far, and grace will lead me home.[452]

---

[448] Hebrews 10:23
[449] Matthew 24:13
[450] Revelation 2:10
[451] 2 Timothy 2:3
[452] "Amazing Grace,' John Newton

Acts 15:22-16:5

Acts 15:28-29 For it seemed good to the Holy Ghost, and to us, to lay upon you no greater burden than these necessary things; That ye abstain from meats offered to idols, and from blood, and from things strangled, and from fornication: from which if ye keep yourselves, ye shall do well. Fare ye well.

The church had endured several kinds of problems in its young life. It faced ongoing persecution from outside. The sin of Ananias and Sapphira was a problem within the body. But, in Acts 15 we find the first conflict over a doctrinal issue. The church was more Jewish than Gentile in nature at the beginning, but that was beginning to change. Many Gentiles were coming to faith in Jesus Christ. What part, if any, of the Jewish Law and customs did these Gentile converts need to follow? That question became a great point of controversy with heated discussion on both sides.

The first major church conference convened and through what must have been a word of wisdom, a solution to the controversy was found.[453] Some relatively minimal restrictions would be placed on the Gentile converts, but they would not have to be circumcised. They must not eat meat sacrificed to idols. They must not drink blood or eat meat from animals improperly killed. They must not engage in sexual immorality.

It was not enough that the decision pleased those who were at the council. It seemed good to us. It must be something that pleased God. It seemed good unto the Holy Ghost. May God grant such wisdom to His church today.

James 1:5 If any of you lack wisdom, let him ask of God, that giveth to all *men* liberally, and upbraideth not; and it shall be given him.

---

[453] 1 Corinthians 12:8

Read Acts 15:22-16:5

Acts 15:39-40 And the contention was so sharp between them, that they departed asunder one from the other: and so Barnabas took Mark, and sailed unto Cyprus; And Paul chose Silas, and departed, being recommended by the brethren unto the grace of God.

In Acts, we have seen the problem of persecution from without, and sin and false doctrine from within the church. Now, we see still another way the enemy attempted to derail the church, a sharp disagreement between brothers in Christ.

Paul and Barnabas had worked together very effectively planting churches. Now, Paul felt they should go back and visit those churches encouraging them in the things of God. Barnabas agreed, but wanted to take John Mark with them. Paul didn't want to take him, because when he was with them before he bailed out on them when they really needed him.[454] The fact that Barnabas and Mark were relatives[455] may have complicated this even more. The disagreement between these two Spirit-filled preachers became so intense that they finally went their separate ways. Barnabas and Mark went one way; Paul and Silas another.

The enemy would like to use petty conflicts to hinder or destroy the work of God. Sadly, in some cases, he has been very effective in doing so. He did not achieve that here. The Lord used both preaching teams and the rift between Paul and Mark was healed by the time he wrote 2nd Timothy. He told Timothy, "When you come bring him (Mark) with you, for he is profitable to me for the ministry[456]!"

Knowing how the enemy tries to use these things, we should take a verse like this one very seriously.

Romans 12:18 If it be possible, as much as lieth in you, live peaceably with all men.

---

[454] Acts 13:13
[455] Colossians 4:10
[456] 2 Timothy 4:11

Read Acts 16:6-24

Acts 16:6-7 Now when they had gone throughout Phrygia and the region of Galatia, and were forbidden of the Holy Ghost to preach the word in Asia, After they were come to Mysia, they assayed to go into Bithynia: but the Spirit suffered them not.

God's timing is perfect.   After preaching and encouraging the churches in Phyrgia and Galatia, the most logical place to preach next would be Ephesus in Asia Minor.[457]   In some miraculous way the Holy Spirit made it very clear that that was not His plan for their next phase of ministry.   Next, they thought they might go north into Bithynia. Once again, in some unmistakable way, the Holy Spirit shut the door.

After facing two closed doors, the Holy Spirit showed them the one door that was open to them.   Paul saw a vision of a man from Macedonia begging them to come to his country and help.   The most important help anyone can receive is the Gospel! They made immediate plans to go to Macedonia, knowing this must surely be God's will!

Rejoice today, knowing that even a closed door can be God's way of directing you toward His perfect will. As His children, we can trust Him to lead us every day.

Romans 8:14 For as many as are led by the Spirit of God, they are the sons of God.

---

[457] Modern-day Turkey.

Acts 16:25-17:9

Acts 16:31 And they said, Believe on the Lord Jesus Christ, and thou shalt be saved, and thy house.

We see in this Scripture the power of the Holy Spirit and the power of a godly testimony. Paul and Silas were beaten and thrown in jail for preaching the Gospel. The Lord released them miraculously in the middle of the night. When their jailer realized that they were free, he was about to take his own life.[458] Death would probably have been his punishment for letting a prisoner escape anyway.

When they assured him they were still there, and had not escaped, the Spirit of God filled his heart with such conviction that he cried out, "What Must I Do to Be Saved!" The answer was clear, "Believe on the Lord Jesus Christ and thou shalt be saved and thy house." After hearing the Gospel, the jailer and his family received Christ and were baptized in water!

Of course, those family members heard the Gospel and received Christ for themselves, but one wonders how powerful the jailer's testimony must have been in influencing his family for Christ. May the Lord help us to lead such faithful lives that our testimony will be like salt, bringing spiritual thirst into the lives of our family members.

Matthew 5:13 Ye are the salt of the earth: but if the salt have lost his savor, wherewith shall it be salted? it is thenceforth good for nothing, but to be cast out, and to be trodden under foot of men.

---

[458] Acts 16:27

Acts 17:10-34

Acts 17:11 These were more noble than those in Thessalonica, in that they received the word with all readiness of mind, and searched the scriptures daily, whether those things were so.

The Christians in Berea were commended for the way they received the ministry of the Word of God.   My prayer is that we will all receive the "good seed" of the Word the same way.

First, they received it with all readiness of mind.   They received it eagerly.   They were joyful as they received what they knew was rich spiritual food for their souls.   It was good news. As we are told in 1st Peter 2:2, they desired the sincere milk of the Word, so they could grow.   Receive the Word of God with eagerness and joy!

Second, they received the ministry of the word carefully.   They searched the Scriptures daily to see if what they were hearing was true to the Word of God.   Sadly, many Christians are lacking in *this* area today.   They lack discernment.   I often tell the folks I preach to week after week to check out what they hear from this, or any other pulpit, by the Word of God.   Search the Scriptures daily.

2 Timothy 2:15 Study to shew thyself approved unto God, a workman that needeth not to be ashamed, rightly dividing the word of truth.

Read Acts 18:1-23

Acts 18:9-10 Then spake the Lord to Paul in the night by a vision, Be not afraid, but speak, and hold not thy peace: 10 For I am with thee, and no man shall set on thee to hurt thee: for I have much people in this city.

Though he was a great man of God, and full of the Holy Spirit, Paul was still a man and faced things that made him afraid. In Thessalonica and Berea where he had ministered before, he had faced tremendous persecution from unbelieving Jews. Now, he was ministering in Corinth, which was probably one of the most wicked city of that day—a city with a *very* unsavory reputation. What would he experience there?

In light of those understandable fears, the Lord gave him a word. Don't be afraid to speak. Don't be afraid to proclaim the Word. You may feel all alone in this wicked place, but I have much people in this city. Have you ever felt like you were all alone in serving God? At your work? In your family? The word God gave Paul applies to you too. You don't have to be afraid, fulfill what He has called you to do in the power of the Holy Spirit and know that He will be with you. You are never alone!

Matthew 28:19-20 Go ye therefore, and teach all nations, baptizing them in the name of the Father, and of the Son, and of the Holy Ghost: Teaching them to observe all things whatsoever I have commanded you: and, lo, **I am with you alway, *even* unto the end of the world**. Amen.

Read Acts 18:24-19:20

Acts 19:2 He said unto them, Have ye received the Holy Ghost since ye believed? And they said unto him, We have not so much as heard whether there be any Holy Ghost.

These folks were apparently followers of Jesus, because they are called disciples. However, they had limited knowledge about some of the truths of the Gospel, including the outpouring of the Holy Spirit. In this way, they may have been like Apollos who received further instruction about some of these things from the husband and wife team of Priscilla and Aquila.[459] Paul's words to the Ephesian disciples can be translated, "Having believed, did you receive the Holy Spirit?" All true believers are indwelt by the Holy Spirit[460], but it is clearly possible to be a believer without having been *baptized* in the Holy Spirit.

They had been baptized, but only "John's baptism," a baptism of repentance, looking forward to the coming of Jesus. They had not been baptized as Jesus commanded after His death and resurrection. Paul baptized them in the Name (by the authority of) the Lord Jesus Christ.[461] Then, when he laid his hands on them, they were filled with the Holy Spirit as many others had been before them at Pentecost,[462] in Samaria,[463] and at the house of Cornelius.[464] This was evidenced by the fact that they spoke in tongues and prophesied.

This continues to emphasize an important theme in the book of Acts. In the last days, the Lord will pour out His Spirit on all flesh. I am glad He is *still* doing so!

Acts 2:17-18 And it shall come to pass in the last days, saith God, I will pour out of my Spirit upon all flesh: and your sons and your daughters shall prophesy, and your young men shall see visions, and your old men shall dream dreams: And on my servants and on my handmaidens I will pour out in those days of my Spirit; and they shall prophesy:

---

[459] Acts 18:24-26
[460] Romans 8:9
[461] Matthew 28:19
[462] Acts 2:1-4
[463] Acts 8:14-17
[464] Acts 10:44-46

Read Acts 19:21-41

Acts 19:21 After these things were ended, Paul **purposed in the spirit,** when he had passed through Macedonia and Achaia, to go to Jerusalem, saying, After I have been there, I **must** also see Rome.

The Apostle Paul was an amazing man of God in many ways. Some have estimated that he traveled more than 10,000 miles carrying the Gospel of the Lord Jesus Christ, much of that on foot. Over the course of those many miles, he encountered many great trials. He was shipwrecked, faced robbers, imprisonment, cold, hunger, weariness, pain and persecution. Besides all that, he had the responsibility of caring for all the churches he started.[465]

Despite many trials, he felt compelled by the Holy Spirit to keep going, to reach one more place for Jesus. He felt he owed a spiritual debt to bring the Gospel to the lost.[466] He had no choice but to heed God's call and preach the Gospel. He once said, "Woe is unto me, if I preach not the Gospel."[467]

When I think of Paul's life and ministry, it reminds me of the words of an old song that some of you may remember.

It may not be on the mountain's height, or over the stormy sea;
It may not be at the battle's front my Lord will have need of me,
But, if by a still, small voice He calls to paths I do not know,
I'll answer dear Lord with my hand in Thine,
"I'll go where you want me to go."
I'll go where you want me to go, dear Lord,
O'er mountain, or plain, or sea;
I'll say what you want me to say, dear Lord,
I'll be what you want me to be.[468]

---

[465] 2 Corinthians 11:25-28
[466] Romans 1:14
[467] 1 Corinthians 9:16
[468] I'll Go Where You Want Me to Go," Mary Brown, Carrie E. Rounsefell

Read Acts 20:1-16

Acts 20:7 And upon the first *day* of the week, when the disciples came together to break bread, Paul preached unto them, ready to depart on the morrow; and continued his speech until midnight.

They were meeting on the Lord's Day for the preaching of the Word and breaking of bread---taking the Lord's Supper together. The early church had already begun to meet for worship on the first day of the week, the Lord's Day, remembering the Resurrection of the Lord Jesus Christ[469] and perhaps even the outpouring of the Spirit at Pentecost, which also took place on the first day of the week. This was also a day for receiving offerings, giving as unto the Lord.[470] John, imprisoned on the Isle of Patmos, says that he was "in the Spirit on the Lord's Day."[471]

Whatever the case, the Lord's people are commanded to come together, to assemble. We cannot obey many of God's commandments in the New Testament without meeting as a body. I pray that the Lord's Day finds you worshiping with other believers. It will be even more important as we draw ever closer to the return of Jesus.

Hebrews 10:25 Not forsaking the assembling of ourselves together, as the manner of some *is*; but exhorting *one another*: and so much the more, as ye see the day approaching.

---

[469] Mark 16:2
[470] 1 Corinthians 16:2
[471] Revelation 1:10

Read Acts 20:17-38

Acts 20:28-29 Take heed therefore unto yourselves, and to all the flock, over the which the Holy Ghost hath made you overseers, to feed the church of God, which he hath purchased with his own blood. For I know this, that after my departing shall grievous wolves enter in among you, not sparing the flock.

Paul is giving some final words to the elders of the church in Ephesus. In the New Testament, the word elder is used synonymously with bishop (overseer) and shepherd (pastor). Here in Acts 20, he emphasizes the shepherding/pastoral role. What is expected of these men? He gives us several duties of shepherds, not necessarily in order of importance.

First, they are to take heed unto themselves. If they are not in right relationship with the Lord themselves, they cannot really lead God's people. Second, they are to oversee the flock of God. This might include some administrative duties and looking out for the spiritual welfare of the church. Third, they are to bring healthy spiritual food to God's sheep[472]. This, of course comes from preaching and teaching the Word of God. Fourth, they are to guard the flock against spiritual wolves, false teachers, that are bound to appear, especially in these last days.

Today, pray that your pastor fulfills each of these roles as God would have him to.

---

[472] 1 Peter 5:1-4

Read Acts 21:1-21

Acts 21:8-9 And the next *day* we that were of Paul's company departed, and came unto Caesarea: and we entered into the house of Philip the evangelist, which was *one* of the seven; and abode with him. And the same man had four daughters, virgins, which did prophesy.

Philip, called "The Evangelist" here was one of the seven chosen in Acts 6 to help distribute food to the widows.   Like Steven, another of that group, he was also a powerful preacher of the Gospel.   He preached the Word in Samaria[473] and later lead a prominent Ethiopian court official to Christ.   The last we saw of him in Acts, the Holy Spirit miraculously transported him from where he was, and he preached his way to Caesarea, where he continued to live.[474]

We know very little of Philip's daughters, except that they were prophets, speaking words of exhortation, edification, and comfort through the power of the Holy Spirit.[475]   In this they were part of a long line of godly women used in such a way.   That list includes women such as Moses' sister, Miriam[476], Deborah,[477] Huldah,[478] and Anna.[479]

Today, we are living in the last days and the Lord is still pouring out His Spirit on all flesh.   If you are one of God's children, male or female, rejoice today that He can pour out His Spirit on you!

Acts 2:17-18 And it shall come to pass in the last days, saith God, I will pour out of my Spirit upon **all flesh**: and your sons and **your daughters** shall prophesy, and your young men shall see visions, and your old men shall dream dreams: And on my servants and on **my handmaidens** I will pour out in those days of my Spirit; and they shall prophesy:

---

[473] Acts 8
[474] Acts 8:39-40
[475] 1 Corinthians 14:3
[476] Exodus 15:20-21
[477] Judges 4:4
[478] 2nd Kings 22:14ff
[479] Luke 2:36ff

Read Acts 21:22—40

Acts 21:39 But Paul said, I am a man *which am* a Jew of Tarsus, *a city* in Cilicia, a citizen of no mean city: and, I beseech thee, suffer me to speak unto the people.

Paul had, once more, been falsely accused,[480] beaten,[481] and chained.[482] This was nothing new. These kinds of things had been a part of his life ever since He began to follow the Savior. He undoubtedly remembered the prophetic word spoken over him a short time earlier by the prophet Agabus. Agabus warned Paul that when he got to Jerusalem he would be bound and turned over to the Gentiles.[483] Paul did not beg for his life, but standing before that angry mob he asked for an opportunity to speak, which he was given. He gave his testimony and preached the Gospel with power and authority despite the great danger to his life.

Everywhere he went, it seems that someone was warning him about the dangers that were ahead. He had a ready answer for those who warned him, "None of these things move me, neither count I my life dear unto me."[484]

May the Lord give us the same kind of faith, that we would also proclaim, "none of these things move me!" I love the words of an old Gospel song taken from Psalm 1.

I shall not be, I shall not be moved, I shall not be, I shall not be moved,
Just like a tree that's planted by the waters, I shall not be moved.

---

[480] Acts 21:28
[481] Acts 21:31-32
[482] Acts 21:33
[483] Acts 21:11
[484] Acts 20:24

Read Acts 22:1-23

Acts 22:16 And now why tarriest thou? arise, and be baptized, and wash away thy sins, calling on the name of the Lord.

Paul is giving his testimony before an angry mob in Jerusalem. He tells them that he is a fellow Jew and has been taught the law of God by one of their most famous rabbis, Gamaliel. He had lived a life that was very devoted to God's law, as had most who listened to him.[485] He zealously persecuted Christians, believing he was doing God a service.

Despite his zeal for God, and devotion to the Law, he was not saved until he had an encounter with the Lord. He admitted that he was a sinner, something we must all do, and he called on the Lord to save him. He made a public declaration by being baptized in water. That is how his sins were washed away, something no amount of zeal or keeping of the Law could do.

Acts 2:21 And it shall come to pass, *that* whosoever shall call on the name of the Lord shall be saved.

---

[485] Acts 22:3

Read Acts 22:24-23:11

Acts 23:11 And the night following the Lord stood by him, and said, Be of good cheer, Paul: for as thou hast testified of me in Jerusalem, so must thou bear witness also at Rome.

Paul was attacked by an angry mob, and beaten by those who hoped he would confess his supposed crime. He was brought before the Sanhedrin, the same group that ordered Jesus' crucifixion, and it would seem his life was in great danger. Yet, the Lord stood by Him and gave him a word. Cheer up Paul! You are going to make it! You are going to preach the Gospel in Rome just as you have preached it here in Jerusalem!

The road to Rome would have many dangers, but the Lord and His promise sustained him. Once, when their ship was wrecked, he comforted the crew and passengers with these words, "Be of good cheer (notice that is what the Lord told *him* in Jerusalem!) for I believe God, that it shall be done even as it was told me."[486] I'm going to make it safely to Rome. That is standing on God's promises!

We are probably not headed to Rome to preach the Gospel, but the Lord has a plan for *our* lives too. I'm thankful today that he has promised us safe passage to our destination. Like Paul, we can stand on His promises!

> Standing on the promises that cannot fail,
> When the howling storms of doubt and fear assail,
> By the living Word of God I shall prevail,
> Standing on the promises of God.[487]

---

[486] Acts 27:25
[487] "Standing on the Promises," Russell Carter, 1886.

Read Acts 24:1-23

Acts 24:16 And herein do I exercise myself, to have always a conscience void of offence toward God, and *toward* men.

Paul not only preached the resurrection of the Lord Jesus Christ, but he also preached the resurrection of the dead, both the just and the unjust[488]. This was nothing new, not a heresy, but something taught in the Old Testament Scriptures, the Law and the Prophets. He knew that he too was going to stand before God some day. That knowledge is what made him do all he could to keep a clear conscience, void of offence, toward both God and men.[489]

The truth is, everyone will stand before God one day. As Christians, we will stand before the Judgment Seat of Christ,[490] those who reject Him will stand before the Great White Throne.[491] There truly is coming a resurrection (and judgment) of both the just and the unjust and all will stand before God. Because of that great truth, my prayer today is this, "May I, like Paul, have a conscience void of offence toward God and men!"

Hebrews 10:22 Let us draw near with a true heart in full assurance of faith, having our hearts sprinkled from an evil conscience, and our bodies washed with pure water.

---

[488] Acts 24:14-15
[489] Acts 24:16
[490] 2 Corinthians 5:10
[491] Revelation 20:11-12

Read Acts 24:1-23

Acts 24:15 And have hope toward God, which they themselves also allow, that there shall be a resurrection of the dead, both of the just and unjust.

Paul was preaching and teaching something that godly Jews should have known from Old Testament Scripture. He was preaching something that the Pharisees, at least, should have believed wholeheartedly. There will be a day of resurrection for both the just *and* the unjust. It was because of that hope that he stood before them that day.[492]

The coming resurrection was Paul's hope and it is our blessed hope too.[493] When Jesus returns *for* His church, those who are in their graves will hear His voice and rise to meet Him.[494] Their bodies will be changed in a moment of time, becoming like Jesus' body after He rose from the dead.[495] Almost simultaneously, those of us who are still alive and remain on this earth will be changed and caught up together with them to meet the Lord in the air.[496] We are to comfort one another with this great hope.[497] This is the resurrection of the just, what the Bible calls the *first* resurrection. If we are a part of that number, the second death[498] can have no power over us![499]

Changed in the twinkling of an eye,
Changed in the twinkling of an eye,
The trumpet shall sound, the dead shall be raised,
Changed in the twinkling of an eye.[500]

---

[492] Acts 24:21
[493] Titus 2:13
[494] John 5:28
[495] 1 Corinthians 15:52, 1 John 3:1-3
[496] 1 Thessalonians 4:15-17
[497] 1 Thessalonians 4:18
[498] Eternal Separation from God.
[499] Revelation 20:6
[500] "Changed in the Twinkling of an Eye," Fanny Crosby and William J. Kirkpatrick

Read Acts 24:24-25:12

Acts 24:25 And as he reasoned of righteousness, temperance, and judgment to come, Felix trembled, and answered, Go thy way for this time; when I have a convenient season, I will call for thee.

Felix and his wife, Drusilla, were living ungodly lives. She is said to have been a very outwardly beautiful woman, and Felix had seduced her away from her husband, so she could become his third wife.[501] They were curious, and wanted to hear what Paul had to say. Anointed by the Holy Spirit, Paul began to speak to them about righteousness (something they knew little about), temperance (self-control), and judgment to come (something they would soon face), very fitting subjects because of how they had been living. There was such great conviction of sin that Felix began to tremble. Had he cried out to God for mercy, he could have been saved, but he did not.

Felix did not repent and turn to Christ, nor did he openly reject Him. He simply sent Paul away and said, "When it's convenient, I will call for you again." So far as we know, neither Felix nor Drusilla ever found that "convenient" time to repent and turn to Christ, dying without Him. Today is the day! We must seek Him while He may be found.

Isaiah 55:6-7 Seek ye the LORD while he may be found, call ye upon him while he is near: Let the wicked forsake his way, and the unrighteous man his thoughts: and let him return unto the LORD, and he will have mercy upon him; and to our God, for he will abundantly pardon.

---

[501] Enduring Word Commentary

Read Acts 25:13-27

Acts 25:23 And on the morrow, when Agrippa was come, and Bernice, with great pomp, and was entered into the place of hearing, with the chief captains, and principal men of the city, at Festus' commandment Paul was brought forth.

Herod Agrippa, the Roman king of Judea, and his sister, Bernice, were visiting the place where Paul was being held.   Agrippa's great-grandfather was the one who tried to kill Jesus at His birth.[502]   His grandfather was the one who ordered John the Baptist beheaded.[503] His father was the one who killed the first apostle, James.[504] Now Paul is about to stand before the next in this long line of evil men.

This was all a part of God's plan for his life. The day he was born again, the Lord gave a word that he would bear the Name of Jesus before kings.[505] That prophetic word was being fulfilled. What a joy it must have been for Paul to give his testimony before this man, knowing it was a "God Thing" a part of something much bigger than what he could see with his eyes.   How wonderful to know that our steps are ordered by the Lord!

Psalm 37:23-24 The steps of a *good* man are ordered by the LORD: and he delighteth in his way. Though he fall, he shall not be utterly cast down: for the LORD upholdeth *him with* his hand.

---

[502] Matthew 2:16-18
[503503] Matthew 14:1-12
[504] Acts 12:1-2
[505] Acts 9:15-16

Read Acts 26:1-23

Acts 26:23 That Christ should suffer, *and* that he should be the first that should rise from the dead, and should shew light unto the people, and to the Gentiles.

Paul recognizes that he is being judged for his belief in the resurrection[506]. It was not a new teaching that God would raise the dead. It was a promise made to their fathers in Old Testament days. Should it be so strange that God would do what He promised to do?[507]

The crucified and resurrected Lord Jesus Christ was always at the center of apostolic preaching, and He must be at the center of our preaching too[508]. Paul could not be disobedient to what the Lord had told him to do.[509] He could not deny that Jesus was alive, because he met him on the road to Damascus.

Jesus was the *first* to experience resurrection, but He will not be the last. He said, because I live, you shall live also![510]

He lives, He lives, Christ Jesus lives today!
He walks with me and talks with me along life's narrow way.
He lives, He lives, salvation to impart!
You ask me how I know He lives?
He lives within my heart.[511]

---

[506] Acts 26:3
[507] Acts 26:8
[508] 1 Corinthians 15:1-6
[509] Acts 26:19
[510] John 14:19
[511] "He Lives," Alfred Henry Ackley

Read Acts 26:24-27:12

Acts 26:27-28 King Agrippa, believest thou the prophets? I know that thou believest. Then Agrippa said unto Paul, Almost thou persuadest me to be a Christian.

Felix heard the Gospel, trembled with conviction, and then put off his decision for a more convenient day that never came.[512] King Agrippa heard the same Gospel truths, and said, "Almost thou persuadest me to be a Christian." Some think this is actually a question, "Do you think you could persuade me to be a Christian in such a short time?" Either way, here are men who heard the truth, could have been gloriously saved, but continued in their sin.

Both Felix and Agrippa squandered their great moment of opportunity. They heard the truth, experienced the conviction of the Holy Spirit, and yet they did not respond to what they heard. Years later, a pastor spoke these words at the end of his message, "He who is almost persuaded is almost saved, and to be almost saved is to be entirely lost."[513] Songwriter, Philip Bliss, sitting in the congregation that day, wrote a song based on the pastor's closing words....ALMOST persuaded.

> "Almost persuaded," now to believe;
> "Almost persuaded," Christ to receive;
> Seems now some soul to say,
> "Go, Spirit, go Thy way,
> Some more convenient day
> On Thee I'll call."
>
> "Almost persuaded," harvest is past!
> "Almost persuaded," doom comes at last!
> "Almost" cannot avail;
> "Almost" is but to fail!
> Sad, sad, that bitter wail,
> "Almost," but lost.[514]

---

[512] Acts 24:25
[513] http://breadsite.org/hymnstories/almostpersuaded.htm
[514] "Almost Persuaded," Philip P. Bliss.

Read Acts 27:13-38

Acts 27:23-25 For there stood by me this night the angel of God, whose I am, and whom I serve, Saying, Fear not, Paul; thou must be brought before Caesar: and, lo, God hath given thee all them that sail with thee. Wherefore, sirs, be of good cheer: for I believe God, that it shall be even as it was told me.

Paul was now on board ship, beginning a trip that would ultimately take him to Rome. He had warned the sailors that continuing to sail as they were would likely lead to disaster, but no one listened.[515] Great difficulty did come, just as he had warned, a terrifying Mediterranean storm, known as Euroclydon, a northeaster, struck. After days of raging seas, and terrifying waves, they had literally given up all hope of being saved.[516]

It was then that Paul received a visit from an angelic messenger, the emissary of the One he belonged to (whose I am) and the One he served (whom I serve). The angel brought a confirmation of a word he had received back in Jerusalem, "Be of good cheer, Paul: for as thou hast testified of me in Jerusalem, so must thou bear witness also at Rome."[517] Because of that confirmation, he was able to speak a word of encouraging faith to those who were with him, "Be of good cheer! I believe God!"

If God gives us an encouragement, or a word of comfort, He expects us to use what He has given to encourage someone else.

2 Corinthians 1:3-4 Blessed *be* God, even the Father of our Lord Jesus Christ, the Father of mercies, and the God of all comfort; Who comforteth us in all our tribulation, that we may be able to comfort them which are in any trouble, by the comfort wherewith we ourselves are comforted of God.

---

[515] Acts 27:10
[516] Acts 27:20
[517] Acts 23:11

Read Acts 27:39-28:10

Acts 28:3-5 And when Paul had gathered a bundle of sticks, and laid them on the fire, there came a viper out of the heat, and fastened on his hand. And when the barbarians saw the venomous beast hang on his hand, they said among themselves, No doubt this man is a murderer, whom, though he hath escaped the sea, yet vengeance suffereth not to live. And he shook off the beast into the fire, and felt no harm.

After weathering a near-fatal shipwreck, they landed on the Island of Malta. Gathering sticks for the fire, Paul faced another adverse situation. He was bitten by a venomous snake. The King James Version calls it a viper, and there is some question as to which snake it actually was, but the citizens of Malta knew it to be very dangerous. They expected Paul to swell up and die, most likely as a punishment for some great sin he had committed (they knew he was a prisoner from the ship). When they saw that he simply shook the snake off his hand and into the fire, they were amazed. They went from thinking him a murderer, to thinking him a god.

This event is a fulfillment of Jesus' words in Mark 16:18, "They shall take up serpents; and if they drink any deadly thing, it shall not hurt them; they shall lay hands on the sick, and they shall recover." Paul was obviously not a "snake handler," but when in the course of ministry, he needed miraculous deliverance from that snake bite, the Lord gave it to him. Even though he was technically a prisoner, that miracle gave him an open door to preach the Gospel and pray for the sick all over the Island of Malta!

What Satan meant for evil, God meant for good!

Genesis 50:20 But as for you, ye thought evil against me; but God meant it unto good, to bring to pass, as it is this day, to save much people alive.

Read Acts 28:11-31

Acts 28:14-15 Where we found brethren, and were desired to tarry with them seven days: and so we went toward Rome. And from thence, when the brethren heard of us, they came to meet us as far as Appii forum, and The three taverns: whom when Paul saw, he thanked God, and took courage.

Paul is nearing the end of a long journey that took him from an arrest in Jerusalem to within miles of his destination—Rome!   There, he will have a two year wait before his promised hearing before Caesar. Though he faced many perils along the way, he was never alone. There was One who promised never to leave or forsake him.

The Lord also sent *people* along the way to encourage him.   He sent a faithful friend in Luke, the one who wrote the book of Acts.   We know that Luke was with him, because he uses the word "we" in this part of Acts.   Luke never left his friend from Caesarea all the way to Rome.[518] Other friends joined them as they neared Rome, some of them traveling as far as fifty miles to meet Paul.   These brothers had probably never met him in person, but had read the letter he had sent them a few years earlier.[519] Their very presence encouraged and cheered his heart!

We are thankful for our Best Friend, the Lord Jesus Christ, but what a blessing it is to know the others He sends along the way to encourage us.   Thank Him for godly friends today.

Proverbs 17:17 A friend loveth at all times, and a brother is born for adversity.

---

[518] Note how Luke starts using "we" again in Acts 27.
[519] Paul's Epistle to the Romans

Read Romans 1:1-17

Romans 1:16-17 16 For I am not ashamed of the gospel of Christ: for it is the power of God unto salvation to every one that believeth; to the Jew first, and also to the Greek. 17 For therein is the righteousness of God revealed from faith to faith: as it is written, The just shall live by faith.

The just shall live by faith!   It must be an important truth, for we find it quoted four times in the Word of God (Habakkuk 2:4, Romans 1:17, Galatians 3:11, and Hebrews 10:38).   In fact, justification by faith is the theme of Romans, and many have come to saving faith while reading this wonderful book!   In Romans, we will learn of our need for salvation and the means of receiving it.   Later, we will learn how the same faith, by which we were saved, is also essential to our sanctification.

What does it mean to be just, or justified?   Some have said that it means "just as if I'd never sinned."   As glorious as that is, it is only half of it.   Spiritually, we are worse than bankrupt.   We are bankrupt, *and* owe a tremendous debt that is impossible to pay.   Justification not only wipes out the debt of sin, it imputes Jesus' perfect righteousness to us. My sins have been forgiven, and I have been made righteous in Him. For this great gift, I will praise Him forever!

> He paid a debt He did not owe,
> I owed a debt I could not pay,
> I needed someone to wash my sins away,
> And now I sing a brand-new song, Amazing Grace!
> Christ Jesus paid the debt that I could never pay. [520]

---

[520] "He Paid a Debt," Ellis J. Crum

Read Romans 1.18-32

Romans 1:18 For the wrath of God is revealed from heaven against all ungodliness and unrighteousness of men, who hold the truth in unrighteousness;

It is a sobering truth, but outside of Jesus Christ, the wrath of a holy God is directed toward sinful humanity. Wrath is defined as God's righteous anger. He is totally righteous, totally just, and totally justified in being angry with sinful human beings. The ultimate end of that righteous anger is eternal judgment in hell, what the Bible calls the second death[521].

Romans 1 declares that the invisible God has revealed Himself to all mankind through His creation[522]. This is like Psalm 19 where we are told that the heavens declare the glory of God[523]. Day and night, the voice of creation speaks of the Creator.[524] It is a voice understood by every language group[525] and in every corner of the world.[526] Only a fool can look at creation and deny the existence of the Creator.[527] Denying what can be known of Him sends mankind on a downward spiral of sin, a spiral described here in Romans 1, and ultimately leading to what He calls a reprobate or depraved mind[528]. Because of the world's rejection of what can be clearly seen, God declares ALL "without excuse."

These are difficult truths to consider, but unless we know that we are lost and without God, we cannot really know our need of a Savior, and when we consider what we are without Him, we are all the more grateful for what He has done!

---

[521] **Revelation 21:8 But** the fearful, and unbelieving, and the abominable, and murderers, and whoremongers, and sorcerers, and idolaters, and all liars, shall have their part in the lake which burneth with fire and brimstone: which is the second death.

[522] **Romans 1:20 For** the invisible things of him from the creation of the world are clearly seen, being understood by the things that are made, *even* his eternal power and Godhead; so that they are without excuse:

[523] **Psalm 19:1** The heavens declare the glory of God; and the firmament sheweth his handiwork.

[524] **Psalm 19:2 Day** unto day uttereth speech, and night unto night sheweth knowledge.

[525] **Psalm 19:3 There** *is* no speech nor language, *where* their voice is not heard.

[526] **Psalm 19:4 Their** line is gone out through all the earth, and their words to the end of the world. In them hath he set a tabernacle for the sun,

[527] **Psalm 14:1** The fool hath said in his heart, *There is* no God. They are corrupt, they have done abominable works, *there is* none that doeth good.

[528] **Romans 1:28 And** even as they did not like to retain God in *their* knowledge, God gave them over to a reprobate mind, to do those things which are not convenient;

Read Romans 2:1-29

Romans 2:1 Therefore thou art inexcusable, O man, whosoever thou art that judgest: for wherein thou judgest another, thou condemnest thyself; for thou that judgest doest the same things.

Romans 2 is still building the case that outside of Christ, all stand inexcusable and condemned. So often the lost seek to justify their behavior by comparing it with that of others. How often I have heard, "At least I'm not as bad as *that* person." In reality, though, without His salvation, no matter how moral we think that we are, we are just as lost as the vilest of sinners.

Those who are self-deceived in this way will not escape God's righteous judgment,[529] but there is good news! God, in His goodness, has been longsuffering with sinners. He has declared that it is not His will that any perish in their sin,[530] and in His goodness, He has given us an opportunity to repent and be saved![531] As I thought about this today, the words of an old hymn came to mind. They are my prayer, and I hope that they are yours too.

> I need Thee every hour, most gracious Lord;
> No tender voice like Thine can peace afford.
> I need Thee, O I need Thee; every hour I need Thee;
> O bless me now, my Savior, I come to Thee.[532]

---

[529] **Romans 2:1-3** 1 Therefore thou art inexcusable, O man, whosoever thou art that judgest: for wherein thou judgest another, thou condemnest thyself; for thou that judgest doest the same things. 2 But we are sure that the judgment of God is according to truth against them which commit such things. 3 And thinkest thou this, O man, that judgest them which do such things, and doest the same, that thou shalt escape the judgment of God?

[530] **2 Peter 3:9** The Lord is not slack concerning his promise, as some men count slackness; but is longsuffering to us-ward, not willing that any should perish, but that all should come to repentance.

[531] **Romans 2:4** Or despisest thou the riches of his goodness and forbearance and longsuffering; not knowing that the goodness of God leadeth thee to repentance?

[532] "I Need Thee Every Hour," Annie Hawks

Read Romans 3:1-31

Romans 3:10-12 10 As it is written, There is none righteous, no, not one: 11 There is none that understandeth, there is none that seeketh after God. 12 They are all gone out of the way, they are together become unprofitable; there is none that doeth good, no, not one.

The Book of Romans makes it very clear that we cannot save ourselves. Neither a moral Gentile nor a devout Jew are truly righteous before God. How many righteous people are there in the world? None! How many are there that naturally seek after God? None! How many have strayed from the path? All! How many do what is good? Not even one! We have all sinned against God, and we come nowhere near His perfect glory.[533]

God's Law cannot save us, but it does reveal our great need.[534] How can unclean human beings be made righteous? It is not through keeping the Law. For one thing, no one, but Jesus, has been able to do that[535]. Offending in one small point of the Law makes us guilty of breaking it all.[536] Even if we could keep it, we would have to do so continually.[537] God calls our righteous deeds filthy rags.[538] We are not justified through carefully following the path, for all of us have strayed from that path of righteousness.[539]

---

[533] **Romans 3:23 For** all have sinned, and come short of the glory of God;
[534] **Romans 3:20 Therefore** by the deeds of the law there shall no flesh be justified in his sight: for by the law *is* the knowledge of sin.
Galatians 3:24-25 24 Wherefore the law was our schoolmaster *to bring us* unto Christ, that we might be justified by faith. 25 But after that faith is come, we are no longer under a schoolmaster.
[535] **Hebrews 4:15 For** we have not an high priest which cannot be touched with the feeling of our infirmities; but was in all points tempted like as *we are, yet* without sin.
[536] **James 2:10 For** whosoever shall keep the whole law, and yet offend in one *point*, he is guilty of all.
[537] **Galatians 3:10 For** as many as are of the works of the law are under the curse: for it is written, Cursed *is* every one that continueth not in all things which are written in the book of the law to do them.
[538] **Isaiah 64:6 But** we are all as an unclean *thing*, and all our righteousnesses *are* as filthy rags; and we all do fade as a leaf; and our iniquities, like the wind, have taken us away.
[539] **Isaiah 53:6 All** we like sheep have gone astray; we have turned everyone to his own way; and the LORD hath laid on him the iniquity of us all.

The only righteousness we really have is that which is given to us through faith in Jesus Christ.[540]   Remember what we have learned about justification? It is not only being forgiven the debt of sin, it is being given the gift of His righteousness.   What an amazing gift!   I think the words of this old hymn say it so very well[541].

1. Rock of Ages, cleft for me,
Let me hide myself in Thee;
Let the water and the blood,
From Thy wounded side which flowed,
Be of sin the double cure,
Save from wrath and make me pure.

2. <u>Not the labor of my hands</u>
<u>Can fulfill Thy law's demands</u>;
Could my zeal no respite know,
Could my tears forever flow,
All for sin could not atone;
Thou must save, and Thou alone.

3. <u>Nothing</u> in my hand I bring,
Simply to Thy cross I cling;
<u>Naked</u>, come to Thee for dress;
<u>Helpless</u>, look to Thee for grace;
Foul, I to the fountain fly;
Wash me, Savior, or I die.

4. While I draw this fleeting breath,
When my eyes shall close in death,
When I rise to worlds unknown,
And behold Thee on Thy throne,
Rock of Ages, cleft for me,
Let me hide myself in Thee.

---

[540] **Romans 3:21-22** 21 But now the righteousness of God without the law is manifested, being witnessed by the law and the prophets; 22 Even the righteousness of God *which is* by faith of Jesus Christ unto all and upon all them that believe: for there is no difference:
[541] "Rock of Ages," Augustus Toplady, 1776.

Read Romans 4:1-25

Romans 4:2-3 For if Abraham were justified by works, he hath *whereof* to glory; but not before God. 3 For what saith the scripture? Abraham believed God, and it was counted unto him for righteousness.

If we are totally lost, separated from God, and without excuse, as Romans 1-3 makes clear, how then can we be made **right** with God? First, it must be clear that we cannot justify ourselves through our own good works or futile attempts at keeping the Law of God.   If we could work to merit our salvation, then salvation would not be a gift of God's grace, but a debt owed to us. [542]   Ephesians 2:9 says that salvation is "not of works, lest any man should boast."

If we are not justified by our own good works, how then does our salvation come? Like Abraham, we believe God and it is *counted* unto us for righteousness.   The Greek word translated "counted" is "logizomai," an accounting term, meaning to credit to one's account. Though we have no righteousness of our own, when we believe, His righteousness is credited to our spiritual account.   When we try to earn, or merit, the blessings of God, then it is as if Jesus Christ died in vain.[543]

> Salvation unto us has come
> By God's free grace and favor;
> Good works cannot avert our doom,
> They help and save us never.
> Faith looks to Jesus Christ alone,
> Who did for all the world atone;
> He is our one Redeemer.[544]

---

[542] **Romans 4:4 Now** to him that worketh is the reward not reckoned of grace, but of debt.
[543] **Galatians 2:21** I do not frustrate the grace of God: for if righteousness *come* by the law, then Christ is dead in vain.
[544] "Salvation Now Has Come to All," Paul Speramus. Speramus was a Roman Catholic priest during the time of the Protestant Reformation. He was sentenced to death, and put in prison for preaching that we are justified by faith, just as the Bible declares.   While in prison, he wrote this hymn.

Read Romans 5:1-21

Romans 5:8 But God commendeth his love toward us, in that, while we were yet sinners, Christ died for us.

In the Gospel of John, Jesus tells us that the greatest demonstration of human love is to lay down one's life for a friend.[545] Most of us would be willing to lay down our lives to save a friend, our spouse, child, or perhaps even an endangered stranger, but what about someone that is our enemy[546]?   The love of God demonstrated by the death of Christ is amazing in that the Father loved us, and Christ died for us, while we were yet sinners[547].   He loved us while we were still His enemies, estranged from Him, and in rebellion. We were worthy of only His great justice and wrath, but in His amazing love He, instead, showed us grace and mercy[548].   Can anything be more wonderful than to know that Jesus loves me!

> I am so glad that our Father in Heav'n
> Tells of His love in the Book He has giv'n;
> Wonderful things in the Bible I see,
> This is the dearest, that Jesus loves me.
> I am so glad that Jesus loves me,
> Jesus loves me, Jesus loves me;
> I am so glad that Jesus loves me,
> Jesus loves even me[549].

---

[545] **John 15:13 Greater** love hath no man than this, that a man lay down his life for his friends.
[546] **Romans 5:7 For** scarcely for a righteous man will one die: yet peradventure for a good man some would even dare to die.
[547] **Romans 5:6 For** when we were yet without strength, in due time Christ died for the ungodly.
[548] **Romans 5:9** Much more then, being now justified by his blood, we shall be saved from wrath through him.
[549] "Jesus Loves Even Me," Philip P. Bliss

Read Romans 6:1-23

Romans 6:23 For the wages of sin *is* death; but the gift of God *is* eternal life through Jesus Christ our Lord.

The wages of sin is death. One of the old commentaries put it this way, ""Every sinner *earns* this by long, sore, and painful service. Oh! What pains do men take to get to hell! Early and late they toil at sin; and would not Divine justice be in their *debt*, if it did not pay them their due wages?" [550] When we are justified by faith in Christ, though, we **DO NOT RECEIVE** those wages, (the penalty) that is justly ours, a penalty that would ultimately mean eternal separation from God. Instead, we rejoice that Jesus paid the debt for us on the cross. That is His great **mercy**!

The gift of God is eternal life. Unlike wages, a gift is not earned or merited. It is simply received. John says, "as many as received him, to them gave he power to become the sons of God, *even* to them that believe on his name[551]." When we are justified by faith in Christ, **WE RECEIVE** a precious gift that we do not deserve--eternal life. That is His great **grace**!

So here in Romans 6 we see two of the most wonderful things we have received through being justified by faith—mercy and grace. How many of you remember this old hymn? It says it so well!

> 1. Years I spent in vanity and pride,
>   Caring not my Lord was crucified,
>   Knowing not it was for me He died
>   On Calvary.

---

[550] <u>Commentary on the New Testament</u>, Adam Clarke.
[551] John 1:12

Refrain:
Mercy there was great, and grace was free;
Pardon there was multiplied to me;
There my burdened soul found liberty
At Calvary.

2. By God's Word at last my sin I learned;
Then I trembled at the law I'd spurned,
Till my guilty soul imploring turned
To Calvary.

3. Now I've giv'n to Jesus everything,
Now I gladly own Him as my King,
Now my raptured soul can only sing
Of Calvary!

4. Oh, the love that drew salvation's plan!
Oh, the grace that brought it down to man!
Oh, the mighty gulf that God did span
At Calvary![552]

---

[552] "At Calvary," William Newell

Read Romans 7:1-25

Romans 7:24 O wretched man that I am! who shall deliver me from the body of this death?

In Romans 7 Paul describes the struggle of trying to live a righteous life in one's own strength and power. Those efforts helped him realize that there was no good at all in his flesh. He *wanted* to do what was right, but did not seem to have the power to do so.[553] His words echo those of all who have tried to live for God the same way, "For the good that I would I do not: but the evil which I would not, that I do."[554] Self-effort, outside the power of the cross, only leads to defeat and despair. Some see Paul's expression "body of death" as describing an ancient means of capital punishment. Spurgeon describes it very graphically, "It was the custom of ancient tyrants, when they wished to put men to the most fearful punishments, to tie a dead body to them, placing the two back to back; and there was the living man, with a dead body closely strapped to him, rotting, putrid, corrupting, and this he must drag with him wherever he went. . .this body of death, a thing as loathsome, as hideous, as abominable to his new life, as a dead stinking carcass would be to a living man."[555] Have you ever felt the weight of that "body of death?"

How horrible if his words were to end with Romans 7:24, but we must know the rest of the story! Deliverance comes through Christ, and His power, alone, "I thank God through Jesus Christ our Lord!"[556] We will find when we come to Romans 8 that there is glorious freedom in Christ! When you think about where He brought you from, it means so much to sing about freedom!

He set me free! Yes, He set me free! He broke the bonds of prison for me!
I'm glory bound, my Jesus to see, for glory to God, He set me free![557]

---

[553] Romans 7:18
[554] Romans 7:19
[555] <u>The Complete Works of Charles Spurgeon</u>, Charles Spurgeon
[556] Romans 7:25
[557] "He Set Me Free," Albert E. Brumley

Read Romans 8:1-22

Romans 8:1 *There is* therefore now no condemnation to them which are in Christ Jesus, who walk not after the flesh, but after the Spirit.

After the despairing cry of Romans 7:24, "Who shall deliver me from the body of this death," we find the wonderful declaration of Romans 8:1, "There is therefore now no condemnation to them which are in Christ Jesus." What a difference it makes when we are "in Him," the glorious position of one who has been justified by faith.

"In Christ" we are promised the indwelling of the Holy Spirit[558], whose presence gives us the assurance that we are truly God's children[559], and who helps us when we don't know how to pray as we should.[560] He will also quicken us, raising and changing our bodies on the day of resurrection.[561]

In the flesh we can never please God, but "in Christ," by the power of the Spirit, we are enabled to do so.

Romans 8:13 For if ye live after the flesh, ye shall die: but if ye through the Spirit do mortify the deeds of the body, ye shall live.

---

[558] **Romans 8:9** But ye are not in the flesh, but in the Spirit, if so be that the Spirit of God dwell in you. Now if any man have not the Spirit of Christ, he is none of his.

[559] **Romans 8:15-16** 15 For ye have not received the spirit of bondage again to fear; but ye have received the Spirit of adoption, whereby we cry, Abba, Father. 16 The Spirit itself beareth witness with our spirit, that we are the children of God:

[560] **Romans 8:26-27** 26 Likewise the Spirit also helpeth our infirmities: for we know not what we should pray for as we ought: but the Spirit itself maketh intercession for us with groanings which cannot be uttered. 27 And he that searcheth the hearts knoweth what *is* the mind of the Spirit, because he maketh intercession for the saints according to *the will of* God.

[561] **Romans 8:11** But if the Spirit of him that raised up Jesus from the dead dwell in you, he that raised up Christ from the dead shall also quicken your mortal bodies by his Spirit that dwelleth in you.

Read Romans 8:24-39

Romans 8:28-29   And we know that all things work together for good to them that love God, to them who are the called according to His purpose. 29 For whom he did foreknow, he also did predestinate to be conformed to the image of his Son, that he might be the firstborn among many brethren.

These verses can bring great peace to the child of God. Because of this, it has been a favorite of mine for many years. All things *do* work together for good, but there are certain conditions that must be met. First, we must love God, a love that is evidenced by a desire to please and obey Him. Second, we must be yielded to His divine will for our lives. It is as Jesus commanded us to pray, "Thy kingdom come, Thy will be done on earth as it is in heaven."

His purpose in all of this is to conform us to His image. Through it all, He is making us more like Jesus, as we are changed from glory to glory![562]

To be like Jesus, to be like Jesus, all I ask is to be like Him,
All through life's journey from earth to glory, all I ask is to be like Him.

---

[562] [2Co 3:18 KJV] 18 But we all, with open face beholding as in a glass the glory of the Lord, are changed into the same image from glory to glory, even as by the Spirit of the Lord.

Read Romans 9:1-22

Romans 9:1-3   I say the truth in Christ, I lie not, my conscience also bearing me witness in the Holy Ghost, 2 That I have great heaviness and continual sorrow in my heart. 3 For I could wish that myself were accursed from Christ for my brethren, my kinsmen according to the flesh:

The first eight chapters of Romans have dealt with our need for a Savior and the salvation that He alone can bring.   In chapters 9-11 the focus changes to the Nation of Israel and God's continuing plan for them.   The great heaviness and painful sorrow in Paul's heart came because his own people, the Jews, had rejected Jesus, their Messiah.

The desire of his heart was that they be saved. If possible, he said, he would wish that he could come under God's curse himself, instead of them facing it, that he could take their place. That, of course, was not possible, because it had already been done.   Jesus already bore the curse for all---Jew and Gentile---when He died on the cross.[563]   Today, let us pray for the peace of Jerusalem, that the Jews will find the Prince of Peace as Messiah, Savior, and Lord.

Psalm 122:6 Pray for the peace of Jerusalem: they shall prosper that love thee.

---

[563] [Gal 3:13 KJV] 13 Christ hath redeemed us from the curse of the law, being made a curse for us: for it is written, Cursed is every one that hangeth on a tree:

Read Romans 9:24-10:4

Romans 10:1 Brethren, my heart's desire and prayer to God for Israel is, that they might be saved.

The desire of Paul's heart and the prayer that was continually on his lips was that his fellow Jews come to faith in Jesus Christ as Savior and Lord. It is not that they were not passionate and sincere about their religious beliefs, most of them were. He says that they had a "zeal of God, but not according to knowledge."[564] The world is full of sincere religious people, truly believing that *their* way will lead them to heaven, but God's Word warns, "there is a way that seems right unto a man, but the end thereof are the ways of death."[565]   Sincerity and zeal, no matter how well-meaning, can never save us. Whether we are Jews or Gentiles, salvation is *only* through faith in Christ. Pray today that those close to you will find the One who is **the** Way!

John 14:6 Jesus saith unto him, I am the way, the truth, and the life: no man cometh unto the Father, but by me.

---

[564] Romans 10:2
[565] **Proverbs 16:25 There** is a way that seemeth right unto a man, but the end thereof *are* the ways of death.

Read Romans 10:5-21

Romans 10:9 That if thou shalt confess with thy mouth the Lord Jesus, and shalt believe in thine heart that God hath raised him from the dead, thou shalt be saved.

At the very beginning of this chapter, Paul expresses his heart's desire, and prayer, that his own people, the Jews, would come to faith in Jesus Christ. Yes, they are very sincere, and very zealous for their faith, but zeal, no matter how well-intentioned, cannot save us. How then *can* they be saved? We are told that we must confess the Lord Jesus Christ with our mouths and that we must believe in our hearts that God raised Him from the dead. If we will call on the Name of the Lord, we will be saved![566]

But, how can someone call on the Name of the Lord, if they have never heard that precious Name? How can they hear unless someone, a preacher of the Gospel, tells them? How can those preachers tell them, if they have not been sent?[567] We may not all go to the ends of the earth with the Gospel, but we can all participate in sending those who do. Be willing to go, but also ask the Lord how you can help send others also.

Matthew 9:37-38 Then saith he unto his disciples, The harvest truly *is* plenteous, but the labourers *are* few; 38 Pray ye therefore the Lord of the harvest, that he will send forth labourers into his harvest.

---

[566] **Romans 10:13** For whosoever shall call upon the name of the Lord shall be saved.
[567] **Romans 10:14-15** 14 How then shall they call on him in whom they have not believed? and how shall they believe in him of whom they have not heard? and how shall they hear without a preacher? 15 And how shall they preach, except they be sent? as it is written, How beautiful are the feet of them that preach the gospel of peace, and bring glad tidings of good things!

Read Romans 11:1-16

Romans 11:1 I say then, Hath God cast away his people? God forbid. For I also am an Israelite, of the seed of Abraham, *of* the tribe of Benjamin.

Paul is still speaking of his own people, the Jews, here. Even though they have rejected the Messiah, that does not mean God has cast them aside forever. He says, "God forbid. . . The Lord has not cast off His people which He foreknew," [568] those that in His foreknowledge He knew would turn to the Lord.

He writes of another time when things looked spiritually bleak for Israel. In Elijah's day, it appeared that all of them had rejected the Lord to serve idols. Elijah himself felt all alone, the only one still serving God. Yet the Lord made it clear to him that He still had seven thousand that had not bowed their knees to false gods. The Bible calls those faithful ones a remnant, that is, a small remaining quantity of something.

Even today, there may be times when God's people feel that so very few are truly serving Him. But, the Lord still has a people who have not bowed their knees to Baal, and by His grace may we be one of that number!

Isaiah 10:21 **The** remnant shall return, *even* the remnant of Jacob, unto the mighty God.

---

[568] Romans 11:2-3

Read Romans 11:17-36

Romans 11:29 For the gifts and calling of God are without repentance.

This chapter refutes replacement theology, a false teaching prevalent in some circles today. It is the belief that the church has somehow replaced Israel in God's plan, and that the Jews are no longer God's chosen people. It is the belief that the covenants and promises given to Israel have all been either rescinded or transferred to the church, and that Israel is now no different than any other nation on earth. However, the Word is clear, the Lord will not forget the promises He made to Israel! Jeremiah says that those promises will continue as long as the sun and moon endure,[569] and as Romans 11:29 declares, God's gifts and callings are without repentance, they are irrevocable!

The point of this chapter is not that Gentiles who receive Christ become Jews, but that believing Jews, not just those who are Jews by ethnic background, will receive the promises. It is as we were told in chapter 9, "They are not all Israel, which are of Israel."[570] The Lord promises a time when all Israel will turn to the Messiah and be saved. We pray for that day!

Romans 11:26 And so all Israel shall be saved: as it is written, There shall come out of Sion the Deliverer, and shall turn away ungodliness from Jacob:

---

[569] Jeremiah 31:35-37
[570] Romans 9:6

Read Romans 12

Romans 12:1-2 I beseech you therefore, brethren, by the mercies of God, that ye present your bodies a living sacrifice, holy, acceptable unto God, *which is* your reasonable service. 2 And be not conformed to this world: but be ye transformed by the renewing of your mind, that ye may prove what *is* that good, and acceptable, and perfect, will of God.

Religion and Christianity are not the same thing. In religion, sacrifices of various kinds are made to obtain God's blessing and mercy. In Christianity, we receive those blessings and mercy *because* of the ultimate sacrifice, the one that has already been made on the cross. Now, we present our bodies (our entire being) to God as a *living* sacrifice, not to obtain His mercy, but gratefully, because we already have!

Because we have obtained His mercy, we do not conform to this world[571]. The word "conform" means to "press into a mold." We are not pressed into the mold of an ungodly world system. Instead, we are being transformed[572] by the renewing[573] of our minds. As I yield myself to Him every day, the change comes.

Many years ago, Frances Havergal composed a hymn that expresses this very well:

Take my life and let it be, consecrated Lord to Thee; Take my hands and let them move at the impulse of Thy love, at the impulse of Thy love.
Take my feet, and let them be, swift and beautiful for Thee; take my voice, and let me sing Always, only, for my King, Always, only for My King.
Take my silver and my gold, not a mite would I withhold; take my moments and my days, let them flow in ceaseless praise, let them flow in ceaseless praise.
Take my will and make it Thine, it shall be no longer mine; take my heart, it is Thine own, it shall be Thy royal throne, it shall be Thy royal throne.

---

[571] 1 John 2:16

[572] Transformed is the Greek word metamorpho, from which we get our English word metamorphosis, the process by which larvae becomes butterflies or tadpoles become frogs. It is a change from one thing to another.

[573] "Renewing" indicates something that is a work in process. We are being changed from glory to glory, even as by the Spirit of the Lord (2nd Corinthians 3:18).

Read Romans 13

Romans 13:8 Owe no man any thing, but to love one another: for he that loveth another hath fulfilled the law.

In the New Covenant, love fulfills the Law of God. Jesus Himself told us that the two great commandments are to first love God with all of our heart, soul, mind, and strength, and second, to love our neighbor as ourselves.[574] The Ten Commandments are clearly about love. The first four are about loving God. (1) Because we love God, we will have no other gods before Him. (2) Because we love Him, will not make any idols. (3) We will not take the Name of One we love in vain. (4) We will respect the day of worship, because we love Him. The last six are about loving our neighbor as ourselves. (5) We honor our mother and father, because we love God and we love them. (6) We do not commit murder, because we love God, and we love our neighbor as ourselves. (7) We do not commit adultery, because we love God, and we love our mate. (8) We do not steal from one that we love. (9) We do not bear false witness against one that we love. (10) We do not covet that which belongs to one that we love. This is not ordinary human love, but supernatural love shed abroad in our hearts by the Holy Spirit.[575]

Galatians 5:14 For all the law is fulfilled in one word, *even* in this; Thou shalt love thy neighbour as thyself.

---

[574] Mark 12:29-31 29 And Jesus answered him, The first of all the commandments *is*, Hear, O Israel; The Lord our God is one Lord: 30 And thou shalt love the Lord thy God with all thy heart, and with all thy soul, and with all thy mind, and with all thy strength: this *is* the first commandment. 31 And the second *is* like, *namely* this, Thou shalt love thy neighbour as thyself. There is none other commandment greater than these.

[575] Romans 5:5   And hope maketh not ashamed; because the love of God is shed abroad in our hearts by the Holy Ghost which is given unto us.

Read Romans 14

Romans 14:12 So then every one of us shall give account of himself to God.

This chapter deals with what the King James Version of the Bible calls "Doubtful Disputations."[576] Another translates it as "quarrels over personal opinions." There are black and white issues of sin and righteousness, but there are also areas of personal conviction. We should not make those areas of personal conviction a matter of quarrelling or arguing.

The specific matters they were arguing about apparently had to do with food and special holy days. Some with tender conscience believed that they could not eat meat at all, because they feared the meat they bought might have been previously sacrificed to a pagan idol, which often happened in those days, or it might not have been kosher according to the Old Covenant. Other Christians, just as sincere in their belief, believed that those things could not harm them.[577] Some viewed certain days as holy days, probably the Sabbaths and Jewish feast days, others believed every day belonged to the Lord.[578]

In the New Covenant, every day does belong to the Lord, and there are no unclean foods,[579] but whatever the issue, we do not flaunt our freedom before those who may have different convictions. To do so is not to walk in the way of love.[580] Each of us will, one day, stand before the Judgment Seat of Christ[581] and we must not be found arguing over "doubtful disputations." (Romans 14:17).

---

[576] **Romans 14:1** Him that is weak in the faith receive ye, *but* not to doubtful disputations.

[577] **Romans 14:2-3** 2 For one believeth that he may eat all things: another, who is weak, eateth herbs. 3 Let not him that eateth despise him that eateth not; and let not him which eateth not judge him that eateth: for God hath received him.

[578] **Romans 14:5** One man esteemeth one day above another: another esteemeth every day *alike*. Let every man be fully persuaded in his own mind.

[579] **Mark 7:18-19** 18 And he saith unto them, Are ye so without understanding also? Do ye not perceive, that whatsoever thing from without entereth into the man, *it* cannot defile him; 19 Because it entereth not into his heart, but into the belly, and goeth out into the draught, purging all meats?

Romans 14:14 I know, and am persuaded by the Lord Jesus, that *there is* nothing unclean of itself: but to him that esteemeth any thing to be unclean, to him *it is* unclean.

1 Timothy 4:1-5 1 Now the Spirit speaketh expressly, that in the latter times some shall depart from the faith, giving heed to seducing spirits, and doctrines of devils; 2 Speaking lies in hypocrisy; having their conscience seared with a hot iron; 3 Forbidding to marry, *and commanding* to abstain from meats, which God hath created to be received with thanksgiving of them which believe and know the truth. 4 For every creature of God *is* good, and nothing to be refused, if it be received with thanksgiving: 5 For it is sanctified by the word of God and prayer.

[580] **Romans 14:15** But if thy brother be grieved with *thy* meat, now walkest thou not charitably. Destroy not him with thy meat, for whom Christ died.

[581] **Romans 14:10** But why dost thou judge thy brother? or why dost thou set at nought thy brother? for we shall all stand before the judgment seat of Christ.

Read Romans 15:1-21

Romans 15:1 We then that are strong ought to bear the infirmities of the weak, and not to please ourselves.

Today we are often encouraged to learn to assert ourselves and look out for "number one." That may be what is expected in the corporate world, but it is certainly not in the kingdom of God. If God has given us strength in an area, it has been given to us to help someone who is not so strong. Living to please self alone is an empty existence indeed.

Our responsibility to our neighbor is to edify them, helping to encourage and build them up in their faith. We are all grateful for those who have done so for us over the years![582] Of course, Jesus Himself is the best example of what it looks like to live that kind of a life.[583] As a young Christian someone told me that the way to joy was this <u>J</u>esus, <u>O</u>thers, and then <u>Y</u>ou. It's still true!

Romans 12:10 *Be* kindly affectioned one to another with brotherly love; in honour preferring one another;

---

[582] **Romans 15:2** Let every one of us please *his* neighbour for *his* good to edification.
[583] **Romans 15:3-4** 3 For even Christ pleased not himself; but, as it is written, The reproaches of them that reproached thee fell on me. 4 For whatsoever things were written aforetime were written for our learning, that we through patience and comfort of the scriptures might have hope.

Read Romans 15:22-16:7

Romans 15:30 Now I beseech you, brethren, for the Lord Jesus Christ's sake, and for the love of the Spirit, that ye strive together with me in *your* prayers to God for me;

Paul is requesting prayer for the continued work of God through his life and ministry. He pleads with them to pray earnestly for Jesus' sake and because of the love they have for him. That, of course, is a love that only the Holy Spirit can bring. "Strive together" is from a Greek word which can mean to agonize together. It is the same kind of praying Jesus did in the Garden of Gethsemane[584]. What he desired from them was more than a simple "God bless Brother Paul," but it was powerful prayer in the Spirit, literally doing battle on their knees!

His need of prayer centered around a planned trip to Jerusalem. He knows that he will be in danger from unbelieving Jews and that even the Christians there may not be accepting of what he is doing. He desperately needs prayer![585] Pray, also, he says, that I will be able to fulfill my desire of visiting you and encouraging you.[586] That prayer was answered in a different way than they probably anticipated. He did finally get to visit Rome, but he was taken there in chains and spent two years under house arrest there preaching, teaching, and encouraging the saints in Rome!

1 Samuel 12:23   Moreover as for me, God forbid that I should sin against the LORD in ceasing to pray for you: but I will teach you the good and the right way:

---

[584] **Luke 22:44**   And being in an agony he prayed more earnestly: and his sweat was as it were great drops of blood falling down to the ground.
[585] **Romans 15:31**   That I may be delivered from them that do not believe in Judaea; and that my service which *I have* for Jerusalem may be accepted of the saints;
[586] **Romans 15:32**   That I may come unto you with joy by the will of God, and may with you be refreshed.

Read Romans 16.8-27

Romans 16:17 Now I beseech you, brethren, mark them which cause divisions and offences contrary to the doctrine which ye have learned; and avoid them.

We are strongly encouraged to mark (take note of) those that cause division. The Lord has made it clear that "sowing discord among brethren" is among those things that He hates.[587]   We are also to beware of those who come preaching false doctrine, doctrine contrary to the clear teaching of the Word of God. False teachers and their teaching can prove disastrous to the body of Christ, drawing people away from the simple message of Jesus.[588]   He reserves the harshest of words for those who would come preaching "another" Gospel.[589]   We are to avoid those who through seductive words, seek to deceive those who are spiritually naïve.[590]

Ephesians 4:2-3   2 With all lowliness and meekness, with longsuffering, forbearing one another in love; 3 Endeavoring to keep the unity of the Spirit in the bond of peace.

Titus 1:9   Holding fast the faithful word as he hath been taught, that he may be able by sound doctrine both to exhort and to convince the gainsayers.

---

[587] **Proverbs 6:16-19** 16 These six *things* doth the LORD hate: yea, seven *are* an abomination unto him: 17 A proud look, a lying tongue, and hands that shed innocent blood, 18 An heart that deviseth wicked imaginations, feet that be swift in running to mischief, 19 A false witness *that* speaketh lies, and <u>he that soweth discord among brethren.</u>

[588] **2 Corinthians 11:1-4** 1 Would to God ye could bear with me a little in *my* folly: and indeed bear with me. 2 For I am jealous over you with godly jealousy: for I have espoused you to one husband, that I may present *you as* a chaste virgin to Christ. 3 But I fear, lest by any means, as the serpent beguiled Eve through his subtilty, so your minds should be corrupted from the simplicity that is in Christ. 4 For if he that cometh preacheth another Jesus, whom we have not preached, or *if* ye receive another spirit, which ye have not received, or another gospel, which ye have not accepted, ye might well bear with *him*.

[589] **Galatians 1:6-9** 6 I marvel that ye are so soon removed from him that called you into the grace of Christ unto another gospel: 7 Which is not another; but there be some that trouble you, and would pervert the gospel of Christ. 8 But though we, or an angel from heaven, preach any other gospel unto you than that which we have preached unto you, let him be accursed. 9 As we said before, so say I now again, If any *man* preach any other gospel unto you than that ye have received, let him be accursed.

[590] **Romans 16:18**   For they that are such serve not our Lord Jesus Christ, but their own belly; and by good words and fair speeches deceive the hearts of the simple.

<u>Read 1 Corinthians 1:1-25</u>

1 Corinthians 1:10 Now I beseech you, brethren, by the name of our Lord Jesus Christ, that ye all speak the same thing, and *that* there be no divisions among you; but *that* ye be perfectly joined together in the same mind and in the same judgment.

Paul received word that there were some divisive cliques in the church at Corinth, groups formed around the personalities of various preachers. All the preachers and teachers were godly men, preaching the same Gospel, but their personalities and preaching styles may have been quite different.

One group was partial to the Apostle Paul, after all he was the founder of the church. Paul made no claim of being an eloquent speaker[591], but Apollos certainly was[592], and some followed him. Perhaps some chose Cephas (Peter), because he was one of the original twelve who walked with the Lord. What about the group that claimed to just follow Jesus? That would seem commendable, but this is what one commentary says about them, "There was the "Jesus Party," who declared "You all are so carnal, following after mere men. We are following in the footsteps of no one less than Jesus Himself. We're the ones really right with God!"[593] These divisions were a mark of carnality in the body.[594]

God poured out the Spirit when His church was in one accord[595], and He will still move when His people come together around His agenda, not their own. Knowing this, Satan has used division and false doctrine from within the body more effectively than any of his other tools. May God help us to make every effort to keep the unity of the spirit in the bond of peace.[596]

Psalm 133:1 Behold, how good and how pleasant *it is* for brethren to dwell together in unity!

---

[591] 1 Corinthians 2:4
[592] Acts 18:24
[593] <u>Enduring Word Commentary</u>, Guzik.
[594] 1 Corinthians 3:1-3
[595] Acts 2:1-4
[596] Ephesians 4:3

Read 1 Corinthians 1.26-2.16

1 Corinthians 2:9 But as it is written, Eye hath not seen, nor ear heard, neither have entered into the heart of man, the things which God hath prepared for them that love him.

This Scripture, a paraphrase of Isaiah 64:6, has often been taken out of context. It is often used to teach that we cannot know the things that God has prepared for us while in this life. We will have to wait until we get to heaven to find out the fullness of what He has prepared for His children. That may be true, but it is *not* what *this* verse is teaching. Reading the surrounding verses shows how important context can be in rightly dividing the Word of Truth. For example, the next verse reads, "BUT GOD has revealed them to us by His Spirit." It is not that He will reveal those things to us in glory alone, but that He has revealed them to us *now*!

In verse 12, he reminds us the Spirit will reveal to us what God has given us. When the child of God opens the Word, the Spirit will reveal amazing truths and wonderful promises. Though the natural man (the unsaved person) cannot receive or understand those truths, thinking they are foolish, God reveals them to us by the Spirit.[597] In light of these things, this is my prayer for you today.

Ephesians 1:18 The eyes of your understanding being enlightened; that ye may know what is the hope of his calling, and what the riches of the glory of his inheritance in the saints,

---

[597] 1 Corinthians 2:14

Read 1 Corinthians 3.1-23

1 Corinthians 3:16-17) 16 Know ye not that ye are the temple of God, and *that* the Spirit of God dwelleth in you? 17 If any man defile the temple of God, him shall God destroy; for the temple of God is holy, which *temple* ye are.

1 Corinthians 6:19-20 19 What? know ye not that your body is the temple of the Holy Ghost *which is* in you, which ye have of God, and ye are not your own? 20 For ye are bought with a price: therefore glorify God in your body, and in your spirit, which are God's.

These two Scriptures would seem to say almost the same thing, but there is an important difference. Unlike English, many other languages, including the Greek of the New Testament, have a second person plural pronoun. If it has been years for you, like it has been for me, since you've taken an English class, let me explain. In English the word "you" can mean either one individual (Second Person Singular) or a group (Second Person Plural). Context reveals whether one person, or a group is being addressed. Southerners have gotten around this by using "y'all" when more than one person is indicated!

In 1 Corinthians 3:16-17 Paul used the second person plural. That means that the church, collectively, is the temple of the Holy Ghost, and there is a strong warning for anyone who would destroy, or harm, the Lord's holy temple, His church. In 1 Corinthians 6:19-20 he uses the second person singular. Every individual believer is also the temple of the Holy Ghost. He dwells in believers as His temple, and because of that we are each called to glorify Him in our bodies and in our spirits, because both belong to God. The church as a whole belongs to the Lord as does each individual member!

1 Peter 2:5 Ye also, as lively stones, are built up a spiritual house, an holy priesthood, to offer up spiritual sacrifices, acceptable to God by Jesus Christ.

Read 1 Corinthians 4.1-21

1 Corinthians 4:1-2 1 Let a man so account of us, as of the ministers of Christ, and stewards of the mysteries of God. 2 Moreover it is required in stewards, that a man be found faithful.

Paul speaks of himself, and others in ministry as "ministers of Christ." The Greek word he uses here was used for a servant who was an underrower on a galley ship. Someone once described an underrower as, "one who acts under direction, and asks no questions, one who does the thing he is appointed to do without hesitation, and one who reports only to the One Who is over him."[598]

Ministry is also described as stewardship, stewardship of the mysteries of God. A steward was a servant responsible for managing the affairs of another. A steward must be faithful with what belongs to his master. We must be faithful to what the Lord has entrusted to us as His ministers—the glorious Gospel of Jesus Christ!

1 Timothy 1:12 And I thank Christ Jesus our Lord, who hath enabled me, for that he counted me faithful, putting me into the ministry;

---

[598] The Corinthian Letters of Paul: An Exposition on I and II Corinthians, G. Campbell Morgan.

Read 1 Corinthians 5:1-13

1 Corinthians 5:1 It is reported commonly *that there is* fornication among you, and such fornication as is not so much as named among the Gentiles, that one should have his father's wife.

A member of the church at Corinth was involved in an open and immoral sexual relationship, involving his step-mother, his father's wife. This was "commonly reported," meaning that apparently everyone knew about it. A professing *Christian* had sin in his life worse than that of those out in the world. Rather than grieving over such an evil and dealing with it, the church seems to have accepted it, even been proud of it (verse 2)! Even today, there are those who seem proud of being "accepting," "non-judgmental," and "inclusive" of things that God has condemned. The *woman* involved was apparently not a church member, because her part in the sin is not even mentioned here. This was a church issue.

We can assume the man was given an opportunity to repent, following the example of Matthew 18:1-5 and Galatians 6:1 and since repentance did not come, Paul's judgment is that the man be "turned over to Satan."   This probably meant he was excommunicated. He was no longer welcome as a part of the fellowship of the church. They were not to even eat with him (verse 9-11).   This was all done with the hope that he would repent and be saved.   Were it not confronted, *his* sin would embolden others in the body to sin.   Sin, like leaven in bread, would permeate the whole church (verse 6-8).   Those within the church are to be judged, not those without (Verses 3, 9-13).

1 Peter 4:17 **For** the time *is come* that judgment must begin at the house of God: and if *it* first *begin* at us, what shall the end *be* of them that obey not the gospel of God?

Read 1 Corinthians 6:1-20

1 Corinthians 6:9-10   Know ye not that the unrighteous shall not inherit the kingdom of God? Be not deceived: neither fornicators, nor idolaters, nor adulterers, nor effeminate, nor abusers of themselves with mankind, 10 Nor thieves, nor covetous, nor drunkards, nor revilers, nor extortioners, shall inherit the kingdom of God.

He gives us a list of those who will *not* enter heaven. That list includes those who are involved in sexual relations outside of marriage, those who worship idols, those who break their marriage vows, those who are involved in homosexual sin, those who are thieves, those who are drunks, and even those who are greedy.   Taken out of its context, this would leave little hope for us, but there is good news in the verses that follow.

Within the Corinthian church there were members who had *once* practiced **all** of those evils, but he uses the past tense, "such ***WERE*** some of you."[599] That was yesterday, this was a new day in Jesus and they had been delivered from the bondage of those sins. The Lord had washed them in his own blood!   He had justified them, removing the debt of sin and giving them His perfect righteousness!   He had sanctified them, setting them apart as holy.   His salvation makes us new creations![600]

Isaiah 1:18 Come now, and let us reason together, saith the LORD: though your sins be as scarlet, they shall be as white as snow; though they be red like crimson, they shall be as wool.

---

[599] 1 Corinthians 6:11
[600] 2 Corinthians 5:17

Read 1 Corinthians 7.1-24

1 Corinthians 7:16 For what knowest thou, O wife, whether thou shalt save *thy* husband? or how knowest thou, O man, whether thou shalt save *thy* wife?

In verses 10-16 he is speaking of the seriousness of the marriage vows. If Christians separate, they are to seek reconciliation or remain single. What about spiritually mixed marriages, where one is a believer and the other is not? Perhaps the believer got saved *after* they were married.   If the non-believer is willing to stay in the marriage, the believer is to remain with them; unbelief alone does not constitute scriptural grounds for divorce.   However, if the unbeliever refuses to remain in that marriage, and leaves, the believer is free and can remarry without sin, so long as it is in the Lord.

Though it may be difficult, remaining with an unbeliever can be the means of winning them to Christ.   Peter says that a believing wife may win her husband, without having said a word, just by the godly life that she lives.[601]   Often our lives preach a far more powerful sermon than anything we say!

1 Peter 3:1 Likewise, ye wives, *be* in subjection to your own husbands; that, if any obey not the word, they also may without the word be won by the conversation [lifestyle] of the wives;

---

[601] 1 Peter 3:1

Read 1 Corinthians 7:25-40

1 Corinthians 7:25-27 Now concerning virgins I have no commandment of the Lord: yet I give my judgment, as one that hath obtained mercy of the Lord to be faithful. 26 I suppose therefore that this is good for the present distress, *I say*, that *it is* good for a man so to be. 27 Art thou bound unto a wife? seek not to be loosed. Art thou loosed from a wife? seek not a wife.

There are groups that view the single, or celibate, state as being holier than the married state, but the entirety of Scripture views marriage as a very honorable thing.[602] It is meant to be an earthly picture of the relationship between Christ and His church,[603] something that God ordained in the Garden of Eden[604]. Despite this, 1 Corinthians 7 reminds us that for some the best path may be remaining single. Paul's remarks were given because of special conditions, something he calls "the present distress," probably a time of great persecution.[605] There was no sin in marrying, but because of the difficult times, remaining single might spare them some grief.[606] If it proved to be God's will for their lives, they could serve and glorify Him as singles, undistracted, for the short time that remained[607]. The key for all of us is this: Whether through a godly marriage, or godly singleness, our goal should be to glorify Him!

1 Corinthians 10:31 Whether therefore ye eat, or drink, or **whatsoever ye do, do all to the glory of God.**

---

[602] Hebrews 13:4
[603] Ephesians 5
[604] Matthew 19:4-5
[605] 1 Corinthians 7:25
[606] 1 Corinthians 7:28
[607] 1 Corinthians 7:29

Read 1 Corinthians 8:1-13

1Co 8:12-13 But when ye sin so against the brethren, and wound their weak conscience, ye sin against Christ. 13 Wherefore, if meat make my brother to offend, I will eat no flesh while the world standeth, lest I make my brother to offend.

The Corinthians had asked Paul a question about meat that had been sacrificed to idols. Some of the meat from animals offered to false gods in pagan temples was then sold. The idol temples were probably an economical place to eat or buy meat. Was there a sin in buying and eating this meat, since it had once been devoted to a false god? Of course the mature Christians in their midst knew that the idol was not really a god, for there is only one true God. For them the idol was just a piece of wood or metal and the meat was just that---meat. Others having come out of idolatry could not go there and eat with a clear conscience. It would probably even offend them to see a brother or sister eating there. It might even bring a temptation to go back to their old life!

Meat sacrificed to idols is not an issue for most of us today, but the *principles* found in this chapter apply to innumerable other life situations. Love for my brothers and sisters in Christ means that I do not consciously do what will wound their conscience or cause them to sin.

1 Peter 1:22 Seeing ye have purified your souls in obeying the truth through the Spirit unto unfeigned love of the brethren, see that ye love one another with a pure heart fervently:

Read 1 Corinthians 9:1-27

1Co 9:14-15 Even so hath the Lord ordained that they which preach the gospel should live of the gospel. 15 But I have used none of these things: neither have I written these things, that it should be so done unto me: for [it were] better for me to die, than that any man should make my glorying void.

In this chapter Paul makes a strong case for the financial support of those in full-time ministry. He uses several illustrations. A soldier does not serve in the army at his own expense. The one who plants a vineyard eats some of the grapes. One does not muzzle an ox as he threshes the grain. He concludes that the Lord has ordained that those who preach the Gospel should live of the Gospel. Though he apparently did receive support at some other places, Paul did not avail himself of that right at Corinth. Instead, he worked alongside his friends, Priscilla and Aquila, who were tentmakers, a trade Paul had apparently known since his youth[608]. Perhaps accusations had been made in Corinth. We are not told. But Paul did not want the slightest hint that he was lazy or "In it for the money." Nothing in his life must hinder the work of God. It was far too important.

1 Timothy 1:12 And I thank Christ Jesus our Lord, who hath enabled me, for that he counted me faithful, putting me into the ministry;

---

[608] Acts 18:1-3

Read 1 Corinthians 10:1-22

1 Corinthians 10:12, "Wherefore let him that thinketh he standeth take heed lest he fall."

We are told that the stories of the Israelites are given to us as examples, sometimes examples of what *not* to do.[609]   Paul begins by telling us of the great blessings that they ALL received.[610]   In spite of the great blessings, because of their own sin and disobedience many[611] of them faced God's judgment and died in the wilderness.

We are warned about falling prey to the same things that brought judgment to them: idolatry, sexual immorality, murmuring, etc.   Even though they ALL received great blessings, they did not all walk in obedience and avail themselves of what God had provided.

The same can be true of us today in the New Covenant.   We have been blessed even more greatly than they.   Yet, we must walk humbly before God and realize that we are not immune to temptation.   We are weakest when we think that we are strongest.   Those temptations that we face are nothing new, they are common to man, faced by all other human beings. Thankfully, the Lord has promised that we will never be tempted in a way that is greater than we are able to bear.   Also, He promises the presence of a way of escape.

1 Corinthians 10:13 There hath no temptation taken you but such as is common to man: but God *is* faithful, who will not suffer you to be tempted above that ye are able; but will with the temptation also make a way to escape, that ye may be able to bear *it*.

---

[609] 1 Corinthians 10:6, 11
[610] 1 Corinthians 10:1-5
[611] Actually most didn't make it to the Promised Land.   Of their original number, only Joshua and Caleb survived to enter Canaan.

Read 1 Corinthians 10:23-11:16

1 Corinthians 10:17 For we *being* many are one bread, *and* one body: for we are all partakers of that one bread.

Several things are shown when we obey the Lord and take Communion together.   We remember His death, what He did for us on the cross. We remember that He is coming again.   Jesus said, "I will not drink of this fruit of the vine, **until** the day when I drink it new with you in my Father's kingdom."[612]   Later Paul will say that we show the Lord's death **until** He comes.[613]   It is also a demonstration of the unity of the church, the body of Christ.

Regardless of the names that may be over the doors of our buildings, there is only one church, one body of Christ, consisting of all those who have been redeemed by His blood.   We are one body, along with every other born again child of God.   We proclaim that truth each time we come to the Lord's table and receive the bread and cup.   For that reason, we should also seek to walk in unity with one another.

Ephesians 4:2-6 With all lowliness and meekness, with longsuffering, forbearing one another in love; 3 Endeavoring[614] to keep the unity of the Spirit in the bond of peace. 4 *There is* ONE body, and ONE Spirit, even as ye are called in ONE hope of your calling; 5 ONE Lord, ONE faith, ONE baptism, 6 ONE God and Father of all, who *is* above all, and through all, and in you all.

---

[612] Matthew 26:29
[613] 1 Corinthians 11:26
[614] Literally, "making every effort."

Read 1 Corinthians 11:17-34

1Co 11:27-29 Wherefore whosoever shall eat this bread, and drink this cup of the Lord, unworthily, shall be guilty of the body and blood of the Lord. 28 But let a man examine himself, and so let him eat of that bread, and drink of that cup. 29 For he that eateth and drinketh unworthily, eateth and drinketh damnation to himself, not discerning the Lord's body.

The Lord's Supper is a time of holy reverence, as we remember the Lord's death until He comes. However, some of the members of the Corinthian church were receiving Communion in an unworthy manner. They were coming together for a common meal, and may have even called it the Lord's Supper, but it had degraded into something far less.[615] They selfishly ate what they brought, without regard to anyone else. Some of them were even drunk, a sin that Paul earlier said could keep them from seeing heaven.[616] Their selfish, and ungodly, attitude toward their brothers and sisters in Christ was seen as not discerning the Lord's body. The Body, of course, is a Bible term used for the church, His people. When we examine ourselves before receiving the Lord's Supper, we should always examine our relationship toward others in the Body of Christ. An improper relationship with them can lead to judgment, sickness, or even an untimely death[617]. Love and unity should always be seen in the Body of Christ, especially at the Lord's Supper!

1 John 4:7-8 Beloved, let us love one another: for love is of God; and every one that loveth is born of God, and knoweth God. 8 He that loveth not knoweth not God; for God is love.

---

[615] 1 Corinthians 11:20
[616] 1 Corinthians 11:21, 1 Corinthians 6:9-11
[617] 1 Corinthians 11:30

Read 1 Corinthians 12.1-27

1 Corinthians 12:1 Now concerning spiritual *gifts*, brethren, I would not have you ignorant.

It is not the Lord's will that we be ignorant about the Gifts of the Holy Spirit. He gives us teaching regarding those gifts here in 1 Corinthians 12-14. In these chapters, we learn that true spiritual gifts are meant to glorify the Lord Jesus Christ, [618] and edify[619] His church. We also learn that it should be our desire to be used in spiritual gifts. The Lord tells us in 1 Corinthians 12:31 that we are to "**earnestly <u>covet</u> the best gifts,**" those that are needed at a given time. In 1 Corinthians 14:1 He tells us that we should **<u>desire</u>** spiritual gifts, particularly the gift of prophecy, and in verse 12 we are told to be **<u>zealous</u>** (eagerly seek) for those gifts that will bring encouragement and edification to the body.[620] If He desires to use us, let us say a resounding Yes!

I'll say Yes, Lord, Yes, to Your will and to Your way,
I'll say, Yes, Lord, Yes, I will trust You and obey,
When Your Spirit speaks to me, with my whole heart I'll agree, and my answer will be Yes, Lord, Yes.[621]

---

[618] John 16:13-14, 1 Corinthians 12:3
[619] To edify means to build up spiritually.
[620] 1 Corinthians 14:12
[621] "I'll Say Yes," Kevin LeVar

Read 1 Corinthians 12.28-13.13

1 Corinthians 12:31 But covet earnestly the best gifts: and yet shew I unto you a more excellent way.

There was a more "excellent way" of exercising the gifts of the Spirt than what was happening in Corinth. Apparently, gifts were manifest without the presence of spiritual fruit, particularly the fruit of love. This leads us right into 1 Corinthians 13, which has been called the "Love Chapter."

Spiritual gifts, as wonderful, and important, as they are, are just ever so much noise if manifest without the fruit of love,[622]   and when the Lord returns (that which is perfect), the gifts will no longer be necessary. Love, however will continue throughout eternity.[623]   Just as we are to desire spiritual gifts, we are to remain in fellowship with Him so His fruit will continue to grow in our lives.

John 15:4-5 4 Abide in me, and I in you. As the branch cannot bear fruit of itself, except it abide in the vine; no more can ye, except ye abide in me. 5 I am the vine, ye *are* the branches: He that abideth in me, and I in him, the same bringeth forth much fruit: for without me ye can do nothing.

Romans 5:5 And hope maketh not ashamed; because the love of God is shed abroad in our hearts by the Holy Ghost which is given unto us.

---

[622] 1 Corinthians 13:1
[623] 1 Corinthians 13:8-10, 13

Read 1 Corinthians 14:1-25

1 Corinthians 14:15 What is it then? I will pray with the spirit, and I will pray with the understanding also: I will sing with the spirit, and I will sing with the understanding also.

Some wrongly think that the Apostle Paul discouraged speaking in tongues in this chapter. On the contrary, he actually *encouraged* it, but in the proper context. The Christians in Corinth loved to speak in tongues, and rightly so, for it edified them. That is, it built them up spiritually, just as other practices do (the Word of God, prayer, etc.).[624] However, in the local church setting, when they met together for public worship, there were other gifts that could better serve the whole body[625]. Remember the problems in Corinth? There was a lack of love and everyone was just looking out for "number one."

The Apostle Paul spoke in tongues more than all of them (and they spoke in tongues a great deal!), but he also said, "Yet in the church (the public gathering of the saints), I had rather speak five words with my understanding (in my native language), that by my voice I might teach others also, than ten thousand words in an unknown tongue."[626] In His devotional and worship life, he must have prayed in the Spirit a great deal, because of the tremendous spiritual benefit that God promised. He prayed in the Spirit, speaking to God in a language known only to God.[627] But, when he met with the people of God, it was far better to speak to them in a language they could all understand!

As a born-again believer, the Lord will baptize you in the Spirit, if you will ask Him to,[628] giving you power to be His faithful witness all the days of your life.[629] When He does, you can expect to speak in tongues just as they all did in the Book of Acts[630]. When He does, pray often in the Spirit! But, in the house of God, seek to lift up your brothers and sisters.

1 Corinthians 14:39-40 39 Wherefore, brethren, covet to prophesy, and forbid not to speak with tongues. 40 Let all things be done decently and in order.

---

[624] 1 Corinthians 14:4
[625] Prophecy, Interpretation of Tongues, Word of Wisdom, Word of Knowledge, Gifts of Healings, Discerning of spirits, Miracles, and Faith.
[626] 1 Corinthians 14:18-19
[627] 1 Corinthians 14:1-2
[628] Luke 11:13
[629] Acts 1:8
[630] Acts 2:1-4, Acts 10:44-46, Acts 19:6

Read 1 Corinthians 14.26-15.11

1 Corinthians 15:1-2 Moreover, brethren, I declare unto you the gospel which I preached unto you, which also ye have received, and wherein ye stand; 2 By which also ye are saved, if ye keep in memory what I preached unto you, unless ye have believed in vain.

Here in 1 Corinthians 15, the Apostle Paul gives us the basic tenets of the Gospel, the good news, the message that he preached, and the one we must preach, if we are to be true to the Lord and His Word. These things are vitally important, essential to our salvation.

First, the Gospel declares that Christ died for our sins. He died in our place on the cross, and His death provided the means by which we can be saved. Second, He was buried. They placed His body in the tomb of Joseph of Arimathea, where it remained for three days. Third, He rose from the dead, for the grave could not hold Him! His resurrection was validated by many eyewitnesses, including a group of more than five hundred who saw Him at one time! We need have no doubt about the resurrection. Most of those eyewitnesses were still alive when Paul wrote this. Anyone could have gone to them and found them all so sure of what they had seen that they were willing to die for it!

Give thanks for the Gospel today, the Good News by which you were saved!

Romans 1:16 For I am not ashamed of the gospel of Christ: for it is the power of God unto salvation to everyone that believeth; to the Jew first, and also to the Greek.

Read 1 Corinthians 15.12-34

1 Corinthians 15:20 But now is Christ risen from the dead, *and* become the firstfruits of them that slept.

Jesus was the first to experience resurrection, rising from the dead with a glorified body, never to die again. However, He was not the last. Our bodies will also experience resurrection at the coming of the Lord! In 1 Corinthians 15, we find some amazing teaching about **our** future resurrection!

Our resurrection is possible, because of His![631] If we deny the future resurrection of believers, it is the same as denying that He rose from the dead. This is extremely important teaching.[632] Without the resurrection our preaching and faith are in vain (empty and meaningless), we are still in our sins, and there is no hope for our loved ones who have already died. How miserable would be our existence, if the end of these few short earthly years marked the end of our existence, but they do not. Paul said, "If in this life *only* we have hope in Christ, we are of all men most miserable."

Jesus said, "Because I live ye shall live also," that is our great and blessed hope![633]

There ain't no grave gonna hold my body down
There ain't no grave gonna hold my body down
When I hear the trumpet sound
Gonna get up outa the ground
There ain't no grave gonna hold my body down.[634]

---

[631] 1 Corinthians 1:12
[632] 1 Corinthians 1:13
[633] John 14:19, Titus 2:13, 1 Peter 1:3
[634] "Ain't No Grave," Claude Ely.

Read 1 Corinthians 15.35-58

1 Corinthians 15:51 Behold I shew you a mystery; We shall not all sleep, but we shall all be changed,

In the New Testament, a mystery is something that was once hidden, but has now been revealed. Such is the case with some of God's wonderful teaching about the resurrection here in 1 Corinthians 15! Sleep here is speaking of the death of our bodies. When a born-again believer dies, their body "sleeps" in the grave, awaiting the resurrection, while their spirit goes to be with the Lord.[635] However, the generation of believers living at the time of the Rapture, when Jesus returns *for* His church, will not face that "sleep" of death, but will experience something else. What will happen to them?

First, the bodies of those who have died in Christ will be raised from the dead and transformed into what the Bible calls incorruptible bodies, bodies no longer subject to death, pain, sickness, or any other result of the curse of sin that has been on this world and its inhabitants. Their spirits, having been with the Lord since death, will rejoin their gloriously changed bodies. A millisecond later, the bodies of living Christians will be changed in the same way. This will all take place in what the Bible calls the twinkling of an eye. Both groups will ascend to meet the Lord in the air. What a wonderful, and glorious, hope this is! I hope you are ready should that trumpet sound today!

1 Thessalonians 4:16-18 For the Lord himself shall descend from heaven with a shout, with the voice of the archangel, and with the trump of God: and the dead in Christ shall rise first: 17 Then we which are alive *and* remain shall be caught up together with them in the clouds, to meet the Lord in the air: and so shall we ever be with the Lord. 18 Wherefore comfort one another with these words.

---

[635] Luke 23:42-43, 2 Corinthians 5:6-8, Philippians 1:23

Read 1 Corinthians 16:1-14

1 Corinthians 16:1-2 Now concerning the collection for the saints, as I have given order to the churches of Galatia, even so do ye. 2 Upon the first *day* of the week let every one of you lay by him in store, as *God* hath prospered him, that there be no gatherings when I come.

The Corinthians had asked Paul about a special offering that was being received. He gives them instruction about that offering here. It was probably being received to help their brothers and sisters back in Jerusalem where things were very difficult.[636] Every Lord's Day, the first day of the week, when the church met for worship, those funds were to be gathered[637]. I am told that the Greek word used here may indicate a special offering, something above their normal giving[638]. The hope was that the offering would be ready for delivery by the time Paul arrived back in Corinth.

A certain level of giving was not mandated. People gave as the Lord had prospered and blessed them. Later he told them that this giving was to be as they purposed in their hearts, one would hope hearts moved upon by the Holy Spirit. Special offerings were not to be given grudgingly or of necessity (forced, mandated, or coerced); they were to be given cheerfully. Giving as unto the Lord is a joyful privilege. It is not that we **HAVE** to give in an offering, it is that we **GET** to give!

2 Corinthians 9:7 Every man according as he purposeth in his heart, *so let him give*; not grudgingly, or of necessity: for God loveth a cheerful giver.

---

[636] Acts 11:27-30, 24:17, Romans 15:26, 2 Corinthians 8:13, 9:9-12.

[637] It is interesting to note that the church was already meeting on Sunday for worship, probably because that is the day the Lord rose from the dead. Also note that they came together on that say for the breaking of bread—the Lord's Supper (Acts 20:7). In Jewish areas, Paul did go to the synagogues on Saturday, because that is when large groups of devout Jews would be meeting, and could be reached with the Gospel.

[638] "The ancient Greek word for **collection** is *logia*. It means, "an extra collection," one that is not compulsory. This was not a "tax" upon the Christians of Corinth. They were free to give as their heart directed them," Enduring Word Commentary, David Guzik

Read 2 Corinthians 1:1-24

2 Corinthians 1:3-4   Blessed *be* God, even the Father of our Lord Jesus Christ, the Father of mercies, and the God of all comfort; 4 Who comforteth us in all our tribulation, that we may be able to comfort them which are in any trouble, by the comfort wherewith we ourselves are comforted of God.

Praise the Lord for the comfort and mercy that only He can bring!   We have all been the recipients of that comfort in times of trials, testing, trouble, and tribulation.   A child of God is never alone in those times.   In fact, there is a wonderful purpose behind the comfort that He brings, a purpose that we may not always think about.   He comforts us so that we can comfort others. When we are comforted by God in our times of trouble, we can then take what He has given us and share it with someone else.   What you have been through personally, and the way the Lord helped you, makes you uniquely equipped to help someone else going through the same thing.

Jesus told Peter, "Satan hath desired *to have* you, that he may sift *you* as wheat: But I have prayed for you, that your faith fail not: and when you are converted, ***Strengthen Your Brethren***.[639]"   Peter failed miserably after this, denying the Lord, but repentance brought restoration.   I believe that for the rest of Peter's life, he was gifted in helping other "failures" come back to God, because of his own personal experience.

May the Lord use **you** to strengthen and comfort others through what He has done in **your** life, making *you* a blessing!

---

[639] Luke 22:31-32

Read 2 Corinthians 2.1-17

2 Corinthians 2:14-16 14 Now thanks *be* unto God, which always causeth us to triumph in Christ, and maketh manifest the savour of his knowledge by us in every place. 15 For we are unto God a sweet savour of Christ, in them that are saved, and in them that perish: 16 To the one *we are* the savour of death unto death; and to the other the savour of life unto life. And who *is* sufficient for these things?

The Greek word translated as 'triumph' here in the King James Version was used for a victory parade. Conquering generals returned home in triumphant procession along with those who had served with them. Of course, Jesus is the Mighty Conqueror! Following along behind those conquerors would be others who had been taken captive in battle, those whose days were numbered. Also marching with them would be priests burning sweet smelling incense as they came into the city. The savour of that incense was cause for rejoicing in those who had triumphed. It was the sweet smell of victory! For the captives, however, it was just the opposite. It spoke to them of their impending doom! This illustrates well the power of the Gospel. The same sweet Gospel that brings victory to those who receive it, will bring judgment to those who reject. In light of this, can't you identify with Paul when he says, "Who is sufficient for these things?" In other words, who is up to the task of sharing a Gospel that has such power!

The following words of Jesus teach us some of the same things. Those who receive the Gospel we preach will have their sins forgiven, but those who do not will face eternal judgment. May God help us!

John 20:23 Whose soever sins ye remit, they are remitted unto them; *and* whose soever *sins* ye retain, they are retained.

Read 2 Corinthians 3.1-18

2 Corinthians 3:17-18 17 Now the Lord is that Spirit: and where the Spirit of the Lord *is*, there *is* liberty. 18 But we all, with open face beholding as in a glass the glory of the Lord, are changed into the same image from glory to glory, *even* as by the Spirit of the Lord.

In the wonderful New Covenant, we have so much that we could not have had under the Old Covenant. For example, we are promised the power and presence of the Holy Spirit.   By His power, we are enabled to live a holy life.   His presence is liberating.   Thank God for that glorious liberty!

By the indwelling Holy Spirit and the Word of God we behold as in a glass (mirror) the glory of the Lord Jesus Christ.   We are being changed into that image, the image of Jesus, by the Spirit of the Lord. That work of sanctification, being conformed to His image, is not instantaneous. We are His work in progress, being changed day by day, and from glory to glory, by the Spirit.

That work will be complete when we see Jesus as He truly is at His return.   That is our great and blessed hope.

1 John 3:1-3   1 Behold, what manner of love the Father hath bestowed upon us, that we should be called the sons of God: therefore the world knoweth us not, because it knew him not. 2 Beloved, now are we the sons of God, and it doth not yet appear what we shall be: but we know that, when he shall appear, we shall be like him; for we shall see him as he is. 3 And every man that hath this hope in him purifieth himself, even as he is pure.

Read 2 Corinthians 4:1-18

2 Corinthians 4:3-4 3 But if our gospel be hid, it is hid to them that are lost: 4 In whom the god of this world hath blinded the minds of them which believe not, lest the light of the glorious gospel of Christ, who is the image of God, should shine unto them.

We all probably know what it is to share the Gospel with a friend or family member, and realize that they are just not "getting it." The word the Bible uses for their condition is so very fitting. . . LOST! They are lost, blind, and wandering in darkness.   In their deception, they often don't even realize that they are lost, so they remain on the same course, a course that only leads to *further* darkness. Even though the light of Jesus is present, they cannot see it, because they are spiritually blind.   This is why we are told in 1 Corinthians 2:14 that the natural man (one who is unsaved) cannot receive the things of the Spirit. They seem foolish to that person, because of the same spiritual blindness.

Salvation is a supernatural work of the Spirit.   We pray that He will open their eyes so that they can receive the light and truth of the Gospel and be saved.   We must continue to witness to them, while praying that their eyes will be opened by the Holy Spirit!

2 Corinthians 4:6 For God, who commanded the light to shine out of darkness, hath shined in our hearts, to *give* the light of the knowledge of the glory of God in the face of Jesus Christ.

Ephesians 1:18 The eyes of your understanding being enlightened; that ye may know what is the hope of his calling, and what the riches of the glory of his inheritance in the saints,

Read 2 Corinthians 5:1-21

2 Corinthians 5:20 Now then we are ambassadors for Christ, as though God did beseech *you* by us: we pray *you* in Christ's stead, be ye reconciled to God.

The word 'ambassador' is a very fitting way to describe the ministry of believers in this world. The word can be defined as one who has been "sent by one nation as its official representative to another nation." This present world is not our true home. The Bible says that we are strangers and pilgrims here and that our true citizenship is in heaven.[640] Living here on planet earth, we are called to represent our King and His kingdom in what can sometimes be hostile territory. How greatly we need His power![641]

When we, empowered by the Holy Spirit, speak the truth of the Gospel, we are speaking on behalf of the King of kings! As divinely called and appointed ambassadors, we serve as His representatives in this fallen world. Our prayer is that the world will see our King manifest through our lives and ministry. How wonderful to be one of his "Sent Ones!"

John 20:21 Then said Jesus to them again, Peace *be* unto you: as *my* Father hath sent me, ***even so send I you.***

---

[640] Philippians 3:20, 1Peter 2:11
[641] Acts 1:8

Read 2 Corinthians 6.1-18

2 Corinthians 6:14 Be ye not unequally yoked together with unbelievers: for what fellowship hath righteousness with unrighteousness? and what communion hath light with darkness?

Paul is using an illustration from the Old Testament where the Israelites were prohibited from using two different kinds of animals together while working their fields.[642] As he indicates here, this has more to do with separation from evil influences than it does agricultural practices. Various applications have been made from these words. Most often, we think of the dangers of a believer dating or marrying a non-believer. That is the only kind of mixed marriage forbidden by the Word of God. It is not that we do not associate with unbelievers. Jesus Himself was often criticized for doing so. What we do not do is enter relationships (yokes) that will likely influence us in a negative way[643]. True Christian fellowship and communion [koinonia] indicate a holy interaction between two believers and the Lord. Friendship may be possible between those who are not followers of Christ, but true communion is virtually impossible.

It is in light of this truth that we find these words at the end of chapter 6.

2 Corinthians 6:17-18 17 Wherefore come out from among them, and be ye separate, saith the Lord, and touch not the unclean *thing*; and I will receive you, 18 And will be a Father unto you, and ye shall be my sons and daughters, saith the Lord Almighty.

---

[642] **Deuteronomy 22:10** **Thou** shalt not plow with an ox and an ass together.
[643] **Mark 2:16-17** 16 And when the scribes and Pharisees saw him eat with publicans and sinners, they said unto his disciples, How is it that he eateth and drinketh with publicans and sinners? 17 When Jesus heard *it*, he saith unto them, They that are whole have no need of the physician, but they that are sick: I came not to call the righteous, but sinners to repentance.

Read 2 Corinthians 7:1-16

2 Corinthians 7:10 For godly sorrow worketh repentance to salvation not to be repented of: but the sorrow of the world worketh death.

Paul speaks of a previous letter that he had written to this church, one that had been sorrowful in nature.[644]   This letter has been called Paul's sorrowful letter. It may be a reference to what we now know as 1 Corinthians, or perhaps to another letter that he wrote between the two. Whatever the case, it involved some strong words that called for repentance on their part.   His words made them sorry, but it was the right kind of sorrow, the kind that leads to repentance.[645]

Sorrow alone does not mean true repentance has taken place. One can be sorry for the consequences of his or her sin without being truly repentant.   True godly sorrow is being sorry that we have sinned against God and then being willing to turn and walk another way.   This is the kind of sorrow that Jesus spoke about in the Sermon on the Mount, "Blessed are they that mourn, for they shall be comforted[646]." The old timers used to call the church altar the "mourner's bench," for good reason. Those who were convicted of their sin, turned from it and found salvation at that altar. Godly sorrow over our sin will ultimately bring the comfort of sins forgiven!

James 4:7-10 7 Submit yourselves therefore to God. Resist the devil, and he will flee from you. 8 Draw nigh to God, and he will draw nigh to you. Cleanse *your* hands, *ye* sinners; and purify *your* hearts, *ye* double minded. 9 Be **_afflicted, and mourn, and weep: let your laughter be turned to mourning, and your joy to heaviness._** 10 Humble yourselves in the sight of the Lord, and he shall lift you up.

---

[644] 2 Corinthians 7:8
[645] 2 Corinthians 7:9
[646] Matthew 5:4

Read 2 Corinthians 8:1-24

2 Corinthians 8:7 Therefore, as ye abound in every *thing, in* faith, and utterance, and knowledge, and *in* all diligence, and *in* your love to us, *see* that ye abound in this grace also.

Paul commends the Christians in Macedonia for their generous giving. An offering was being received for their suffering brothers and sisters in Jerusalem[647]. In spite of their own personal difficulties, they gave very generously in that offering.   They gave as they were able, and even beyond, giving sacrificially. They found, as many have, that one cannot out give the Lord!

Paul uses their wonderful example to encourage their neighbors, the Corinthians, to give generously in that offering also. He does not command them to give, that is not how New Testament giving works. He simply relates how others have been generous, and prays that they, like their neighbors in Macedonia, will abound in the same grace of giving.   As we have seen before, giving is not something we **HAVE** to do, it is something that we **GET** to do.

2 Corinthians 9:7 **Every** man according as he purposeth in his heart, *so let him give*; not grudgingly, or of necessity: for God loveth a cheerful giver.

---

[647] 1 Corinthians 16:1-4

Read 2 Corinthians 9.1-15

2 Corinthians 9:6-7 6 But this *I say*, He which soweth sparingly shall reap also sparingly; and he which soweth bountifully shall reap also bountifully. 7 Every man according as he purposeth in his heart, *so let him give*; not grudgingly, or of necessity: for God loveth a cheerful giver.

Just as in the previous chapter, Paul is speaking to them about a special offering, an offering for their needy brothers and sisters in the church at Jerusalem.   They had been encouraged in chapter 8 to give as generously as those in nearby Macedonia had already done

In continuing to speak of this special offering, he gives some important Biblical principles about giving in such offerings.   **First**, giving is compared to sowing seeds[648].   A wise farmer would not think of getting ahead, by keeping all of his seed in the barn.   Initially, he might seem to have more than others, but at harvest time[649], he would have far less than the wise one who had sown much.   He knows that he must sow seed in order to reap a harvest.   We do not gain, in the long run, by hanging on to all that we have. Abundant giving, ultimately, brings an abundant spiritual harvest.

Second, this giving is not forced[650].   That would make it more like taxation than Christian giving. Each was to give as he purposed in his heart, one would hope a heart moved upon by the Holy Spirit!   I am thankful that along with our tithes, the Holy Spirit touches our hearts about giving in other ways.

---

[648] 2 Corinthians 9:6
[649] Harvest time for Christians will ultimately come at the Judgment Seat of Christ.
[650] 2 Corinthians 9:7

Third, the offering is not given grudgingly[651]. Giving is a privilege. It is not something we do because we feel that we are obligated, or because everyone else is doing it, or because we feel that someone is "twisting our arm."

Fourth, we do not give of necessity[652], or because we have to. We give, because we want to. The Holy Spirit is the One who will give us that godly desire to give

Fifth, we give cheerfully[653]. We give with a joyful heart, because we know that it is God's work and that His harvest is coming!

Sixth, the Lord will take care of the needs of that one who is generous. They will not do without. As we seek His kingdom first, all of the other things that we need will be added to us.[654]

Seventh, the Lord will multiply the "seed" that we sow. As we are obedient to the Holy Spirit, the Lord will multiply what we have sown into the kingdom of God.[655] This is much like the way the Lord took the loaves and fishes given by a young boy, and multiplied them for the multitudes[656]! Little is much when God is in it.

When the Lord gives you an opportunity to be a blessing through giving, rejoice and know that harvest is coming!

Luke 6:38 Give, and it shall be given unto you; good measure, pressed down, and shaken together, and running over, shall men give into your bosom. For with the same measure that ye mete withal it shall be measured to you again.

---

[651] Ibid.
[652] Ibid.
[653] 2 Corinthians 9:7
[654] Matthew 6:33
[655] 2 Corinthians 9:10
[656] John 6:1-14

Read 2 Corinthians 10.1-18

2 Corinthians 10:3 For though we walk in the flesh, we do not war after the flesh:

We walk in the flesh; we do not yet have our glorified bodies. However, the battles that we face cannot be fought by our own human abilities.   We cannot use carnal (fleshly) weapons to fight spiritual battles.[657]   This is in keeping with what Paul told the Ephesians, "we wrestle not against flesh and blood, but against principalities, against powers, against the rulers of the darkness of this world, against spiritual wickedness in high *places*."[658]   He was speaking of our unseen enemies, satanic beings in the spiritual realm. That is why we are told to be strong in the Lord and in the power of **HIS** might.[659]   The Lord has provided us with spiritual armor and at least one very powerful weapon, the Word of God.[660] With the Word of God we can pull down strongholds, areas where the enemy has been allowed to make inroads.   With the same powerful sword, the Word of God, we can cast down what the King James Version calls imaginations.   The Greek word is logismos, what we might call worldly arguments.   He calls them "high things that exalt themselves against the knowledge of God," proud things contrary to the Word.   Most of us will agree that our greatest battles take place in the arena of our minds.   So many troubles come, because of various forms of deception. We sometimes believe what is not true, but He says we can bring those deceptive thoughts "captive to the obedience of Christ!" His truth will make, and keep, us free!

John 8:31-32 31 Then said Jesus to those Jews which believed on him, if ye continue in my word, *then* are ye my disciples indeed; 32 And ye shall know the truth, and the truth shall make you free.

---

[657] 1 Corinthians 10:4
[658] Ephesians 6:12
[659] Ephesians 6:10
[660] Ephesians 6:13-19

Read 2 Corinthians 11.1-28

2 Corinthians 11:2 For I am jealous over you with godly jealousy: for I have espoused you to one husband, that I may present *you as* a chaste virgin to Christ.

Human jealousy can be an ungodly thing, but God's jealousy toward His people is always pure and holy. Beginning with the Ten Commandments we are warned about idolatry, because our God is a jealous God[661]. The relationship we have with God is compared to a marriage covenant. Idolatry is a breaking of that covenant and is spoken of as adultery or even whoredom in the Word of God. We must have no other gods before Him.

He also warns us that just as Eve was deceived by Satan, we can be deceived also. False teachers, then and now, preach a "Jesus" and a "gospel" that is not the One revealed to us in the Word. False teachers bringing "another Gospel" may have even knocked at your door! Stay faithful to the Word of God and to the Savior revealed in its pages.

Galatians 1:6-9 6 I marvel that ye are so soon removed from him that called you into the grace of Christ unto another gospel: 7 Which is not another; but there be some that trouble you, and would pervert the gospel of Christ. 8 But though we, or an angel from heaven, preach any other gospel unto you than that which we have preached unto you, let him be accursed. 9 As we said before, so say I now again, if any *man* preach any other gospel unto you than that ye have received, let him be accursed.

---

[661] Exodus 20

Read 2 Corinthians 11:29-12:19

2 Corinthians 12:7 And lest I should be exalted above measure through the abundance of the revelations, there was given to me a thorn in the flesh, the messenger of Satan to buffet me, lest I should be exalted above measure.

The question of just what Paul's "thorn in the flesh" was has long been a matter of conjecture. It must not be important that we know those details, because God did not see fit to include them in His Word. At the beginning of the chapter, Paul describes an amazing spiritual experience.   Someone, most believe it was Paul himself, was caught up to heaven!   Though, he did not boast about this experience, he certainly could have. He saw things he was not at liberty to share with them, and he waited fourteen years before even sharing what he did here.

In light of that glorious vision, something was allowed in his life, something he called a thorn in the flesh.   We still use that term today to speak of some chronic trial or trouble in our lives.   It may have even been a person who troubled Paul, someone he called the messenger of Satan. It was his belief that the Lord allowed this to keep him from being "exalted above measure." Whatever it was, it kept him humble and trusting in God. He prayed for God's deliverance on at least three occasions.   It is not that he did not receive an answer. He received a powerful answer, just not the one he might have wanted at the time.   Rather than immediately removing this thorn from Paul's life, the Lord promised His sustaining grace. He said, "My grace is sufficient for you!" Until the day deliverance came, God's grace and mercy was going to be enough!   That is true today for all of us. God has promised to deliver you from affliction[662], but until that deliverance comes, rejoice in His sustaining grace! If you have Jesus, you have all you really need.

He's more than enough
More than enough
He is El Shaddai
The God of plenty
The all sufficient One
God Almighty
He is more than enough.[663]

---

[662] Psalm 34:19
[663] "More than Enough," David Ingles, David Ingles Music, 1978.

Read 2 Corinthians 12:20-13:13

2 Corinthians 13:5 Examine yourselves, whether ye be in the faith; prove your own selves. Know ye not your own selves, how that Jesus Christ is in you, except ye be reprobates?

Paul had visited this church on two occasions, and a third visit was planned. His first visit had been when he founded the church. His second visit had been brief, and sorrowful; as he dealt with some difficult issues. Now he is planning a third visit, and if there is no repentance in the areas he addressed before, he will have to deal harshly with some situations. When he comes the next time, he will not spare. Some of them seemed to doubt that Paul had the authority to deal with these issues and questioned whether the Lord was truly speaking through him. Perhaps they were like some today who say, "No one can tell me what to do!" Regardless, they would find out when he arrived. Someone paraphrased his words this way, "You want to see proof of Christ speaking in me? Fine. When I come the third time, you will see the power of God in my rebuke as I clean house. So, clean it up before I come."[664]

Rather than criticizing the Apostle Paul, they were to look at their own lives, examining themselves to see if they were truly in the faith. The word used here for "examine" was used for assaying metal to see if the gold or silver was pure, or whether it had been adulterated with some lesser metal. They were to put themselves to the test. Were they the true gold of one who was "in the faith", one with Christ within, or were they something less?

We should all do the same thing. Rather than criticizing and examining others, we should prayerfully examine our own lives. When we do, I know we will all find ourselves greatly in need of His grace and mercy! It reminds me of the words of an old spiritual song.

Not my brother or my sister, but it's me, O Lord,
standing in the need of prayer!

---

[664] <u>Enduring Word Commentary</u>, 2 Corinthians, David Guzik.

Read Galatians 1

Galatians 1:6 I marvel that ye are so soon removed from him that called you into the grace of Christ unto another gospel:

The Christians in Galatia had not been saved very long. Sadly, however, in that length of time, some of them had left the good news of the grace of God for another "gospel." It had to do with a teaching that some brought to them, a teaching that insisted that they, as Gentile believers, must be circumcised and come under Old Testament Law in order to be right with God. Sometimes those who taught this are called the Judaizers, because they insisted that Gentile believers in Christ must first become Jews before they can really become Christians. Even though this issue was settled at the Jerusalem Council in Acts 15, it has never completely gone away to this day. He told them that it was not really a gospel (good news) at all. In fact, it was a perversion of the Good News. It took them away from the message of the grace of God into something else.[665] That false teaching, or any other, must not be received no matter how enticing or how charismatic the teacher or alluring his words. Paul said, "even if I start preaching it, don't believe it." Even if an angel from heaven preaches it[666], don't believe it. He uses the strongest word imaginable when condemning those who would bring "another gospel" into the church. He says, "let them be accursed." That is the Greek word *anathema*, meaning to come under God's divine curse[667]. If there were no repentance, it would likely include separation from God in hell. This is such an important thing that it is repeated in verse 9[668]. The Gospel of Christ has always, and will always be under attack. That is why we are told to earnestly contend for the faith[669], and continually preach the Word!

2 Timothy 4:2-4 2 Preach the word; be instant in season, out of season; reprove, rebuke, exhort with all longsuffering and doctrine. 3 For the time will come when they will not endure sound doctrine; but after their own lusts shall they heap to themselves teachers, having itching ears; 4 And they shall turn away *their* ears from the truth, and shall be turned unto fables.

---

[665] Galatians 1:7 Which is not another; but there be some that trouble you, and would pervert the gospel of Christ.

[666] Mormonism, for example, is a non-Christian cult supposedly brought by angelic messenger, but it is quite obviously "another Gospel," not the Gospel as revealed in the New Testament Scriptures.

[667] Deuteronomy 27

[668] Galatians 1:9 As we said before, so say I now again, If any man preach any other gospel unto you than that ye have received, let him be accursed.

[669] **Jude 1:3 Beloved**, when I gave all diligence to write unto you of the common salvation, it was needful for me to write unto you, and exhort *you* that ye should earnestly contend for the faith which was once delivered unto the saints.

Read Galatians 2

Galatians 2:11-12 11 But when Peter was come to Antioch, I withstood him to the face, because he was to be blamed. 12 For before that certain came from James, he did eat with the Gentiles: but when they were come, he withdrew and separated himself, fearing them which were of the circumcision.

Peter should have known better. After all, he was the *first* to bring the Gospel to the Gentiles. After receiving a vision from God, he went to a Gentile home and preached Jesus Christ. That entire household turned to the Lord, were baptized in the Holy Spirit, evidenced by speaking in tongues, and they were baptized in water[670]. The Lord's message to Peter in all of this was clear, "Do not call what I have made clean unclean." Entering a Gentile home and enjoying fellowship with them would have been unthinkable for most Jews, but Peter had a word from the Lord that changed his outlook.

Later, the first church council convened in Jerusalem to discuss what parts of the Law should be binding on Gentiles who came to Christ. Some were unsure that Gentiles could even be saved, but Peter was one who gave testimony that they could. Speaking of that first preaching experience in a Gentile home, he said, "God, which knoweth the hearts, bare them witness, giving them the Holy Ghost, even as *he did* unto us; And put no difference between us and them, purifying their hearts by faith."[671] The Gentiles became brothers and sisters through faith in Christ, not through adhering to the Law.

In spite of all of that, Peter let the fear of what other people might think, dictate his actions. When visiting the church at Antioch, he ate freely with the Gentiles sharing fellowship with them as members of the family of God. That changed, though, when some of the Jewish Christians came down from Jerusalem. Fearing what they might think, Peter pulled away from the Gentiles[672]. Several others, sadly, followed his lead and Paul was forced to confront him about it. We trust that that Peter repented of his hypocrisy, but his actions surely remind us of the truth found in Proverbs 29:25.

The fear of man bringeth a snare: but whoso putteth his trust in the LORD shall be safe.

---

[670] Acts 10
[671] Acts 15:8-9
[672] Some believe that this may have even included refusing to take the Lord's Supper with them.

Read Galatians 3:1-20

Galatians 3:3   Are ye so foolish? having begun in the Spirit, are ye now made perfect by the flesh?

As we learned in Galatians 1, some of the Galatian Christians had given in to the false teaching of the Judaizers, those who would have them leave simple faith in Christ and come back under the Law.[673] How foolish that was in light of what they knew!   The Lord's sacrifice had once been so clear to them, now they had lost sight of the cross and the power of the Holy Spirit. They were so deceived, it was almost as if they had been 'bewitched.'[674]

How could something begun as a miracle made possible by the cross and the power of the Holy Spirit be perfected by the flesh? By the flesh he means our vain efforts at being made righteous through keeping the Law. The answer is clear.   We cannot possibly be made righteous through the keeping of the Law. It is foolish to believe that we can. Like Abraham, who lived long before the Law was given, we receive our righteousness through faith in Jesus Christ.

Galatians 3:6-7   6 Even as Abraham believed God, and it was accounted to him for righteousness. 7 Know ye therefore that they which are of faith, the same are the children of Abraham.

---

[673] Galatians 1:6-9
[674] Galatians 3:1

Read Galatians 3.21-4.7

Galatians 4:4-5 4 But when the fulness of the time was come, God sent forth his Son, made of a woman, made under the law, 5 To redeem them that were under the law, that we might receive the adoption of sons.

Jesus Christ was, and is, both God and man.   As the Son of God, He is Immanuel, God come in human flesh. As one 'made of a woman," he is a perfect human being. He was also a Jew, one "made under the Law."   All of this was necessary so that in becoming one of us, giving His life, and rising again, He might make a way for us to be adopted into *His* Royal Family!

As adopted children, we have all the rights and privileges of one born into a family[675]!   That includes being indwelt by His Holy Spirit, coming to our Father on an intimate basis[676], and standing to receive a glorious inheritance in heaven[677]. We are heirs to all that is His, children of the King of kings!

My Father is rich in houses and lands,
He holdeth the wealth of the world in His hands!
Of rubies and diamonds, of silver and gold,
His coffers are full, He has riches untold.

I'm a child of the King,
A child of the King:
With Jesus my Savior,
I'm a child of the King.[678]

---

[675] **Romans 8:17**   And if children, then heirs; heirs of God, and joint-heirs with Christ; if so be that we suffer with *him*, that we may be also glorified together.
[676] It has been said by some that "Abba" the Aramaic word for father is, perhaps, even more like our word 'daddy."
[677] **Colossians 3:24**   Knowing that of the Lord ye shall receive the reward of the inheritance: for ye serve the Lord Christ.
[678] "A Child of the King," Harriet E. Buell

Read Galatians 4:8-31

Galatians 4:9-11 9 But now, after that ye have known God, or rather are known of God, how turn ye again to the weak and beggarly elements, whereunto ye desire again to be in bondage? 10 Ye observe days, and months, and times, and years. 11 I am afraid of you, lest I have bestowed upon you labour in vain.

After sharing the wonderful blessings of what it is to be a child of the King and to enjoy the freedom of that relationship, Paul marvels at how the Galatian Christians would want to go back into bondage. He was referring to the bondage of a system of any kind that makes our good works the means of salvation or sanctification. He knew that all of the preaching and teaching he had done in their midst was in vain, if they left the Gospel and went back to a system of works.   If you will remember, the false teaching prevalent in Galatia was that the Gentile Christians must come under all of the Old Testament Law including circumcision, special diet, holy days, etc.   It is very clear from the Word of God that none of those things can save us or make us more holy. Other churches of that day, such as the one in Colossae were facing the same kinds of issues. The false teachers there were judging Gentile Christians, because they did not follow "the rules." Paul said to them, "Let no man therefore judge you in meat, or in drink, or in respect of an holyday, or of the new moon, or of the sabbath *days*: Which are a shadow of things to come; but the body *is* of Christ."[679]   Jesus Christ and His salvation are the reality behind all of those shadows.   Why follow a shadow when we can know the real thing!

Marvelous grace of our loving Lord,
Grace that exceeds our sin and our guilt!
Yonder on Calvary's mount outpoured,
There where the blood of the Lamb was spilled.

Grace, grace, God's grace,
Grace that will pardon and cleanse within;
Grace, grace, God's grace,
Grace that is greater than all our sin![680]

---

[679] Colossians 2:16-17
[680] "Grace Greater than our Sin," Julia Johnston

Read Galatians 5

Galatians 5:14   For all the law is fulfilled in one word, *even* in this; Thou shalt love thy neighbour as thyself.

In chapter 5 we are called to stand fast in the freedom we have in Christ.[681]   We are told that to leave that liberty and go back under the Law as a means of salvation is to fall from grace.[682]   However, that does *not* mean that we are free to live ungodly lives.[683]   We fulfill God's Law by walking in love[684].   This can only be done through the power of the Holy Spirit[685].   In fact, it can be said that the nine fruits of the Spirit spoken of in this chapter are actually manifestations of that one all-important fruit—love.   May the Lord so fill our hearts that we will do those things that please him motivated by His holy love.   Fill my way, every day, with love!

Galatians 5:22-23   22 But the fruit of the Spirit is love, joy, peace, longsuffering, gentleness, goodness, faith, 23 Meekness, temperance: against such there is no law.

---

[681] **Galatians 5:1**   Stand fast therefore in the liberty wherewith Christ hath made us free, and be not entangled again with the yoke of bondage.

[682] **Galatians 5:4**   Christ is become of no effect unto you, whosoever of you are justified by the law; ye are fallen from grace.

[683] **Galatians 5:13**   For, brethren, ye have been called unto liberty; only *use* not liberty for an occasion to the flesh, but by love serve one another.

[684] **Galatians 5:14**   For all the law is fulfilled in one word, *even* in this; Thou shalt love thy neighbour as thyself.

[685] **Romans 5:5**   And hope maketh not ashamed; because the love of God is shed abroad in our hearts by the Holy Ghost which is given unto us.

Galatians 5:16   *This* I say then, Walk in the Spirit, and ye shall not fulfil the lust of the flesh.

Read Galatians 6

Galatians 6:9   And let us not be weary in well doing: for in due season we shall reap, if we faint not.

Seeds are miraculous things. It is amazing that something that appears so dead and dry can, when given the right conditions, grow and ultimately produce fruit and more seeds like itself. Here in Galatians 6 he is speaking of another kind of seed, those seeds that are sown through what we do with our lives. We can do those things that please our fleshly nature, or we can do those things that please the Spirit. Whichever seed we sow, there will be consequences, or a time of reaping.   To think that there will not be is to mock God and what He says.[686]

We know that reaping follows sowing, but it is not always immediate. Some seeds take a long time to germinate, but, ultimately, they do. An ungodly person may sow wicked seeds and think that there will be no consequences. It may appear that there are not any, but the day will come when he will have to answer for what he has done.   In the same way, a godly person may continue to sow good seeds, and then question why the promised blessings do not seem to appear.   God encourages us to keep sowing that good seed. The promised harvest will come, if we do not give up! I remember the words of an old hymn that was often sung when I was a child.

1. Sowing in the morning, sowing seeds of kindness,
    Sowing in the noontide and the dewy eve;
    Waiting for the harvest, and the time of reaping,
    We shall come rejoicing, bringing in the sheaves.

    o *Refrain:*
    Bringing in the sheaves, bringing in the sheaves,
    We shall come rejoicing, bringing in the sheaves;
    Bringing in the sheaves, bringing in the sheaves,
    We shall come rejoicing, bringing in the sheaves.

2. Sowing in the sunshine, sowing in the shadows,
    Fearing neither clouds nor winter's chilling breeze;
    By and by the harvest, and the labor ended,
    We shall come rejoicing, bringing in the sheaves.[687]

---

[686] **Galatians 6:7** Be not deceived; God is not mocked: for whatsoever a man soweth, that shall he also reap.
[687] "Bringing in the Sheaves," Knowles Shaw

Read Ephesians 1.1-14

Ephesians 1:13-14 13 In whom ye also *trusted*, after that ye heard the word of truth, the gospel of your salvation: in whom also after that ye believed, ye were sealed with that holy Spirit of promise, 14 Which is the earnest of our inheritance until the redemption of the purchased possession, unto the praise of his glory.

The Holy Spirit takes up residence in us when we are born again.[688]   In Ephesians 1, His indwelling presence is compared to both a seal and the earnest of an inheritance. In ancient times, something was sealed in order to prevent tampering. For example, Jesus' tomb was secured with a seal[689]. A seal also showed ownership of something. Ancient kings marked their property with their personal seal. The Holy Spirit on the inside is a mark, or seal, of God's ownership of our lives. Someone once said that that seal serves as a spiritual "no trespassing sign" to the devil. He dare not tamper with what clearly belongs to the Lord. The Spirit is also the earnest of our inheritance. Earnest money is like a down payment. His presence reveals to us the glories that are yet to come when we receive our full heavenly inheritance from the Savior.[690] We have not yet experienced the glories that lie ahead, but the Holy Spirit gives us just a little taste of them today. I'm glad that I have been sealed as "belonging to Jesus!"

Now I Belong to Jesus[691]
Jesus, my Lord will love me forever,
From Him no pow'r of evil can sever,
He gave His life to ransom my soul;
Now I belong to Him;

Now I belong to Jesus,
Jesus belongs to me,
Not for the years of time alone,
But for eternity.

---

[688] **Romans 8:9** But ye are not in the flesh, but in the Spirit, if so be that the Spirit of God dwell in you. Now if any man have not the Spirit of Christ, he is none of his.

[689] **Matthew 27:66** So they went, and made the sepulcher sure, sealing the stone, and setting a watch.

[690] **1 Corinthians 2:12** Now we have received, not the spirit of the world, but the spirit which is of God; that we might know the things that are freely given to us of God.

[691] "Now I Belong to Jesus," Norman J. Clayton

272

Read Ephesians 1:15-2:10

Ephesians 2:7   That in the ages to come he might shew the exceeding riches of his grace in *his* kindness toward us through Christ Jesus.

Grace, God's unmerited favor, is truly an amazing thing.   Some have called grace <u>G</u>od's <u>R</u>iches at <u>C</u>hrist's <u>E</u>xpense, and we will continue to marvel at the wonders of that grace in the endless eons of eternity.

God's grace is available to all, but we can only experience it through faith in Christ.   The gift has already been purchased, but we must receive it for ourselves.[692]   We cannot take any credit for this gift.   We cannot boast about what we have done to earn it, because it is a gift given, in grace, to those who truly do not deserve it.[693]   We cannot earn God's grace, but we must also remember that it is not a license to do evil.   God's Word says, "Shall we continue in sin that grace may abound? God forbid!"[694]   Our works will not save us, but it is expected that a soul saved by grace will begin to live differently.   We are His workmanship created <u>unto</u> good works.[695]   John Newton wrote a song that has been called the theme song of the Christian faith—Amazing Grace. I wonder if we will still be singing it a million years from today!

Amazing grace! How sweet the sound
That saved a wretch like me!
I once was lost, but now am found;
Was blind, but now I see.

---

[692] **Ephesians 2:8**   For by grace are ye saved through faith; and that not of yourselves: *it is* the gift of God:
John 1:12   But as many as received him, to them gave he power to become the sons of God, *even* to them that believe on his name:
Romans 6:23   For the wages of sin *is* death; but the gift of God *is* eternal life through Jesus Christ our Lord.
[693] **Ephesians 2:9**   Not of works, lest any man should boast.
[694] **Romans 6:1-2**   1 What shall we say then? Shall we continue in sin, that grace may abound? 2 God forbid. How shall we, that are dead to sin, live any longer therein?
[695] **Ephesians 2:10**   For we are his workmanship, created in Christ Jesus unto good works, which God hath before ordained that we should walk in them.

Read Ephesians 2:11-22

Ephesians 2:13 But now in Christ Jesus ye who sometimes were far off are made nigh by the blood of Christ.

As Gentiles, the Ephesians had been far from God. The description of their (our) spiritual state outside of Christ is very clear. They were spiritually dead (Ephesians 2:1), walking as Satan would have them to walk (Ephesians 2:2). Their very nature was to be a child of wrath, not a child of God (Ephesians 2:3). They were aliens, foreigners, not a part of God's kingdom and family (Ephesians 2:12). One thing changed all of that! Those who *were* far off, have been made nigh through the blood of Christ. It is by that same blood, His sacrificial death, that Jew and Gentile can be made one. We have been made nigh! How close are we? He says that His church is now a habitation of God through the Spirit (Ephesians 2:22). We are in Him, and He is in us. You can't get much closer than that!

Why not make this hymn your prayer today!

I am Thine, O Lord, I have heard Thy voice,
And it told Thy love to me;
But I long to rise in the arms of faith
And be closer drawn to Thee.

Draw me nearer, nearer blessed Lord,
To the cross where Thou hast died;
Draw me nearer, nearer, nearer blessed Lord,
To Thy precious, bleeding side.

Consecrate me now to Thy service, Lord,
By the power of grace divine;
Let my soul look up with a steadfast hope,
And my will be lost in Thine.

Oh, the pure delight of a single hour
That before Thy throne I spend,
When I kneel in prayer, and with Thee, my God
I commune as friend with friend!

Read Ephesians 3

Ephesians 3:14 For this cause I bow my knees unto the Father of our Lord Jesus Christ,

Paul is praying for his brothers and sisters in Christ. What is he praying?   He is praying for things that are God's will for our lives too. He prays that they would receive inner strength from the Holy Spirit,[696] that Jesus would live in their hearts, by faith, and that their spiritual roots, their foundation, would be the love of God.[697] He prayed that they would know that love in all of its dimensions of breadth, length, depth, and height, and that they would be filled with all the fulness of God. [698]

Is God able to do all those things in our lives? Oh, yes!   He can do that and much, much more. Let us rejoice in what He says about God's ability.

Ephesians 3:20-21   20 Now unto him that is able to do exceeding abundantly above all that we ask or think, according to the power that worketh in us, 21 Unto him *be* glory in the church by Christ Jesus throughout all ages, world without end. Amen.

My God can do anything, anything, anything,
My God can do anything!
He made the world in all its fulness, and all that time shall bring,
My God can do anything[699]!

---

[696] **Ephesians 3:16**   That he would grant you, according to the riches of his glory, to be strengthened with might by his Spirit in the inner man;
[697] **Ephesians 3:17**   That Christ may dwell in your hearts by faith; that ye, being rooted and grounded in love,
[698] **Ephesians 3:18-19**   18 May be able to comprehend with all saints what *is* the breadth, and length, and depth, and height; 19 And to know the love of Christ, which passeth knowledge, that ye might be filled with all the fulness of God.
[699] "My God Can Do Anything," Vep Ellis.

Read Ephesians 4

Ephesians 4:11 And he gave some, apostles; and some, prophets; and some, evangelists; and some, pastors and teachers;

These gifts, given to the church by the Lord, are often called the five-fold ministry gifts, even though there may, actually, be only four of them. The word 'apostle' means 'sent ones', they are often the ones carrying the Gospel into new territory, preaching the Word with miraculous signs following[700]. Some missionaries, serving unreached people groups, could have what we might call an apostolic ministry. Prophets are those who speak an anointed word from the Lord. It is not necessarily "foretelling" some future event, but what some have called "forthtelling." We are told that their ministry should bring exhortation, edification, and comfort to the body[701]. Those who study this in the original language tell us that pastors and teachers should probably be translated pastor-teachers and that it is actually one ministry. Those who serve as shepherds in local churches should also be "apt to teach.[702]"

We are clearly told what the purpose of these ministries is in Ephesians 4. Their ministry is meant to equip the saints, the believers in every local church, for the work of the ministry. Their ministry is meant to edify the body of Christ, that is to help Christians grow in their relationship with the Lord. Their ministry is meant to bring us to the "unity of the faith," that is following sound doctrine, not tossed about by "every *wind* of doctrine." Motivated by love they should speak the truth, not necessarily what people want to hear, but what they need to hear. Of course, the ultimate goal is that God's people become mature in their faith[703].

2 Peter 3:18 But grow in grace, and *in* the knowledge of our Lord and Saviour Jesus Christ. To him *be* glory both now and forever. Amen.

---

[700] **2 Corinthians 12:12 Truly** the signs of an apostle were wrought among you in all patience, in signs, and wonders, and mighty deeds.

[701] **1 Corinthians 14:3 But** he that prophesieth speaketh unto men *to* edification, and exhortation, and comfort.

[702] **1 Timothy 3:2 A** bishop then must be blameless, the husband of one wife, vigilant, sober, of good behaviour, given to hospitality, apt to teach; (Note that the words overseer, bishop, pastor, and elder are used synonymously in the New Testament).

2 Timothy 2:24 And the servant of the Lord must not strive; but be gentle unto all *men*, apt to teach, patient,

[703] **Ephesians 4:12-16** 12 For the perfecting of the saints, for the work of the ministry, for the edifying of the body of Christ: 13 Till we all come in the unity of the faith, and of the knowledge of the Son of God, unto a perfect man, unto the measure of the stature of the fulness of Christ: 14 That we *henceforth* be no more children, tossed to and fro, and carried about with every wind of doctrine, by the sleight of men, *and* cunning craftiness, whereby they lie in wait to deceive; 15 But speaking the truth in love, may grow up into him in all things, which is the head, *even* Christ: 16 From whom the whole body fitly joined together and compacted by that which every joint supplieth, according to the effectual working in the measure of every part, maketh increase of the body unto the edifying of itself in love.

Read Ephesians 5

Ephesians 4:29-30 29 Let no corrupt communication proceed out of your mouth, but that which is good to the use of edifying, that it may minister grace unto the hearers. 30 And grieve not the holy Spirit of God, whereby ye are sealed unto the day of redemption.

The Scriptures speak a great deal about what we say. Jesus said that our words are a measure of what is in our hearts[704] and that we will be judged for every idle word that we speak[705]. James speaks of our tongue as a deadly poison, a wildfire, a vicious animal that cannot be tamed[706]. We know that our tongue has the ability to speak both life and death[707].

Here we are told that no corrupt communication should come out of our mouths. Corrupt is the Greek word sapros, which can refer to something dead, dying, or rotting, a very fitting description of evil speech. Christians should be known for their clean speech, because they have clean hearts, hearts cleansed by the blood of Jesus. Our speech should lift up rather than tear down. It should, like salt, bring a pleasant "seasoning" to our environment[708]. By allowing evil speech to come from our lips, we are grieving the Holy Spirit that lives within us. Perhaps David's prayer should be our prayer today.

Psalm 19:14 Let the words of my mouth, and the meditation of my heart, be acceptable in thy sight, O LORD, my strength, and my redeemer.

---

[704] **Matthew 12:34** O generation of vipers, how can ye, being evil, speak good things? for out of the abundance of the heart the mouth speaketh.

[705] **Matthew 12:36-37** 36 But I say unto you, That every idle word that men shall speak, they shall give account thereof in the day of judgment. 37 For by thy words thou shalt be justified, and by thy words thou shalt be condemned.

[706] **James 3:6-8** 6 And the tongue *is* a fire, a world of iniquity: so is the tongue among our members, that it defileth the whole body, and setteth on fire the course of nature; and it is set on fire of hell. 7 For every kind of beasts, and of birds, and of serpents, and of things in the sea, is tamed, and hath been tamed of mankind: 8 But the tongue can no man tame; *it is* an unruly evil, full of deadly poison.

[707] **Proverbs 18:21** **Death** and life *are* in the power of the tongue: and they that love it shall eat the fruit thereof.

[708] **Colossians 4:6** **Let** your speech *be* alway with grace, seasoned with salt, that ye may know how ye ought to answer every man.

Read Ephesians 5:16-6:4

Ephesians 5:18 And be not drunk with wine, wherein is excess; but be filled with the Spirit;

It is an imperative, a command, that we be filled with the Spirit. The verb used here actually means to keep on being filled. The *experience* of being filled with the Spirit is wonderful, but now we must seek to daily, and continually, *walk* in the Spirit. That will influence every part of our lives.

He contrasts this with drunkenness. Yielding one's life to the power of alcohol leads to excess (every kind of sin and evil imaginable and unimaginable). Alcohol probably causes more sin and evil, ruins more lives, and destroys more homes and families than anything else in this world. It is tragic that so many have invited this evil into their homes! Yielding our lives to the Holy Spirit, on the other hand, will give us power to live overcoming lives. As we shall see in this chapter and the one to follow, being continually filled with the Spirit will impact our personal lives, our marriages, our families, and our work.

Galatians 5:25 If we live in the Spirit, let us also walk in the Spirit.

Read Ephesians 6:5-24

Ephesians 6:10-11 Finally, my brethren, be strong in the Lord, and in the power of his might. Put on the whole armour of God, that ye may be able to stand against the wiles of the devil.

Paul wrote the Book of Ephesians from prison. He was likely shackled to a Roman soldier. As he observed that soldier, the Holy Spirit began to give him an analogy between the soldier's armor and the spiritual armor that is worn by believers. Spiritual armor is necessary, because of the wiles (tricks and deceit) of our enemy.   He is a spiritual foe. We recognize that the real battle and the real enemy is the one we cannot see with our physical eyes.[709]   In the evil day, that day we are under attack, we can stand, because of God's armor![710]

When you pray today, thank Him that He has provided His armor for you.

Thank you, Lord, that my loins are girded about with Your truth.
With Your help, I will walk in the truth of the Word of God today,[711]
And I will rely on the power of the Holy Spirit,
The Spirit of Truth[712].
Thank you, Lord, that I am wearing the breastplate of righteousness.
I am in right standing with You, because of the blood of Jesus.
Like Abraham, I believe God,
And it has been counted unto me for righteousness[713]!
Thank you, Father, that my feet are shod
With the preparation of the Gospel of peace.
You have enabled and prepared me for all that lies ahead.
Your Word says that I am complete in You[714].
Thank you that you have provided for me the shield of faith,
And that you open your Word to me to help my faith to grow.

---

[709] **Ephesians 6:12**   For we wrestle not against flesh and blood, but against principalities, against powers, against the rulers of the darkness of this world, against spiritual wickedness in high *places*.

[710] **Ephesians 6:13 Wherefore** take unto you the whole armour of God, that ye may be able to withstand in the evil day, and having done all, to stand.

[711] **John 17:17 Sanctify** them through thy truth: thy word is truth.

[712] **John 16:13 Howbeit** when he, the Spirit of truth, is come, he will guide you into all truth: for he shall not speak of himself; but whatsoever he shall hear, *that* shall he speak: and he will shew you things to come.

[713713] **Galatians 3:6-7**   6 Even as Abraham believed God, and it was accounted to him for righteousness. 7 Know ye therefore that they which are of faith, the same are the children of Abraham.

[714] **Colossians 2:10 And** ye are complete in him, which is the head of all principality and power:

When I need a particular Word for a particular situation,
Your Spirit reminds me[715].
Thank you that you have provided for me the helmet of salvation.
You offer protection to my head,
Where the battles of thoughts and emotions often take place[716].
Thank you, Father!
Thank you for what I can hold in my hand, and in my heart,
The Bible, the Word of God.
Like Jesus did when He was tempted,
I can put the enemy to flight with the truth of the Word of God[717]!
Help me not to forget to pray in the Spirit,
An important part of putting on Your armor[718]!

Ephesians 6:18 Praying always with all prayer and supplication in the Spirit, and watching thereunto with all perseverance and supplication for all saints;

---

[715] **Romans 10:17 So** then faith *cometh* by hearing, and hearing by the word of God.
John 14:26 But the Comforter, *which is* the Holy Ghost, whom the Father will send in my name, he shall teach you all things, and bring all things to your remembrance, whatsoever I have said unto you.
[716] **Philippians 4:5-7** 5 Let your moderation be known unto all men. The Lord *is* at hand. 6 Be careful about nothing; but in everything by prayer and supplication with thanksgiving let your requests be made known unto God. 7 And the peace of God, which passeth all understanding, shall keep your hearts and minds through Christ Jesus.
[717] **Hebrews 4:12 For** the word of God *is* quick, and powerful, and sharper than any twoedged sword, piercing even to the dividing asunder of soul and spirit, and of the joints and marrow, and *is* a discerner of the thoughts and intents of the heart.
[718] **Jude 1:20 But** ye, beloved, building up yourselves on your most holy faith, praying in the Holy Ghost,

Read Philippians 1:1-20

Philippians 1:6 Being confident of this very thing, that he which hath begun a good work in you will perform IT until the day of Jesus Christ:

Eleven years before, Paul, along with Silas, had been the founder of the church at Philippi. The first convert on the European continent was Lydia, a wealthy businesswoman they met along the riverbank there in Philippi. The second notable convert was a girl delivered from demon possession. She was gloriously set free by the power of God, but her deliverance brought terrible persecution against Paul and Silas. There were those who made money off her supposed occult powers. Of course, as a saved person, she was no longer able to tell fortunes or give psychic readings! Paul and Silas were thrown in jail, where they saw a third amazing conversion. When God delivered them from their chains, the jailer, amazed by what he saw, came to Christ, along with his family! Ministry in Philippi had been glorious, with a great openness, among some, to the Gospel. But, after being released from jail, they left town, probably sooner than they would have liked. Now, eleven years later, Paul is undoubtedly thinking of those converts, and those that had come to faith in Christ since. One thing he was sure about was this: God had begun a good work in them and He would complete that work! I am glad that the Lord is both the Author (beginning) and the Finisher (the one who completes) of my faith.

Hebrews 12:2 Looking unto Jesus the author and finisher of OUR faith; who for the joy that was set before him endured the cross, despising the shame, and is set down at the right hand of the throne of God.

Read Philippians 1:21-2:11

Philippians 1:21   For to me to live is Christ, and to die is gain.

Though his earthly life was in danger, the Apostle Paul was not afraid. The Lord was with Him here on earth, and if he went to heaven, that would be the most glorious thing of all.   But, to remain where he could minister to, and help, the ones that he loved, that was important too.

Ultimately, he would give his life for the faith, most likely in the city of Rome, but in the meantime, he had the assurance that he was going to stay around for a while and continue to bless the saints in Philippi.   The wonderful assurance of a child of God is this: Living or dying, I belong to the Lord! Living or dying, I am His and He is mine.   Living or dying, He will never leave me. He will never forsake me! I am in the hollow of His hand.

Romans 8:38-39 38 For I am persuaded, that <u>neither death, nor life</u>, nor angels, nor principalities, nor powers, nor things present, nor things to come, 39 Nor height, nor depth, nor any other creature, <u>shall be able to separate us from the love of God, which is in Christ Jesus our Lord.</u>

Read Philippians 2.12-30

Philippians 2:12 Wherefore, my beloved, as ye have always obeyed, not as in my presence only, but now much more in my absence, work out your own salvation with fear and trembling.

Paul has full confidence that the Philippians will take heed to what he is telling them. They have always been ready to obey the Word, not just when he was with them, but also when he was absent. His command for them was this: "Work out your own salvation with fear and trembling." We cannot work to achieve our salvation, that would go against the entirety of New Testament teaching. But, once we are saved, we give our relationship with God the fullest effort, and we do so with godly fear and reverence.

Context is very important in understanding the Word of God. The verse that comes immediately after this one reminds us **_how_** we are able to do this. We can only "work out our own salvation," because He is working in us by His mighty power. He is the one, as we were told in the beginning of the book, that will complete His work in us[719]. Someone once said, "Work like it all depends on you, but pray like it all depends on God," for it truly does. Without Him working in me, I could never work out my salvation!

Philippians 2:13 For it is God which worketh in you both to will and to do of *his* good pleasure.

---

[719] **Philippians 1:6 Being** confident of this very thing, that he which hath begun a good work in you will perform *it* until the day of Jesus Christ:

Read Philippians 3

Philippians 3:13 Brethren, I count not myself to have apprehended: but *this* one thing *I do*, forgetting those things which are behind, and reaching forth unto those things which are before,

When a Christian believes they have reached the pinnacle of perfection, they are in a very dangerous place indeed. Even the apostle Paul, one of the greatest men of God who ever lived, recognized his own great need. He had not yet reached full maturity in Christ. In light of this, he must forget the successes and failures of yesterday and continue to reach toward the goal.[720] He must continually press toward that mark.[721] Someone put it this way, "Just as a little child is a perfect human being, but still is far from perfect in all his development as a man, so the true child of God is also perfect in all his parts, although not yet perfect in all the stages of his development in faith."[722] It reminds me of the words of a children's song from long ago.

He's still working on me
To make me what I ought to be
It took him just a week to make the moon and stars
The sun and the earth and Jupiter and Mars
How loving and patient He must be
'Cause He's still workin' on me
There really ought to be a sign upon my heart
Don't judge him yet, there's an unfinished part
But I'll be perfect just according to His plan
Fashioned by the Master's loving hands[723].

---

[720] **Philippians 3:12 Not** as though I had already attained, either were already perfect: but I follow after, if that I may apprehend that for which also I am apprehended of Christ Jesus.
[721] **Philippians 3:14** I press toward the mark for the prize of the high calling of God in Christ Jesus."
[722] Unknown. Possibly, George Muller.
[723] "He's Still Working on Me," Joel Hemphill

Read Philippians 4:3-23

Philippians 4:6-7 Be careful for nothing; but in every thing by prayer and supplication with thanksgiving let your requests be made known unto God. 7 And the peace of God, which passeth all understanding, shall keep your hearts and minds through Christ Jesus.

The word 'careful' here does not mean 'cautious' as the word is usually defined today. It means 'full of care." We might say worried or anxious. A good paraphrase of the first part of this verse would be, "Don't worry about anything, but thankfully pray about everything!" The words 'prayer' and 'supplication' are similar. Prayer is communication with God in general, while supplication is specifically asking for what we need. The Lord has given us both the command and the privilege of asking many times in the New Testament![724] We are told here to ask with thanksgiving, thanking Him for His faithfulness, His goodness, and, by faith, thanking Him for the answers which we believe He will bring.

What are we promised until the answer comes? We are promised a peace that passes all understanding. Our hearts and minds may tend toward worry and fear when we are beset by trials, but when we leave those needs with Him in prayer, we are promised a peace that will <u>keep</u> our hearts and minds. The Greek word translated 'keep' can mean to surround as with a garrison of soldiers. It is the same word used in 1 Peter 1:5 where it says we are "kept by the power of God."   Someone put it this way, "God's peace, like a garrison of soldiers, will keep guard over your thoughts and feelings so that they will be as safe against the assaults of worry and fear as any fortress."[725] I rejoice in that peace today!

Isaiah 26:3   Thou wilt keep *him* in perfect peace, *whose* mind *is* stayed *on thee*: because he trusteth in thee.

---

[724] Matthew 7:7-11, Matthew 18:19, Matthew 21:22, Luke 11:9-13, John 14:14, John 15:7, John 15:16 , John 16:23, Ephesians 3:20, James 1:5-6, James 4:2, 1 John 3:22, 1 John 5:14-16.
[725] <u>Word Biblical Commentary: Philippians</u>, Gerald Hawthorne

Read Colossians 1:1-20

Colossians 1:13   Who hath delivered us from the power of darkness, and hath translated *us* into the kingdom of his dear Son:

His glorious full salvation is a deliverance, a salvation to the uttermost![726]   There are only two kingdoms in this universe, the kingdom of darkness and the kingdom of God.   Everyone is living in one or the other.   Outside of Jesus Christ, we are, by default, living in the kingdom of darkness.   We have a fallen, sinful nature, and God says that we love darkness rather than light, because our deeds are evil.[727] Satan, the one called the "god of this world" seeks to keep our eyes blinded to the liberating truth of the Gospel[728].

But, when we are born again, many amazing things happen. We are given a new heart, and the Spirit writes God's Law on our hearts[729]. We begin to love those things we once hated, and hate those things we once loved.   We are delivered, miraculously snatched, from Satan's kingdom, and placed as full citizens in God's kingdom[730].   What an amazing and wonderful thing salvation truly is!

Philippians 3:20   For our conversation [citizenship] is in heaven; from whence also we look for the Saviour, the Lord Jesus Christ:

---

[726] **Hebrews 7:25** Wherefore he is able also to save them to the uttermost that come unto God by him, seeing he ever liveth to make intercession for them.

[727] **John 3:18-21** 18 He that believeth on him is not condemned: but he that believeth not is condemned already, because he hath not believed in the name of the only begotten Son of God. 19 And this is the condemnation, that light is come into the world, and men loved darkness rather than light, because their deeds were evil. 20 For every one that doeth evil hateth the light, neither cometh to the light, lest his deeds should be reproved. 21 But he that doeth truth cometh to the light, that his deeds may be made manifest, that they are wrought in God.

[728] **2 Corinthians 4:3-4** 3 But if our gospel be hid, it is hid to them that are lost: 4 In whom the god of this world hath blinded the minds of them which believe not, lest the light of the glorious gospel of Christ, who is the image of God, should shine unto them.

[729] **Jeremiah 31:33-34** 33 But this *shall be* the covenant that I will make with the house of Israel; After those days, saith the LORD, I will put my law in their inward parts, and write it in their hearts; and will be their God, and they shall be my people. 34 And they shall teach no more every man his neighbour, and every man his brother, saying, Know the LORD: for they shall all know me, from the least of them unto the greatest of them, saith the LORD: for I will forgive their iniquity, and I will remember their sin no more.

[730] **Ephesians 2:19** Now therefore ye are no more strangers and foreigners, but fellowcitizens with the saints, and of the household of God;

Read Colossians 1.21-2.7

Colossians 1:21-23 21 And you, that were sometime alienated and enemies in *your* mind by wicked works, yet now hath he reconciled 22 In the body of his flesh through death, to present you holy and unblameable and unreproveable in his sight: 23 If ye continue in the faith grounded and settled, and *be* not moved away from the hope of the gospel, which ye have heard, *and* which was preached to every creature which is under heaven; whereof I Paul am made a minister;

Our wickedness alienated us from God. Outside of His salvation, we were God's enemies. The good news is that Jesus has reconciled us to God by what He did for us on the cross. Glory to God! The word "reconcile" has been defined as "to make friendly again, to restore to fellowship, or to bring back to harmony." We are told elsewhere that we now have "peace with God,"[731] something we never had before. His plan is to, one day, present us holy, unblameable, and unreproveable before the Father.[732] We will be like Him someday, seeing Him as He truly is![733]

Until then, we *continue* in the faith, rooted and grounded, knowing that the One who reconciled and saved us, will also keep us by His mighty power! Praise the One that has saved you, reconciling you to the Father!   Praise the One that now keeps you by His power! Praise Him now and forever!

Jude 1:24-25 24 Now unto him that is able to keep you from falling, and to present *you* faultless before the presence of his glory with exceeding joy, 25 To the only wise God our Saviour, *be* glory and majesty, dominion and power, both now and ever. Amen.

---

[731] **Romans 5:1 Therefore** being justified by faith, we have peace with God through our Lord Jesus Christ:

[732] **2 Corinthians 11:2 For** I am jealous over you with godly jealousy: for I have espoused you to one husband, that I may present *you as* a chaste virgin to Christ.
Ephesians 5:27 That he might present it to himself a glorious church, not having spot, or wrinkle, or any such thing; but that it should be holy and without blemish.
Colossians 1:28 Whom we preach, warning every man, and teaching every man in all wisdom; that we may present every man perfect in Christ Jesus:
Jude 1:24 Now unto him that is able to keep you from falling, and to present *you* faultless before the presence of his glory with exceeding joy,

[733] **1 John 3:1-3 1** Behold, what manner of love the Father hath bestowed upon us, that we should be called the sons of God: therefore the world knoweth us not, because it knew him not. 2 Beloved, now are we the sons of God, and it doth not yet appear what we shall be: but we know that, when he shall appear, we shall be like him; for we shall see him as he is. 3 And every man that hath this hope in him purifieth himself, even as he is pure.

Read Colossians 2:8-23

Colossians 2:16-17 16 Let no man therefore judge you in meat, or in drink, or in respect of an holyday, or of the new moon, or of the sabbath *days*: 17 Which are a shadow of things to come; but the body *is* of Christ.

As more and more Gentiles became followers of the Lord, there were issues with their brothers and sisters who came from a Jewish background. There were questions about the Gentile Christians' relationship to Old Testament Law. Many questions were being asked. Is it necessary for a Gentile man who receives Christ to be circumcised as a Jew also? Is it necessary for a Gentile family to adopt a Kosher diet when they become Christians? Are Gentile Christians required to keep the feasts, new moons[734], holy days, and sabbaths[735] of Judaism? Even though the issue should have been settled forever at the Jerusalem Council in Acts 15, there were those, sometimes called the Judaizers, who insisted that Gentile Christians *must* adhere to all of these things. Some of the Judaizers were apparently passing judgment on the Christians in Colossae, because of this. As wonderful as these things are, they are but shadows of what we have in Christ. Christ is the fulfillment, the reality behind the shadow. We see the same truth in Hebrews 10:1, "For the law having a **shadow** of good things to come, *and* **not the very image of the things**, can **never** with those sacrifices which they offered year by year continually make the comers thereunto perfect." To leave Christ and go back under the shadow is to fall from grace[736]. How wonderful to serve the One who is the reality behind it all!

He is my everything! He is my all!
He is my everything, both great and small!
He gave His life for me! He makes everything new! He is my everything!
None other will do![737]

---

[734] The Jewish Feasts are timed around the appearance of the New Moon, which indicates the beginning of a new month.

[735] Not only the weekly sabbath on Saturday, but sabbatical years, and other special sabbaths.

[736] **Galatians 5:1-4** 1 Stand fast therefore in the liberty wherewith Christ hath made us free, and be not entangled again with the yoke of bondage. 2 Behold, I Paul say unto you, that if ye be circumcised, Christ shall profit you nothing. 3 For I testify again to every man that is circumcised, that he is a debtor to do the whole law. 4 Christ is become of no effect unto you, whosoever of you are justified by the law; ye are fallen from grace.

[737] "He is My Everything," William Harrison Tyner

Read Colossians 3:1-17

Colossians 3:1-4 1 If ye then be risen with Christ, seek those things which are above, where Christ sitteth on the right hand of God. 2 Set your affection on things above, not on things on the earth. 3 For ye are dead, and your life is hid with Christ in God. 4 When Christ, *who is* our life, shall appear, then shall ye also appear with him in glory.

We identify with Christ in His death and resurrection. Baptism, as we have already seen, is a graphic representation of that truth[738]. We live as though that old person we once were is dead, and now we are living as one who has been raised to new life with Christ. We live a new kind of life, a life of ministry empowered by the Holy Spirit, a life that seeks to honor Jesus, a life that anticipates our ultimate union with Him in heaven, the day we will appear with Him in glory!

Because of this, we are told that certain sins must be dealt with very severely. They must be mortified, or put to death.[739] Sin must be put off, as one would take off a soiled garment.[740] Because we are a "new man" a new creation in Christ, we cannot live as we once did.[741] We are new creations[742]. I love the very biblical words of a chorus I once heard. They celebrate this truth very well.

> I'm a new creation, I'm a brand-new man,
> Old things have passed away,
> I've been born again,
> More than a conqueror, that's who I am,
> I'm a new creation, I'm a brand-new man[743].

---

[738] **Colossians 2:12 Buried** with him in baptism, wherein also ye are risen with *him* through the faith of the operation of God, who hath raised him from the dead.

[739] **Colossians 3:5-7** 5 Mortify therefore your members which are upon the earth; fornication, uncleanness, inordinate affection, evil concupiscence, and covetousness, which is idolatry: 6 For which things' sake the wrath of God cometh on the children of disobedience: 7 In the which ye also walked some time, when ye lived in them.

[740] **Colossians 3:8-9** 8 But now ye also put off all these; anger, wrath, malice, blasphemy, filthy communication out of your mouth. 9 Lie not one to another, seeing that ye have put off the old man with his deeds;

[741] **Colossians 3:10 And** have put on the new *man*, which is renewed in knowledge after the image of him that created him:

[742] **2 Corinthians 5:17 Therefore** if any man *be* in Christ, *he is* a new creature: old things are passed away; behold, all things are become new.

[743] "I'm a New Creation," David Ingles

Read Colossians 3.17-4.18

Colossians 3:17 And whatsoever ye do in word or deed, *do* all in the name of the Lord Jesus, giving thanks to God and the Father by him.

The new life we now live in Christ changes every human relationship for the better. He speaks of several of those relationships here: husbands and wives; parents and children; and, masters and slaves. A godly wife will submit to her husband's leadership. This is, of course, made easier, when the godly husband loves his wife and is kind to her as God commands.[744] Godly children will obey their parents, but those parents must not provoke them or discourage them.[745] Discipline that is given should, ultimately, encourage, rather than discourage.   Servants (employees) are to do their jobs as if they are working for the Lord (because they are!),[746] while Christian masters (employers) are to be just and fair with their workers, knowing that they will have to answer to God for what they do.[747] It is easy to see that living for Jesus will alter every part of how we live our lives.

Colossians 3:23 And whatsoever ye do, do *it* heartily, as to the Lord, and not unto men;

---

[744] **Colossians 3:18-19** 18 Wives, submit yourselves unto your own husbands, as it is fit in the Lord. 19 Husbands, love *your* wives, and be not bitter against them.

[745] **Colossians 3:20-21** 20 Children, obey *your* parents in all things: for this is well pleasing unto the Lord. 21 Fathers, provoke not your children *to anger*, lest they be discouraged.

[746] **Colossians 3:22-25** 22 Servants, obey in all things *your* masters according to the flesh; not with eyeservice, as menpleasers; but in singleness of heart, fearing God: 23 And whatsoever ye do, do *it* heartily, as to the Lord, and not unto men; 24 Knowing that of the Lord ye shall receive the reward of the inheritance: for ye serve the Lord Christ. 25 But he that doeth wrong shall receive for the wrong which he hath done: and there is no respect of persons.

[747] **Colossians 4:1 Masters**, give unto *your* servants that which is just and equal; knowing that ye also have a Master in heaven.

Read Thessalonians 1:1-2:11

1 Thessalonians 1:6 And ye became followers of us, and of the Lord, having received the word in much affliction, with joy of the Holy Ghost:

We are not promised an easy road in this life. In fact, it is promised that we will make it to heaven through *much tribulation*.[748]   True to Jesus' promise, the Thessalonians faced great afflictions when they came to faith in Jesus Christ. Despite their troubles, they walked in holy joy, and we can too, through the power of the Holy Spirit. Joy is one of the fruit of the Spirit,[749] and, unlike ordinary happiness, is not dependent upon outward circumstances.

The Lord calls us to rejoice when we are persecuted, [750] when we fall into various kinds of temptations,[751] and even when we face fiery trials.[752]   This is impossible without the help of the Holy Spirit. May we be so filled with the Spirit, that God's holy joy is evident in every part of our lives.   Let's make David's prayer in Psalm 51 *our* prayer today!

Psalm 51:11-12 Cast me not away from thy presence; and take not thy holy spirit from me. Restore unto me the joy of thy salvation; and uphold me *with thy* free spirit.

---

[748] Acts 14:22
[749] Galatians 5:22
[750] Matthew 5:11-12
[751] James 1:2
[752] 1 Peter 4:12-13

Read 1 Thessalonians 2:12-3:13

1 Thessalonians 2:13 For this cause also thank we God without ceasing, because, when ye received the word of God which ye heard of us, ye received *it* not *as* the word of men, but as it is in truth, the word of God, which effectually worketh also in you that believe.

Paul rejoiced every day, as any good pastor should, because of how the Thessalonians, received the Word of God.   First, they received it as God speaking to *them*.   Someone once remarked, "I've never heard God speak to me."   That could only be true, had they never opened their Bibles. He will speak to us through His Word daily, if we will give Him that opportunity.   Second, they allowed the Word to "effectually work" in their lives. The Greek word used here (energeo) is most often used for the power of God's Spirit.   The Word is the tool the Holy Spirit uses to work mightily in our lives!   Third, we must believe the Word. The Spirit can only use the Word in our lives, if we believe it.   I pray today that just as in the words of this little chorus, "The Word is Working Mightily in You!"

> The Word is working mightily in me!
> The Word is working mightily in me!
> No matter what the circumstances, what I feel or see,
> The Word is working mightily in me![753]

---

[753] The Word is Working Mightily in Me," David Ingles

Read 1 Thessalonians 4:1-18

1 Thessalonians 4:13 But I would not have you to be ignorant, brethren, concerning them which are asleep, that ye sorrow not, even as others which have no hope.

Sleep is one of the metaphors the Bible uses to describe the death of a child of God.   Upon the death of a Christian, their body 'sleeps' in the grave, awaiting the day of resurrection, while their spirit goes immediately into the presence of the Lord.[754]   That is why, even though we sorrow when a believing loved one dies, our sorrow is tempered by the knowledge that they are with Him!

This Scripture speaks of the wonderful hope we have in Christ.   At the resurrection (rapture), the bodies of those who died in Christ will be raised and glorified, joining their spirits which are now present with the Lord.   Those of us who are living at that time will be changed and caught up with them to meet the Lord in the air.   All of this will only take a fraction of a second, what the Bible calls the twinkling of an eye.[755] This is our Blessed Hope,[756]   and these words are given that we might comfort one another.

1 Thessalonians 4:18   Wherefore comfort one another with these words.

---

[754] Luke 23:43, 2 Corinthians 5:8
[755] 1 Corinthians 15:51-52
[756] Titus 2:13

Read 1 Thessalonians 5:1-28

1 Thessalonians 5:4 But ye, brethren, are not in darkness, that that day should overtake you as a thief.

We often hear that the Lord will return like a thief in the night.[757] A thief does not announce himself. He comes unexpectedly. Jesus' coming will be unexpected in that no one knows the day, nor the hour of His return.[758] Over the centuries, many have, unscripturally, set dates for His return. Obviously, all of those dates have been proven untrue. For believers, though, there is something else to consider. Though we do not know the day nor the hour of His return, we will not be taken by surprise, because we are always ready.

We do not find the Lord telling us to "get ready" in the New Testament Scriptures, but to "be ready."   Jesus says, "Be ye also ready for in such an hour as you think not the Son of Man cometh."[759] He is returning for those who are looking for Him, those who are ready.

Hebrews 9:28 So Christ was once offered to bear the sins of many; and **unto them that look for him** shall he appear the second time without sin unto salvation.

---

[757] Matthew 24:43, Luke 12:39, 1 Thessalonians 5:2.
[758] Matthew 24:36, Matthew 25:13, Mark 13:32, Luke 12:46
[759] Matthew 24:44

Read 2 Thessalonians 1:1-2:8

2 Thessalonians 2:7 For the mystery of iniquity doth already work: only he who now letteth *will let*, until he be taken out of the way.

A very troubling false teaching had risen in the church at Thessalonica. Some were teaching that the Day of the Lord, the time of the Great Tribulation, had already come. This might have been easy to believe, because of the great persecution they were already facing. There were apparently even supposed gifts of the Spirit and a forged letter claiming to be from Paul himself that made these claims.[760] Paul, inspired by the Holy Spirit, needed to set the record straight.

That day will not arrive until the Antichrist, the Man of Sin, is revealed. He will set himself up to be worshipped in the temple of God in Jerusalem. There has been no temple in Jerusalem since AD 70, but we know that one must be built before that day. How will that happen, since both Jews and Muslims lay claim to that hotly contested piece of real estate—the Temple Mount? Perhaps, making it happen will be one of the things that help the Antichrist rise to power

The spirit behind all of this is already at work in the world, the mystery of iniquity. The KJV says that there is something that now "lets." That sounds strange to us, but the word is used in a way that it is not normally used in the 21st century. In context, it means to hinder. Something is hindering the spirit of antichrist. Something is keeping that great evil from being fully manifest in our world. I believe that is the Spirit-filled church—God's salt and light in this world. When the true church is raptured, there will be nothing to prevent the rise of Antichrist. We are not looking for the Antichrist, we are looking for the coming of Jesus Christ!

Titus 2:13 Looking for that blessed hope, and the glorious appearing of the great God and our Saviour Jesus Christ;

---

[760] 2 Thessalonians 2:2

Read 2 Thessalonians 2:9-3:18

2 Thessalonians 2:9-12   9 Even *him*, whose coming is after the working of Satan with all power and signs and lying wonders, 10 And with all deceivableness of unrighteousness in them that perish; because they received not the love of the truth, that they might be saved. 11 And for this cause God shall send them strong delusion, that they should believe a lie: 12 That they all might be damned who believed not the truth, but had pleasure in unrighteousness.

This is a sobering word for those who presume to live as they please now and then get right with God later, if they miss the Rapture.   The Scriptures reveal that there will certainly be a great number saved during the Great Tribulation, but it would seem that those who have heard and rejected the truth of the Gospel now are very unlikely to receive it then.   This Scripture speaks of those who chose not to receive the knowledge of the truth.   They heard the true Gospel of Jesus Christ, but did not do anything about it. Should they continue in that rejection, they can become so deluded and hardened that, ultimately, when he is revealed, they will believe the lie of the Antichrist, following him, and receiving his mark[761], rather than receiving and following the Lord Jesus Christ.

Praise the Lord, we are not yet living in that terrible day. We are still living in the day of salvation, the time when the Gospel is being preached, the Spirit is calling us to salvation, and we can call on the Name of the Lord and be saved.   This is a glorious day, the day of salvation!

2 Corinthians 6:2b, "Behold, NOW *is* the accepted time; behold, NOW *is* the day of salvation."

---

[761] Revelation 13:16-18

Read 1 Timothy 1

1 Timothy 1:13   Who was before a blasphemer, and a persecutor, and injurious: but I obtained mercy, because I did *it* ignorantly in unbelief.

Paul wrote this to Timothy, a young pastor serving the church in Ephesus.   He gives Timothy a little bit of his personal testimony, a testimony that still brings great encouragement to those open to being used by God.   Though he is thankful for the privilege of being in ministry, it is not something he chose for himself.   He is doing what he is doing because of the call of God.

Like most of us, he felt very unworthy of that call.   After all, though perhaps ignorantly and with good intentions, he had done some very evil things.   He had been a blasphemer, a persecutor of the church.   In fact, he was responsible for the death of Stephen, the first Christian martyr.[762]   By his own admission, he was the "chiefest of sinners," but God, in His mercy saved Him and called Him to serve.[763] His grace and mercy are still so amazing[764]!

He wanted his life, and testimony, to be a pattern, an example to others, an example of just what God can do in spite of us, an example of just what can happen through the mercy and grace of God.   That example still reminds us that in spite of the failures of yesterday, God can use us today!

1 Timothy 1:16   Howbeit for this cause I obtained mercy, that in me first Jesus Christ might shew forth all longsuffering, for a pattern to them which should hereafter believe on him to life everlasting.

---

[762] **Acts 7:58**   And cast *him* out of the city, and stoned *him*: and the witnesses laid down their clothes at a young man's feet, whose name was Saul.
Acts 8:1   And Saul was consenting unto his death. And at that time there was a great persecution against the church which was at Jerusalem; and they were all scattered abroad throughout the regions of Judaea and Samaria, except the apostles.
[763] **Galatians 1:15**   But when it pleased God, who separated me from my mother's womb, and called *me* by his grace,
[764] **1 Timothy 1:14**   And the grace of our Lord was exceeding abundant with faith and love which is in Christ Jesus.

Read 1 Timothy 2

1 Timothy 2:1-2 1 I exhort therefore, that, first of all, supplications, prayers, intercessions, *and* giving of thanks, be made for all men; 2 For kings, and *for* all that are in authority; that we may lead a quiet and peaceable life in all godliness and honesty.

"First of all" lets us know that this is of utmost importance. God's people should always be known as people of prayer, and there are various kinds of prayer enumerated here. Supplication means "making a request."   The New Testament gives us many promises regarding asking and receiving!   Prayers is from a word meaning to pray earnestly. We "mean business" when we pray!   Intercession has to do with praying for others. Do others know they can call on you to pray? And, of course, giving of thanks should always be included in our prayers.

Praying Christians should be praying for everyone, because everyone needs prayer. That includes praying for government leaders.   How much better would things be, if we did more praying and less complaining?   When this was written, a Roman Caesar was king, a very ungodly man, yet prayer was to be offered for him, and for all others who were in authority.   The ultimate goal of this kind of praying is that they be saved and come to the knowledge of the truth.   How long since you have prayed for the president, for congress, for supreme court justices, and governors?   God would have every one of them to be saved and to walk in His truth.

1 Timothy 2:4 Who will have all men to be saved, and to come unto the knowledge of the truth.

Read 1 Timothy 3

1 Timothy 3:1 This is a true saying, If a man desire the office of a bishop, he desireth a good work.

In 1 Timothy 3 Paul gives Timothy the spiritual qualifications for those who would serve as bishops or deacons in a local church. The term bishop, though often associated with a "high ranking" church official today is, in the New Testament, simply the pastor or overseer of a local church. It is clear from the New Testament that the words Bishop, Elder, Overseer, and Pastor are used interchangeably to speak of different aspects of the very same ministry.

He also gives the qualifications for another church office, that of the deacon. The Greek word translated "deacon" speaks of one who serves. The first deacons were apparently those chosen in Acts 6 to oversee the local church feeding program.[765] This freed up more time for the apostles to pray and preach the Word.

Some of the first deacons also had powerful preaching ministries. Steven and Philip, for example, were both deacons *and* powerful preachers of the Word. What are some Bible qualifications for those serving as deacons in a local church setting?

Qualifications for Deacons
1. Grave-The deacon must show proper respect toward God and man.

2. Not Double-Tongued-He speaks the truth at all times. He is a man of his word. Today we use the expression that someone "speaks out of both sides of their mouth." That must never be said of a deacon.

3. Not Given to Much Wine-Like the Bishop, he must not abuse alcohol (or drugs by implication in our society). Christians in general should abstain from alcohol[766].

4. Not Greedy of Filthy Lucre-Like the bishop, he must not be motivated by the love of money.

5. Holding the Mystery of the Faith in a Pure Conscience-By his life and teaching, the truth of the Gospel and sound doctrine are proclaimed.

---

[765] Acts 6:1-6
[766] Proverbs 20:1, Proverbs 23:29-35, Ephesians 5:18

6. Proved-He is someone who has proven himself by his godly behavior. This would also indicate that, like the bishop, he must not be a novice, one who is a new convert.

7. Husbands of One Wife-Like a bishop, he must be faithful to his marriage vows. He is a "one-woman man."

8. Ruling their Children and House Well-For the same reasons as the bishop, deacons must have godly order in their own homes.

What about their Wives?

Verse 13 speaks of their wives. The original Greek gives room for two interpretations of this. It could refer to the wives of the deacons. We all know how important the mate of one in ministry can be. It can also speak of one who is a deaconess. There is at least one such person spoken of in Scripture. Phebe was a servant, literally deacon, of a local church.[767] Whichever interpretation is correct, what is added about the qualifications of these women?

1. Grave-Like their husbands, they show prosper respect toward God and others.

2. Not a Slanderer-The word is "diabolos," sometimes translated "devil." They are not devilish in the sense of slandering others. What a very strong word!

3. Sober- They are watchful and spiritually alert, careful about what they do and say.

4. Faithful in All Things-Faithfulness is required of all who serve the Lord[768]!

These qualifications should be a matter of prayerful concern for all of us, even if we are not bishops or deacons. They are marks of godly character in general, and we should all strive, through the power of the Holy Spirit, to have them in evidence in our lives. May God help us!

---

[767] **Romans 16:1**   I commend unto you Phebe our sister, which is a servant [diaconos – deacon] of the church which is at Cenchrea:

[768] **1 Corinthians 4:1-2** 1 Let a man so account of us, as of the ministers of Christ, and stewards of the mysteries of God. 2 Moreover it is required in stewards, that a man be found faithful.

Read 1 Timothy 4

1 Timothy 4:1 Now the Spirit speaketh expressly, that in the latter times some shall depart from the faith, giving heed to seducing spirits, and doctrines of devils;

How important is sound teaching and sound doctrine? It is vitally important! We are warned that in the last days some will turn from the truth, and will instead follow demonic doctrines, doctrines coming from Satan and his demons, *not* from the Word of God. False doctrine can be alluring, even seductive, note that those deceptive demons are called "seducing spirits!" False teaching can sound good to fleshly ears, and may even "seem right" to those same ears, but we are reminded in Proverbs, "There is a way which seems right unto a man, but the end thereof are the ways of death."[769]

The false teaching Timothy faced in Ephesus had to do with some who were adding rules and regulations beyond those of the New Testament. For example, they prescribed a certain diet for "Spiritual" reasons. They also did not allow marriage, perhaps teaching that the single state was somehow more holy. Although the "face" of false doctrine may vary somewhat in every generation, then as now, *anything* that adds to or takes away from the simple faith of the New Testament should be viewed as something hellish and dangerous!

Even the pastor of the church, Timothy, was not immune to deception. He is warned to continue in sound doctrine himself. In doing so, he can save himself and also those to whom he ministers. It is vitally important in these last days that we be students of the Word of God, and those who are seeking to have spiritual discernment.

1 Timothy 4:16 Take heed unto thyself, and unto the doctrine; continue in them: for in doing this thou shalt both save thyself, and them that hear thee.

---

[769] Proverbs 14:12

Read 1 Timothy 5

1 Timothy 5:3   Honour widows that are widows indeed.

The plight of widows in Biblical days was far more severe than today. There were no safety nets of any kind to help them.   There was no social security, no welfare system of any kind.   It was, rightly, the responsibility of the church to make sure that godly widows were not doing without, but there were some stipulations before the church acted.

First, if the widow has family, it is their responsibility *first* to look after their elderly relatives. [770]   Though it is not found in the Scriptures, the proverb, "Charity begins at home," is certainly a Biblical principle.   Anyone who does not see that their loved ones are taken care of is said to have denied the faith and is worse than an infidel.[771]

Second, she must be of good moral character, a woman of godliness, faith, and prayer.[772]

Third, she must be above the age of sixty.   It was believed that the younger widows would probably marry again.[773]   Some of those younger widows were apparently not living upright lives in the Ephesian church, and it was thought best that most of them should marry and have families rather than depend on the church for support.[774]

Though the fate of widows and the elderly is much different today, God's command still holds true.

Exodus 20:12   Honour thy father and thy mother: that thy days may be long upon the land which the LORD thy God giveth thee.

---

[770] **1 Timothy 5:4**   But if any widow have children or nephews [the word can also mean grandchildren], let them learn first to shew piety at home, and to requite their parents: for that is good and acceptable before God.
1 Timothy 5:16   If any man or woman that believeth have widows, let them relieve them, and let not the church be charged; that it may relieve them that are widows indeed.
[771] **1 Timothy 5:8**   But if any provide not for his own, and specially for those of his own house, he hath denied the faith, and is worse than an infidel.
[772] **1 Timothy 5:5-7** 5 Now she that is a widow indeed, and desolate, trusteth in God, and continueth in supplications and prayers night and day. 6 But she that liveth in pleasure is dead while she liveth. 7 And these things give in charge, that they may be blameless. **1 Timothy 5:10**   Well reported of for good works; if she have brought up children, if she have lodged strangers, if she have washed the saints' feet, if she have relieved the afflicted, if she have diligently followed every good work.
[773] **1 Timothy 5:9**   Let not a widow be taken into the number under threescore years old, having been the wife of one man,
[774] **1 Timothy 5:14**   I will therefore that the younger women marry, bear children, guide the house, give none occasion to the adversary to speak reproachfully.

Read 1 Timothy 6

1 Timothy 6:11-12   11 But thou, O man of God, **FLEE** these things; and **FOLLOW** after righteousness, godliness, faith, love, patience, meekness. 12 **FIGHT** the good fight of faith, lay hold on eternal life, whereunto thou art also called, and hast professed a good profession before many witnesses.

The words of admonition given to young Pastor Timothy here are important words for every one of us today.   First, there are certain sins so dangerous that we are told to **FLEE** from them. One of them is spoken of here--the love of money.   Elsewhere in the New Testament we are also told to flee from fornication and idolatry[775].   What has destroyed more lives and testimonies than the love of money, sexual immorality, and idolatry?   Second, we must **FOLLOW** the Lord in such a way that the fruit of the Spirit, His character, will begin to be seen in our lives.[776]   Third, we must never forget that we are called to be His soldiers, and that fierce battles are raging. We must **FIGHT** the good fight of faith, standing true for the Lord and the Word of God.[777]

---

[775] **1 Corinthians 6:18**   Flee fornication. Every sin that a man doeth is without the body; but he that committeth fornication sinneth against his own body.
1 Corinthians 10:14   Wherefore, my dearly beloved, flee from idolatry.
1 Timothy 6:11   But thou, O man of God, flee these things; and follow after righteousness, godliness, faith, love, patience, meekness.
2 Timothy 2:22   Flee also youthful lusts: but follow righteousness, faith, charity, peace, with them that call on the Lord out of a pure heart.
[776] **Mark 6:1**   And he went out from thence, and came into his own country; and his disciples follow him.
Mark 8:34   And when he had called the people *unto him* with his disciples also, he said unto them, Whosoever will come after me, let him deny himself, and take up his cross, and follow me.
John 10:27   My sheep hear my voice, and I know them, and they follow me:
Philippians 3:12   Not as though I had already attained, either were already perfect: but I follow after, if that I may apprehend that for which also I am apprehended of Christ Jesus.
1 Peter 2:21   For even hereunto were ye called: because Christ also suffered for us, leaving us an example, that ye should follow his steps:
[777] **2 Corinthians 10:4**   (For the weapons of our warfare *are* not carnal, but mighty through God to the pulling down of strong holds;)
1 Timothy 1:18   This charge I commit unto thee, son Timothy, according to the prophecies which went before on thee, that thou by them mightest war a good warfare;
2 Timothy 2:3-4   3 Thou therefore endure hardness, as a good soldier of Jesus Christ. 4 No man that warreth entangleth himself with the affairs of *this* life; that he may please him who hath chosen him to be a soldier.
2 Timothy 4:7   I have fought a good fight, I have finished *my* course, I have kept the faith:

Today, let us pray that He will help us to Flee from all that which is evil, to follow more closely than ever before, and fight the good fight of faith. I am reminded today of the words of an old Gospel song.

If you're in the battle for the Lord and right,
Keep on the firing line;
If you win, my brother, surely you must fight,
Keep on the firing line;
There are many dangers that we all must face,
If we die still fighting it is no disgrace;
Cowards in the service will not find a place,
So keep on the firing line.
Oh, you must fight, be brave against all evil,
Never run, nor even lag behind;
If you would win for God and the right,
Just keep on the firing line[778].

---

[778] "Keep on the Firing Line," Bessie Hatcher

Read 2 Timothy 1

2 Timothy 1:6-7 6 Wherefore I put thee in remembrance that thou stir up the gift of God, which is in thee by the putting on of my hands. 7 For God hath not given us the spirit of fear; but of power, and of love, and of a sound mind.

Timothy was pastor of the church at Ephesus, one of the largest churches of that day. It appears that some, because of his youth, did not respect his leadership as they should have[779]. We are not told how old he was, but he was apparently younger than some of the church members. It also appears that he was, by nature, a somewhat shy or timid person. Some have counted over twenty times in 1st and 2nd Timothy where Paul encourages him to be bold and to stand strong. This was apparently a great need in this young brother's life, as it can be in ours also.

In light of this, Timothy needed to remember God's touch on His life. He had received a gift through the laying on of Paul's hands. This could have been when he was baptized in the Holy Spirit, empowering him for a life of witness[780]. It could have been when he was ordained, set apart by God and the church, through the laying on of hands, for a particular ministry[781]. Of course, that also involves the touch of the Holy Spirit. Either way, the gift must be encouraged; it is compared to a flame which must be stirred up, literally "fanned into flame." Though it was part of his temperament, Timothy's natural fearfulness did not come from God. Along with Timothy, we are to remember three things that God *has* given to us through the power of the Holy Spirit.

First, He has given us power, just as we are promised in Acts 1:8, the power to be His witnesses in life and in death. Second, He has given us holy love, just as promised in Romans 5:5, a Spirit-empowered love by which we can fulfill all that God calls us to. Third, He has given us a sound mind, which could be translated as a "disciplined mind." One commentary puts it this way, "The ancient Greek word here had the idea of a calm, self-controlled mind, in contrast to the panic and confusion that rushes in when in a fearful situation[782]." By the power of the Spirit, we can be "cool, calm, and collected" no matter what comes our way! Let's praise Him today because He has given *us* POWER, LOVE, and a SOUND MIND!

> We've got the power in the Name of Jesus,
> We've got the power in the Name of the Lord,
> Though Satan rages, we will not be defeated,
> We've got the power in the Name of the Lord.

---

[779] **1 Timothy 4:12** Let no man despise thy youth; but be thou an example of the believers, in word, in conversation, in charity, in spirit, in faith, in purity.

[780] **Acts 8:17** Then laid they *their* hands on them, and they received the Holy Ghost.
Acts 19:6 And when Paul had laid *his* hands upon them, the Holy Ghost came on them; and they spake with tongues, and prophesied.

[781] **Acts 13:2-3** 2 As they ministered to the Lord, and fasted, the Holy Ghost said, Separate me Barnabas and Saul for the work whereunto I have called them. 3 And when they had fasted and prayed, and laid *their* hands on them, they sent *them* away.

[782] <u>Enduring Word Commentary</u>, Guzik

Read 2 Timothy 2

2 Timothy 2:21   If a man therefore purge himself from these, he shall be a vessel unto honour, sanctified, and meet for the master's use, *and* prepared unto every good work.

The life of a Christian is to be a sanctified life.   We have been separated, set apart, for His holy purpose.   God's church is compared here to a great house, a house having various kinds of vessels (pots, glasses, pitchers, bowls, etc.).[783]   Some of the vessels in a large house might be used for some honorable purpose, such as a gold vase or a beautiful plate.   Others are dishonorable, think of something like a garbage can or an ashtray. We must purge ourselves from spiritually dishonorable things, realizing that God has something far better for our lives.   We are His vessels of honor!   There is something far better, far more honorable, than the corruption of sin.

First, this means that we have been sanctified, set apart for His use.   In the Old Testament the vessels used in the Tabernacle and Temple were said to be sanctified, that is they were anointed with oil, symbolizing that they had been set apart for a particular holy purpose. Because of that anointing, they were not to be used like ordinary vessels.   The Holy Spirit in our lives, like that anointing oil, sets *us* apart for His purpose.   Second, we are meet for the master's use, that means that we can be useful to Him and His kingdom. We are of no use to Him while living in sin and without the sanctification of the Spirit. A sanctified life is useful to God.   Third, we are prepared unto every good work.   A sanctified life is spiritually prepared to do His bidding.

In light of this, here is the prayer I am praying for all of us today.

1 Thessalonians 5:23-24 23 And the very God of peace sanctify you wholly; and *I pray God* your whole spirit and soul and body be preserved blameless unto the coming of our Lord Jesus Christ. 24 Faithful *is* he that calleth you, who also will do *it*.

---

[783] **2 Timothy 2:20**   But in a great house there are not only vessels of gold and of silver, but also of wood and of earth; and some to honour, and some to dishonour.

Read 2 Timothy 3

2 Timothy 3:15-17 15 And that from a child thou hast known the holy scriptures, which are able to make thee wise unto salvation through faith which is in Christ Jesus. 16 All scripture *is* given by inspiration of God, and *is* profitable for doctrine, for reproof, for correction, for instruction in righteousness: 17 That the man of God may be perfect, thoroughly furnished unto all good works.

The Word of God had been a part of Pastor Timothy's life from an early age. He had the benefit of a godly mother and grandmother who must have instilled that in his young life[784].   He is reminded that the Scriptures are inspired, which literally means "God breathed."   Because the Bible, the Word of God, is inspired, it is also infallible and inerrant.   That makes it very spiritually profitable for every believer, and we are told of four specific ways that the Word of God is profitable to us.

First, it is profitable for doctrine, that is teaching. Sound doctrine tells us what we should believe and how we should walk. The Word of God is the standard by which we know those things. Second, the Word of God is profitable for reproof. When we stray from that path, the Word of God will reprove us. It will show us where we have strayed.   Third, the Word of God is profitable for correction. Reproof tells us where we have strayed, but correction helps us get back on the right path.   Fourth, the Word of God is profitable for instruction in righteousness. It gives us instruction as to how to *remain* on the right path.

The ultimate goal of these works of the Word of God is Christian maturity (that the man of God may be perfect), thoroughly furnished (completely prepared) unto all good works.

Psalm 19:7-11   7 The law of the LORD *is* perfect, converting the soul: the testimony of the LORD *is* sure, making wise the simple. 8 The statutes of the LORD *are* right, rejoicing the heart: the commandment of the LORD *is* pure, enlightening the eyes. 9 The fear of the LORD *is* clean, enduring forever: the judgments of the LORD *are* true *and* righteous altogether. 10 More to be desired *are they* than gold, yea, than much fine gold: sweeter also than honey and the honeycomb. 11 Moreover by them is thy servant warned: *and* in keeping of them *there is* great reward.

---

[784] **2 Timothy 1:5**   When I call to remembrance the unfeigned faith that is in thee, which dwelt first in thy grandmother Lois, and thy mother Eunice; and I am persuaded that in thee also.

Read 2 Timothy 4

2 Timothy 4:6-8 6 For I am now ready to be offered, and the time of my departure is at hand. 7 I have fought a good fight, I have finished *my* course, I have kept the faith: 8 Henceforth there is laid up for me a crown of righteousness, which the Lord, the righteous judge, shall give me at that day: and not to me only, but unto all them also that love his appearing.

  This is the Apostle Paul's final written testimony. He says that he is ready to be offered. The word used here means to be poured out like a drink offering. The final drops of his earthly life will be given to the Lord as an offering of praise. He will be departing from this world and going on to the next, and he is able to say three things about his life as he faces the end of its earthly segment. I pray that we will be able to say the same three things when we come to the time of *our* departure!

  First, he said, "I have fought a good fight." He has faced many battles over the years, and with the Lord's help, he has been a good soldier of Jesus Christ, just as he instructed young Timothy[785]. Second, he said, "I have finished my course." Not only is the Christian life compared to a battle, it is compared to a race. The writer of Hebrews tells us that we must run that race with patience (perseverance). We do not give up, but we keep going, with our eyes on Him[786]. Third, he said, "I have kept the faith." That is, I have remained true to the Word of God. I have continued in sound teaching. This too is something he has encouraged Timothy, and others, to do.[787] He knows that a reward, the crown of righteousness, is awaiting on the other side! When I think of the words of this old Gospel song, they remind me of Paul's words of testimony!

Am I a soldier of the cross,
A follower of the Lamb,
And shall I fear to own His cause,
Or blush to speak His name?

---

[785] **2 Timothy 2:3** Thou therefore endure hardness, as a good soldier of Jesus Christ.

[786] **Hebrews 12:1-2** 1 Wherefore seeing we also are compassed about with so great a cloud of witnesses, let us lay aside every weight, and the sin which doth so easily beset *us*, and let us run with patience the race that is set before us, 2 Looking unto Jesus the author and finisher of *our* faith; who for the joy that was set before him endured the cross, despising the shame, and is set down at the right hand of the throne of God.

[787] **2 Timothy 4:1-5** 1 I charge *thee* therefore before God, and the Lord Jesus Christ, who shall judge the quick and the dead at his appearing and his kingdom; 2 Preach the word; be instant in season, out of season; reprove, rebuke, exhort with all longsuffering and doctrine. 3 For the time will come when they will not endure sound doctrine; but after their own lusts shall they heap to themselves teachers, having itching ears; 4 And they shall turn away *their* ears from the truth, and shall be turned unto fables. 5 But watch thou in all things, endure afflictions, do the work of an evangelist, make full proof of thy ministry.

And when the battle's over
We shall wear a crown!
Yes, we shall wear a crown!
Yes, we shall wear a crown!
And when the battle's over
We shall wear a crown
In the new Jerusalem

Wear a crown (wear a crown)
Wear a crown (wear a crown)
Wear a bright and shining crown;
And when the battle's over
We shall wear a crown
In the new Jerusalem.

Must I be carried to the skies
On flowery beds of ease,
While others fought to win the prize,
And sailed through bloody seas?
Are there no foes for me to face?
Must I not stem the flood?
Is this vile world a friend to grace,
To help me on to God?[788]

---

[788] "When the Battle's Over," Isaac Watts

Read Titus 1

Titus 1:5 **For** this cause left I thee in Crete, that thou shouldest set in order the things that are wanting, and ordain elders in every city, as I had appointed thee:

Paul writes this letter to Titus a pastor sent to the Island of Crete to minister to the churches there and to equip each of those local churches with godly leaders. The New Testament uses several words to identify the spiritual leadership in a local church. The words are used interchangeably for the same men, but they may indicate different aspects of their ministry. Elder, Bishop, and Pastor clearly speak of the same individuals. Paul shares some things Titus must look for as he ordains these men. Their ministry is very important on Crete, as it is elsewhere, because of the presence of false teachers and false doctrine. As one appointed over a local assembly, I find these qualifications very sobering.

1. Blameless-This is not sinless perfection, but it does assume that though the minister will be accused at times, there should be no grounds for those accusations.
2. The Husband of One Wife-He is a one-woman man, true to His wife, true to His vows, faithful.
3. Faithful Children-If his own children did not serve God, it could indicate that he was not able to lead others to Christ. Of course, we recognize that when children come of age, they may make wrong choices, because they have been given free will.
4. A Blameless Steward of God-He has been entrusted with the Gospel, and with God's people, and He must be a good steward of what truly belongs to God Himself.
5. Not Self-willed-Though he has God-given authority in the local assembly, he must not be one who has the "my way or the highway" type of attitude.
6. Not Soon Angry-There is a time for anger, but he must not be one who "flies off the handle" quickly.

7. <u>Not Given to Wine</u>-Abstinence should be the standard for all of God's people, especially those in leadership.

8. <u>No Striker</u>-This speaks of violence. He must not be violent. He is not quick to pick a fight.

9. <u>Not Given to Filthy Lucre</u>-He must not be motivated by, or captivated by, money and possessions.

10. <u>Love of Hospitality</u>-The word hospitality literally meant "lover of strangers." He shows love and concern to all.

11. <u>Lover of Good Men</u>-He loves God and loves people.

12. <u>Sober</u>-This means sober-minded. He takes the things of God seriously.

13. <u>Just</u>-He is fair and even handed toward others.

14. <u>Holy</u>-He is seeking, as we all should, to be like Jesus.

15. <u>Temperate</u>-He is self-controlled.

16. <u>Holding Fast the Faithful Word</u>-The Word of God should be the standard for what he preaches and teaches.

17. <u>Sound Doctrine</u>-In the midst of false teaching, he must be a strong champion for sound teaching, and sound doctrine.

Reading these sobering qualifications, it would be fitting to take some time to pray for those whom God has called. Pray specifically for the one standing behind the pulpit every week in your church.

Ephesians 6:18-20 18 Praying always with all prayer and supplication in the Spirit, and watching thereunto with all perseverance and supplication for all saints; 19 And **for me**, that utterance may be given unto me, that I may open my mouth boldly, to make known the mystery of the gospel, 20 For which I am an ambassador in bonds: that therein I may speak boldly, as I ought to speak.

Read Titus 2

Titus 2:1 But speak thou the things which become sound doctrine:

Sound, or healthy doctrine, will lead to sound and healthy Christian living.   Paul reminds Titus, and us, how Biblical teaching impacts the relationships and interaction between various groups within the church. The older are to be teachers of the younger.   By their godly example, older brothers and sisters in the church are to model what it is to be a man or woman of God.   Because we do not automatically know what it is to be a good husband, wife, or parent, God's plan is for these things to be taught, by example.

Older women, for example, are to be teachers of good things, teaching the younger women important skills they could not learn anywhere else, teaching them what it means to love their husbands and children, teaching them principles for marriage, raising children, modesty, and even homemaking.   In the same way, older men are to be examples for the younger men in the way *they* live *their* lives, teaching them what it is to be self-controlled, serious, wise, strong in faith, love, and patience.   These are all things that should be learned in a Christian family, but with the fragmentation of so many families today, it is even more important to see these things lived out in the church family.

Titus 2:11-12   11 For the grace of God that bringeth salvation hath appeared to all men, 12 Teaching us that, denying ungodliness and worldly lusts, we should live soberly, righteously, and godly, in this present world;

Read Titus 3

Titus 3:5   Not by works of righteousness which we have done, but according to his mercy he saved us, by the washing of regeneration, and renewing of the Holy Ghost;

 Christianity, unlike the multitude of man-made religions in the world, is not a system of works that lead to salvation. We are saved, not because of what we do, but because of what He has done for us on the cross. It is not our good works that save us, but His!   Through Him, we receive mercy and grace. Mercy means that we do not receive the punishment that we are due, because of our sin. Grace, on the other hand, means that we receive great undeserved blessings. Mercy says that I don't have to go to hell!   Grace says that I can spend my eternity in heaven with Him!

 However, this does NOT mean that good works are unimportant. Later, in this same chapter, we are told that those who believe should also be careful to maintain good works.[789]   Good works, though not the source of our salvation, are certainly the result of it. We are reminded of these very truths in Ephesians 2, where it says that we are saved by grace through faith "<u>unto</u> good works."[790]   Jesus makes it clear, though, that even when those good works are "shining" in our lives, there is only one who should receive the credit and the glory!

Matthew 5:16   Let your light so shine before men, that they may see your good works, and <u>glorify your Father which is in heaven.</u>

---

[789] **Titus 3:8**   *This is* a faithful saying, and these things I will that thou affirm constantly, that they which have believed in God might be careful to maintain good works. These things are good and profitable unto men.

[790] **Ephesians 2:8-10** 8 For by grace are ye saved through faith; and that not of yourselves: *it is* the gift of God: 9 Not of works, lest any man should boast. 10 For we are his workmanship, created in Christ Jesus unto good works, which God hath before ordained that we should walk in them.

Read Philemon

Philemon 1:11 Which in time past was to thee unprofitable, but now profitable to thee and to me:

Now we come to the short, twenty-five verse letter of Paul to Philemon. Paul writes to him as a friend and brother in Christ asking for a favor. One of Philemon's servants, Onesimus, had apparently stolen from him, and then fled. He ran all the way from Colossae, where Philemon lived, to Rome where Paul was in prison, a tremendous distance in those days. By a wonderful miracle of God's providence, he met Paul there in Rome, and Paul led him to the Lord! After his conversion he became a wonderful help and encouragement to Paul, more like a son than anything. Paul uses a play on words to describe the change in Onesimus. His name means profitable, but he certainly hadn't been. Now, he is finally living up to his name, instead of being the unprofitable servant he had once been.

As a saved man, Onesimus must go back to his former master, and make restitution for what he has done. Paul himself is willing to help him make it right. Before he had just been a servant, now he is returning as a brother in Christ. Some question why the New Testament does not make strong statements against the institution of slavery, which was a major part of society in that time. But, it is very clear that Christian principles would ultimately make slavery impossible. How could Onesimus continue as Philemon's slave when they were now brothers in Christ. Someone once said, "The ground is level at the foot of the cross[791]." What happened when Onesimus went back to make things right? We are not told here, but I believe that Philemon must have received him back with open arms as a brother in Christ. Later, a man named Onesimus went on to become the bishop[792] of the church in Ephesus and many believe he was the very same man!

Like Onesimus, we were slaves. In our case, we were slaves to sin. Now that we are saved, we have become servants of the Lord Jesus Christ. May we, like Onesimus, always be profitable servants for our Lord.

Romans 6:17-18 17 But God be thanked, that ye were the servants of sin, but ye have obeyed from the heart that form of doctrine which was delivered you. 18 Being then made free from sin, ye became the servants of righteousness.

---

[791] **Galatians 3:28** There is neither Jew nor Greek, there is neither bond nor free, there is neither male nor female: for ye are all one in Christ Jesus.

[792] The terms bishop, overseer, elder, and pastor are used interchangeably in the New Testament.

Read Hebrews 1:1-14

Hebrews 1:1-2 1 God, who at sundry times and in divers manners spake in time past unto the fathers by the prophets, 2 Hath in these last days spoken unto us by *his* Son, whom he hath appointed heir of all things, by whom also he made the worlds;

The Father spoke to this world many times in days gone by, speaking through His prophets. However, His best communication in these last days[793] has been through Jesus, the Word become flesh.[794] He is the One who spoke the universe into existence[795], and now holds it together by His word[796]. He is the brightness of the Father's glory and the express image of His person[797]. The Greek word indicates an exact likeness, a carbon copy. He was the perfect sacrifice for sin. Unlike the Old Testament sacrifices, which could only cover sins, His sacrifice purged them, taking them away! Verse three expresses one of the most important doctrines of the New Testament, the Finished Work of the Cross. After Jesus purged our sins, He sat down at the Father's right hand. He could sit down, because His work was complete, there would never be a need for another sacrifice. That's why He could shout, "It is Finished!"[798].

Hebrews 1:3 Who being the brightness of *his* glory, and the express image of his person, and upholding all things by the word of his power, when he had by himself purged our sins, sat down on the right hand of the Majesty on high;

---

[793] The Last Days began at Pentecost when God began to pour out His Spirit on all flesh (Acts 2).

[794] **Hebrews 1:1-2** 1 God, who at sundry times and in divers manners spake in time past unto the fathers by the prophets, 2 Hath in these last days spoken unto us by *his* Son, whom he hath appointed heir of all things, by whom also he made the worlds;

[795] **John 1:1-3** 1 In the beginning was the Word, and the Word was with God, and the Word was God. 2 The same was in the beginning with God. 3 All things were made by him; and without him was not anything made that was made.

[796] **Colossians 1:15-17** 15 Who is the image of the invisible God, the firstborn of every creature: 16 For by him were all things created, that are in heaven, and that are in earth, visible and invisible, whether *they be* thrones, or dominions, or principalities, or powers: all things were created by him, and for him: 17 And he is before all things, and by him all things consist [all things are held together].

[797] **John 14:9** Jesus saith unto him, Have I been so long time with you, and yet hast thou not known me, Philip? he that hath seen me hath seen the Father; and how sayest thou *then*, Shew us the Father?

[798] **John 19:30** When Jesus therefore had received the vinegar, he said, It is finished: and he bowed his head, and gave up the ghost.

Read Hebrews 2

Hebrews 2:18   For in that he himself hath suffered being tempted, he is able to succor them that are tempted.

Jesus was tempted in every way that we are, yet without sin.[799] He overcame the same kinds of temptations Adam and Eve faced in the Garden of Eden, temptations we face every day too. He overcame the lust of the flesh, the lust of the eyes, and the pride of life,[800] overcoming in every way that our first parents failed.   Because of that, the King James Version says that He is able to "succor them that are tempted." "Succor" is an old word that means to help, to come to the aid of, or to assist.   Because He overcame, we now have the power to be overcomers too.   Praise Him today for His help in overcoming temptation!

James 1:12   Blessed *is* the man that endureth temptation: for when he is tried, he shall receive the crown of life, which the Lord hath promised to them that love him.

---

[799] **Hebrews 4:15**   For we have not an high priest which cannot be touched with the feeling of our infirmities; but was in all points tempted like as *we are, yet* without sin.

[800] **Genesis 3:1-5** 1 Now the serpent was more subtil than any beast of the field which the LORD God had made. And he said unto the woman, Yea, hath God said, Ye shall not eat of every tree of the garden? 2 And the woman said unto the serpent, We may eat of the fruit of the trees of the garden: 3 But of the fruit of the tree which *is* in the midst of the garden, God hath said, Ye shall not eat of it, neither shall ye touch it, lest ye die. 4 And the serpent said unto the woman, Ye shall not surely die: 5 For God doth know that in the day ye eat thereof, then your eyes shall be opened, and ye shall be as gods, knowing good and evil.

Matthew 4:1-11 1 Then was Jesus led up of the Spirit into the wilderness to be tempted of the devil. 2 And when he had fasted forty days and forty nights, he was afterward an hungred. 3 And when the tempter came to him, he said, If thou be the Son of God, command that these stones be made bread. 4 But he answered and said, It is written, Man shall not live by bread alone, but by every word that proceedeth out of the mouth of God. 5 Then the devil taketh him up into the holy city, and setteth him on a pinnacle of the temple, 6 And saith unto him, If thou be the Son of God, cast thyself down: for it is written, He shall give his angels charge concerning thee: and in *their* hands they shall bear thee up, lest at any time thou dash thy foot against a stone. 7 Jesus said unto him, It is written again, Thou shalt not tempt the Lord thy God. 8 Again, the devil taketh him up into an exceeding high mountain, and sheweth him all the kingdoms of the world, and the glory of them; 9 And saith unto him, All these things will I give thee, if thou wilt fall down and worship me. 10 Then saith Jesus unto him, Get thee hence, Satan: for it is written, Thou shalt worship the Lord thy God, and him only shalt thou serve. 11 Then the devil leaveth him, and, behold, angels came and ministered unto him.

1 John 2:15-17 15 Love not the world, neither the things *that are* in the world. If any man love the world, the love of the Father is not in him. 16 For all that *is* in the world, the lust of the flesh, and the lust of the eyes, and the pride of life, is not of the Father, but is of the world. 17 And the world passeth away, and the lust thereof: but he that doeth the will of God abideth for ever.

Read Hebrews 3:1-19

Hebrews 3:13   But exhort one another daily, while it is called To day; lest any of you be hardened through the deceitfulness of sin.

Can one be a Christian without being a part of a local church?   One thing is certain, there are many Scriptures that we cannot obey without close fellowship with other believers.   Much of the New Testament has to do with our relationship with "one another."   Hebrews 3:13 is a clear example of that kind of Scripture.   The Hebrews were warned about developing hard hearts as their ancestors did back in the days of Moses.   Sadly, because of that hardness of heart, most of that earlier generation did not enter God's rest in the Promised Land.   In light of what can happen through a hardened heart, we must take heed to our own spiritual lives, and we must also be willing to encourage brothers and sisters who may also be struggling along the way.   It is clear, we need God, but we also need one another.   This is yet another reason, I am so thankful for the family of God!

> You will notice we say "brother and sister" 'round here,
> It's because we're a family and these folks are so near;
> When one has a heartache, we all share the tears,
> And rejoice in each victory in this family so dear.[801]

---

[801] "The Family of God,"   Bill and Gloria Gaither.

Read Hebrews 4:1-13

Hebrews 4:10   For he that is entered into his rest, he also hath ceased from his own works, as God *did* from his.

In Hebrews 4 we learn about the New Covenant implications of the Sabbath. If you will remember, the Hebrews were in danger of going back under the Law. To do so would keep them from the sweet rest they could have in Jesus.

As we read the story of creation, we find that the account of the seventh day, the day God rested from His work of creation, does not include the phrase "evening and morning" as do the accounts of the other six days.   Had sin not entered the picture, it may well have been not just twenty-four hours, but an eternal sabbath, an eternal "day" of rest and blessing.[802]   Hebrews 4 compares this with the rest we now have in Jesus.   God rested on the seventh day, because His work of creation was complete.   Now we rest **in** the work that Jesus finished for us on the cross[803].   This also explains the importance we find in the New Testament of Jesus being seated at the Father's right hand[804].   He was able to sit down, because the work of salvation was complete.   It is not that we do not do good works, we no longer do them as a means of salvation.   We rest in the work that He has already done for us, a salvation planned from before the world began![805]

Some might ask, "Do you keep the Sabbath?"   We can joyfully say, "Jesus, my Sabbath, keeps me!"   I entered His rest when I received His salvation, and I look forward to enjoying that sweet rest in the eons of eternity future!

Matthew 11:28-30 28 Come unto me, all *ye* that labour and are heavy laden, and I will give you rest. 29 Take my yoke upon you, and learn of me; for I am meek and lowly in heart: and ye shall find rest unto your souls. 30 For my yoke *is* easy, and my burden is light.

---

[802] **Genesis 2:1-3** 1 Thus the heavens and the earth were finished, and all the host of them. 2 And on the seventh day God ended his work which he had made; and he rested on the seventh day from all his work which he had made. 3 And God blessed the seventh day, and sanctified it: because that in it he had rested from all his work which God created and made.

[803] **John 19:30**   When Jesus therefore had received the vinegar, he said, It is finished: and he bowed his head, and gave up the ghost.

[804] **Hebrews 1:3**   Who being the brightness of *his* glory, and the express image of his person, and upholding all things by the word of his power, when he had by himself purged our sins, sat down on the right hand of the Majesty on high;

Hebrews 10:11-12 11 And every priest standeth daily ministering and offering oftentimes the same sacrifices, which can never take away sins: 12 But this man, after he had offered one sacrifice for sins for ever, sat down on the right hand of God;

[805] **Hebrews 4:3**   For we which have believed do enter into rest, as he said, As I have sworn in my wrath, if they shall enter into my rest: although the works were finished from the foundation of the world.

Read Hebrews 4:14-5:14

Hebrews 4:16   Let us **therefore** come boldly unto the throne of grace, that we may obtain mercy, and find grace to help in time of need.

When you read the Word of God, you should always take note of words like "therefore."   They direct us to context, to what came before.   It is in light of something else that we now have access to the throne of grace.   What is it?   It is that we have a Great High Priest in Jesus Christ.

The work of earthly high priests was never complete.   They offered the same sacrifices again and again.   Jesus, on the other hand, offered one perfect sacrifice forever, and then sat down, His work being complete.[806]   Earthly high priests were sinners, just like those to whom they ministered.   Our high priest, Jesus Christ, understands us and our weakness,[807]   and unlike every other priest, He lived a perfect, sinless life.   He was tempted in every way that we are as human beings, yet He never sinned.   It is through that Perfect, Holy High Priest and His Finished Work on the Cross that we now have access to the Throne of Grace! Thank God for Calvary!

Years I spent in vanity and pride,
Caring not my Lord was crucified,
Knowing not it was for me He died
On Calvary.

---

[806] **Hebrews 10:9-12** 9 Then said he, Lo, I come to do thy will, O God. He taketh away the first, that he may establish the second. 10 By the which will we are sanctified through the offering of the body of Jesus Christ once *for all*. 11 And every priest standeth daily ministering and offering oftentimes the same sacrifices, which can never take away sins: 12 But this man, after he had offered one sacrifice for sins for ever, sat down on the right hand of God;

[807] **Hebrews 4:15**   For we have not an high priest which cannot be touched with the feeling of our infirmities; but was in all points tempted like as *we are, yet* without sin.

Mercy there was great, and grace was free;
Pardon there was multiplied to me;
There my burdened soul found liberty
At Calvary.

By God's Word at last my sin I learned;
Then I trembled at the law I'd spurned,
Till my guilty soul imploring turned
To Calvary.

Now I've giv'n to Jesus everything,
Now I gladly own Him as my King,
Now my raptured soul can only sing
Of Calvary!

Oh, the love that drew salvation's plan!
Oh, the grace that brought it down to man!
Oh, the mighty gulf that God did span
At Calvary![808]

---

[808] "At Calvary," William R. Newell

Read Hebrews 6:1-20

Hebrews 6:4-6 4 For *it is* impossible for those who were once enlightened, and have tasted of the heavenly gift, and were made partakers of the Holy Ghost, 5 And have tasted the good word of God, and the powers of the world to come, 6 If they shall fall away, to renew them again unto repentance; seeing they crucify to themselves the Son of God afresh, and put *him* to an open shame.

This is obviously an important and fearful Scripture, but what does it really mean?   First, we must recognize that he is speaking of those who have been enlightened, that is, those who have "seen the light" of the Gospel and received the gift of salvation, those who have tasted, that is experienced, the glories of the Word of God. They have known what it is to have the ministry of the precious Holy Spirit in their lives, the powers of the world to come!   There seems to be no doubt that they have been truly born again.

Second, we remember that, in context, Hebrews was written to Christians with a Jewish (Hebrew) background.   Because of persecution, some of them were tempted to go back to Judaism and the Law, thereby denying the cross as the only means of salvation.   It is not that the person who turns away *cannot* come back to Jesus, but if they do turn their backs on Him, there is certainly no hope anywhere else. Salvation is impossible outside of Him. He is the only Way.

Acts 4:12   Neither is there salvation in any other: for there is none other name under heaven given among men, whereby we must be saved.

Read Hebrews 7:1-19

Hebrews 7:11   If therefore perfection were by the Levitical priesthood, (for under it the people received the law,) what further need *was there* that another priest should rise after the order of Melchisedec, and not be called after the order of Aaron?

Under the Old Covenant, there was the need for an earthly priesthood. The descendants of Aaron were God's High Priests. They represented God before the people and the people before God. They were the only ones who could enter the Holy of Holies, the place of God's manifest power and presence on the earth at that time.   They served as mediators between sinful human beings and a holy God, offering multitudes of sacrifices, sacrifices that could temporarily cover sin, but could never perfect anyone. The earthly high priest could only minister over the course of a lifetime, and then another would take his place repeating the same sacrifices for another lifetime.

Jesus, however, is our great high priest, the final and perfect Mediator between God and human beings.[809]   His sacrifice does not just cover sin, but it removes it as far as the east is from the west.   His priesthood did not end with His death, for He rose again; He is our Great High Priest *forever!*[810]   Through His sacrifice on the cross, He did what the Old Covenant and the Old Covenant priesthood could never do.

Hebrews 7:19   For the law made nothing perfect, but the bringing in of a better hope *did*; by the which we draw nigh unto God.

Hebrews 10:14   For by one offering he hath perfected forever them that are sanctified.

---

[809] **1 Timothy 2:5**   For *there is* one God, and **one mediator** between God and men, the man Christ Jesus;
[810] **Hebrews 7:17**   For he testifieth, Thou *art* **a priest for ever** after the order of Melchisedec.

Read Hebrews 7:20-8:6

Hebrews 8:1 Now of the things which we have spoken *this is* the sum: We have such an high priest, who is set on the right hand of the throne of the Majesty in the heavens;

This part of Hebrews is still reminding us of how wonderful it is that Jesus Christ is our Great High Priest.   As a priest, He intercedes for us before the Father,[811] and unlike every earthly priest, He is perfect in every way.[812]

Hebrews 8:1 begins a summary of all that has been said about Jesus' priesthood here in Hebrews. The Old Testament system with its priests was a shadow[813] of the reality we now have in Jesus Christ![814] When He offered Himself as the perfect sacrifice, offering His blood as payment in full for the debt of sin, He was able to do what no previous priest could ever do in the course of their duties. He sat down at the right hand of the Father!   We are told that there were no chairs, or places to sit, in the tabernacle of old. Old Testament priests had no time to sit, because the sacrifices were unending. Jesus, however, sat down, because He offered one perfect sacrifice with eternal consequences. Let us give glory to God now and forever that our Great High Priest is seated, having made payment in full for our debt of sin!

Hebrews 10:10-14 10 By the which will we are sanctified through the offering of the body of Jesus Christ **ONCE FOR ALL**. 11 And every priest standeth daily ministering and offering oftentimes the same sacrifices, which can never take away sins: 12 But this man, after he had offered **ONE SACRIFICE FOR SIN FOR EVER** sat down on the right hand of God; 13 From henceforth expecting till his enemies be made his footstool. 14 For by **ONE OFFERING** he hath **PERFECTED FOR EVER** them that are sanctified.

---

[811] **Hebrews 7:25** Wherefore he is able also to save them to the uttermost that come unto God by him, seeing he ever liveth to make intercession for them.

[812] **Hebrews 7:26** For such an high priest became us, *who is* holy, harmless, undefiled, separate from sinners, and made higher than the heavens;

[813] The concept of the Old Testament Law and Rituals being only a shadow of what we have in Christ is seen several places in the New Testament (Colossians 2:16-17, Hebrews 8:5, Hebrews 10:1).

[814] **Hebrews 8:5** Who serve unto the example and shadow of heavenly things, as Moses was admonished of God when he was about to make the tabernacle: for, See, saith he, *that* thou make all things according to the pattern shewed to thee in the mount.

Read Hebrews 8:7-9:7

Hebrews 8:13 In that he saith, A new *covenant*, he hath made the first old. Now that which decayeth and waxeth old *is* ready to vanish away.

    The entire Book of Hebrews builds a strong case for the New Covenant that we now have in Christ. There is an interesting Greek word in verse 13. When he says, "He hath made the first old," speaking of the Old Covenant, the Greek word translated as "old" is palaioō which means "to make obsolete". The Old Covenant has now become obsolete, because of the new. The system of priests, sacrifices, and rituals is no longer needed.

    We have better promises under the New Covenant (remember the word "better" is the key word in Hebrews).[815] The New Covenant can do things that the Old could never do.[816] The Old Covenant, written on stone tablets, was broken continually from the day that God gave it. It did not offer us the power to keep God's Law. One of the "better promises" of the New Covenant is that He will write His Law upon our hearts.[817] We know from elsewhere in Scripture that by the love of God placed in our hearts; His Law is fulfilled.[818] These wonderful "better" things were prophesied way back in the Book of Jeremiah,[819] where the Lord says, "I will forgive their iniquity, and I will remember **their sin no more."**

---

[815] **Hebrews 8:6** But now hath he obtained a more excellent ministry, by how much also he is the mediator of a better covenant, which was established upon better promises.

[816] **Hebrews 8:7** For if that first *covenant* had been faultless, then should no place have been sought for the second.

[817] **Hebrews 8:10** For this *is* the covenant that I will make with the house of Israel after those days, saith the Lord; I will put my laws into their mind, and write them in their hearts: and I will be to them a God, and they shall be to me a people:

[818] **Romans 5:5** And hope maketh not ashamed; because the love of God is shed abroad in our hearts by the Holy Ghost which is given unto us.

Romans 13:8-10 8 Owe no man any thing, but to love one another: for he that loveth another hath fulfilled the law. 9 For this, Thou shalt not commit adultery, Thou shalt not kill, Thou shalt not steal, Thou shalt not bear false witness, Thou shalt not covet; and if *there be* any other commandment, it is briefly comprehended in this saying, namely, Thou shalt love thy neighbour as thyself. 10 Love worketh no ill to his neighbour: therefore love *is* the fulfilling of the law.

Galatians 5:13-14 13 For, brethren, ye have been called unto liberty; only *use* not liberty for an occasion to the flesh, but by love serve one another. 14 For all the law is fulfilled in one word, *even* in this; Thou shalt love thy neighbour as thyself.

James 2:8 If ye fulfil the royal law according to the scripture, Thou shalt love thy neighbour as thyself, ye do well:

[819] **Jeremiah 31:31-34** 31 Behold, the days come, saith the LORD, that I will make a new covenant with the house of Israel, and with the house of Judah: 32 Not according to the covenant that I made with their fathers in the day *that* I took them by the hand to bring them out of the land of Egypt; which my covenant they brake, although I was an husband unto them, saith the LORD: 33 But this *shall be* the covenant that I will make with the house of Israel; After those days, saith the LORD, I will put my law in their inward parts, and write it in their hearts; and will be their God, and they shall be my people. 34 And they shall teach no more every man his neighbour, and every man his brother, saying, Know the LORD: for they shall all know me, from the least of them unto the greatest of them, saith the LORD: for I will forgive their iniquity, and I will remember their sin no more.

Read Hebrews 9:8-22

Hebrews 9:22   And almost all things are by the law purged with blood; and without shedding of blood is no remission.

Some churches today have eliminated any reference to the blood of Christ, because they believe it is a concept that may be difficult for outsiders to understand.   Some have even suggested that it is an outdated doctrine, something meant for an earlier day!   However, without the blood, salvation is impossible.   From the beginning God has ordained that the penalty for sin is death and that there can be no remission of sins without the shedding of blood.   Today, we know that this all directs us to Jesus shedding His blood, giving His life for us on the cross.   Far from being an outdated concept, we will rejoice forever in what He did for us there, shedding His blood. In the endless eons of eternity we will worship Jesus as the Lamb that was slain[820]! I will be rejoicing, because of His blood, a million years from today!

Romans 5:8-9   8 But God commendeth his love toward us, in that, while we were yet sinners, Christ died for us. 9 Much more then, being now **justified by his blood**, we shall be saved from wrath through him.

Ephesians 1:7   In whom we have **redemption through his blood**, the forgiveness of sins, according to the riches of his grace;

Ephesians 2:13   But now in Christ Jesus ye who sometimes were far off are **made nigh by the blood** of Christ.

Colossians 1:20   And, having **made peace through the blood of his cross,** by him to reconcile all things unto himself; by him, *I say*, whether *they be* things in earth, or things in heaven.

---

[820] **Revelation 5:12**   Saying with a loud voice, Worthy is the Lamb that was slain to receive power, and riches, and wisdom, and strength, and honour, and glory, and blessing.

Hebrews 9:14   <u>How much more shall the blood of Christ</u>, who through the eternal Spirit offered himself without spot to God, <u>**purge your conscience**</u> from dead works to serve the living God?

Hebrews 10:19   Having therefore, brethren, <u>**boldness to enter into the holiest by the blood of Jesus,**</u>

1 Peter 1:18-19 18 Forasmuch as ye know that ye were not redeemed with corruptible things, *as* silver and gold, from your vain conversation *received* by tradition from your fathers; 19 <u>**But with the precious blood of Christ,**</u> as of a lamb without blemish and without spot:

1 John 1:7   But if we walk in the light, as he is in the light, we have fellowship one with another, and <u>**the blood of Jesus Christ his Son cleanseth us from all sin**</u>.

Revelation 12:11   And <u>**they overcame him by the blood of the Lamb,**</u> and by the word of their testimony; and they loved not their lives unto the death.

The blood that Jesus shed for me
Way back on Calvary
The blood that gives me strength
From day to day
It will never lose its power
It reaches to the highest mountain
It flows to the lowest valley
The blood that gives me strength
From day to day
It will never lose its power[821]

---

[821] "The Blood Will Never Lose its Power," Andrae Crouch.

Read Hebrews 9:23-10:10

Hebrews 9:28   So Christ was **once offered** to bear the sins of many; and unto them that look for him shall he appear the second time without sin unto salvation.

I love the emphasis in Hebrews on the "once for all" sacrifice of Jesus Christ on the cross.   The words 'once' and 'one' appear repeatedly in that context, including the reference here in Hebrews 9:28.   Jesus came to the earth to give His life, and He will never have to do that again. His work of redemption is complete. When He returns, it will be for a *different* purpose. I invite you to rejoice in just a few of the "once for all" Scriptures today!

Hebrews 7:27   Who needeth not daily, as those high priests, to offer up sacrifice, first for his own sins, and then for the people's: **FOR THIS HE DID ONCE**, when he offered up himself.

Hebrews 9:12   Neither by the blood of goats and calves, but by his own blood **HE ENTERED IN ONCE** into the holy place, having obtained eternal redemption *for us*.

Hebrews 10:10   By the which will we are sanctified through the offering of the body of Jesus Christ **ONCE FOR ALL**.

Hebrews 10:12   But this man, after he had offered **ONE SACRIFICE FOR SINS FOREVER**, sat down on the right hand of God;

 Hebrews 10:14   **FOR BY ONE OFFERING** he hath perfected forever them that are sanctified.

The Lord came one time to bear my sins to the cross. When He returns for me, He will not be dying again, but will be bringing the final consummation of my salvation!

Read Hebrews 10:11-31

Hebrews 10:24-25 24 And let us consider one another to provoke unto love and to good works: 25 Not forsaking the assembling of ourselves together, as the manner of some *is*; but exhorting *one another*: and so much the more, as ye see the day approaching.

There are those today, who don't think the local church is important. They believe that they can worship God just as well at home, on the lake, at the golf course, or in a deer stand as they can in fellowship with other believers. Apparently, that kind of thinking was prevalent when the Book of Hebrews was written. He said that it was the "manner of some." It is still the "manner of some," but thankfully, not all! One can and should worship God wherever they are, but we cannot be obedient to many of the New Testament admonitions unless we find those times of assembling ourselves together. Whenever that happens, we are to be considerate of one another, and we are to provoke (encourage) one another in the things of God, including love and good works. We are to exhort one another, that means to build one another up spiritually. This was important when Hebrews was written, but it is even more important now, because we are that much closer to the "approaching day," the day that Jesus returns!

1 Corinthians 14:26 How is it then, brethren? **WHEN YE COME TOGETHER**, every one of you hath a psalm, hath a doctrine, hath a tongue, hath a revelation, hath an interpretation. Let all things be done unto edifying.

Read Hebrews 10:32-11:7

Hebrews 11:6 But without faith it is impossible to please him: for he that cometh to God must believe that he is, and that he is a rewarder of them that diligently seek him.

Hebrews 11 is the Faith Chapter. Verse 1 gives us a **definition** for faith, "Faith is the substance of things hoped for, the evidence of things not seen." We may not yet see the fulfillment of all of God's promises, but, by faith, we know that we will. Verse 6 tells us the **importance** of faith, "Without faith it is **impossible** to please God." It does not say that it is difficult, but that it is impossible!

The kind of faith that pleases God is more than just believing that He exists. There are very few true atheists. Down deep most probably believe that a Supreme Being exists, but that alone is not saving faith. James tells us that even the demons believe that much[822]. The faith that pleases God is the faith that "diligently seeks Him." What is the reward for those who seek Him in that way? The greatest reward of all is the Lord Himself.

Deuteronomy 4:29 But if from thence thou shalt seek the LORD thy God, thou shalt find him, if thou seek him with all thy heart and with all thy soul.

---

[822] **James 2:19** Thou believest that there is one God; thou doest well: the devils also believe, and tremble.

Read Hebrews 11:8-19

Hebrews 11:13   These all died in faith, not having received the promises, but having seen them afar off, and were persuaded of *them*, and embraced *them*, and confessed that they were strangers and pilgrims on the earth.

One of the characteristics of men and women of faith is that they live like strangers and pilgrims on the earth.   They are living in this world, but they realize that it is not their eternal home.   They are looking forward to living in their eternal destination, the Heavenly City.   Like them, we look for a city with foundations, a city built by God Himself.[823] That is the place Jesus said that He went to prepare for us.[824]

We are told in the Word of God that as believers our citizenship is already in that heavenly city, the city we see ahead by faith.[825] It is often rightly said that we are in this world, but we are not of it[826] and that we are ambassadors, representing the kingdom of heaven in a dark and sinful world.[827]   These truths are why we can sing with great joy....

This world is not my home, I'm only passing through, my treasures are laid up, somewhere beyond the blue, the angels beckon me from heaven's open door, and I can't feel at home in this world any more.[828]

---

[823] **Hebrews 11:10**   For he looked for a city which hath foundations, whose builder and maker *is* God.
Revelation 21:18-23 18 And the building of the wall of it was *of* jasper: and the city *was* pure gold, like unto clear glass. 19 And **THE FOUNDATIONS** of the wall of the city *were* garnished with all manner of precious stones. The first foundation *was* jasper; the second, sapphire; the third, a chalcedony; the fourth, an emerald; 20 The fifth, sardonyx; the sixth, sardius; the seventh, chrysolite; the eighth, beryl; the ninth, a topaz; the tenth, a chrysoprasus; the eleventh, a jacinth; the twelfth, an amethyst. 21 And the twelve gates *were* twelve pearls; every several gate was of one pearl: and the street of the city *was* pure gold, as it were transparent glass. 22 And I saw no temple therein: for the Lord God Almighty and the Lamb are the temple of it. 23 And the city had no need of the sun, neither of the moon, to shine in it: for the glory of God did lighten it, and the Lamb *is* the light thereof.
[824] **John 14:1-3** 1 Let not your heart be troubled: ye believe in God, believe also in me. 2 In my Father's house are many mansions: if *it were* not *so*, I would have told you. I go to prepare a place for you. 3 And if I go and prepare a place for you, I will come again, and receive you unto myself; that where I am, *there* ye may be also.
[825] **Philippians 3:20**   For our conversation [citizenship] is in heaven; from whence also we look for the Saviour, the Lord Jesus Christ:
[826] **John 17:16**   They are not of the world, even as I am not of the world.
[827] **2 Corinthians 5:20**   Now then we are ambassadors for Christ, as though God did beseech *you* by us: we pray *you* in Christ's stead, be ye reconciled to God.
[828] "This World is Not My Home,"   Albert Edward Brumley

Read Hebrews 11.20-40

Hebrews 11:37-38 37 They were stoned, they were sawn asunder, were tempted, were slain with the sword: they wandered about in sheepskins and goatskins; being destitute, afflicted, tormented; 38 (Of whom the world was not worthy:) they wandered in deserts, and *in* mountains, and *in* dens and caves of the earth.

We read of the mighty deliverances received by those who were men and women of faith.   However, we also read of those who faced great troubles in this world.   As believers we are never promised that we will leave this world without facing tests and trials.   Paul told the Christians in a place called Derbe that they would enter the kingdom of God through "much tribulation[829]."

Though we may face great trials, as many of God's choice servants have over the centuries, we can face both life and death in the power of the Spirit and in the victory of faith.   Paul tells us that the shield of faith will quench all of Satan's fiery darts[830], and John tells us that faith is the victory that overcomes the world[831]!   Wherever He leads me, by faith I know that He will sustain me.

Encamped along the hills of light,
Ye Christian soldiers, rise,
And press the battle ere the night
Shall veil the glowing skies.
Against the foe in vales below
Let all our strength be hurled;
Faith is the victory, we know,
That overcomes the world.

[829] **Acts 14:22**   Confirming the souls of the disciples, *and* exhorting them to continue in the faith, and that we must through much tribulation enter into the kingdom of God.
[830] **Ephesians 6:16**   Above all, taking the shield of faith, wherewith ye shall be able to quench all the fiery darts of the wicked.
[831] **1 John 5:4-5**   4 For whatsoever is born of God overcometh the world: and this is the victory that overcometh the world, *even* our faith. 5 Who is he that overcometh the world, but he that believeth that Jesus is the Son of God?

Faith is the victory!
Faith is the victory!
Oh, glorious victory,
That overcomes the world.

His banner over us is love,
Our sword the Word of God;
We tread the road the saints above
With shouts of triumph trod.
By faith, they like a whirlwind's breath,
Swept on o'er every field;
The faith by which they conquered death
Is still our shining shield.

On every hand the foe we find
Drawn up in dread array;
Let tents of ease be left behind,
And onward to the fray.
Salvation's helmet on each head,
With truth all girt about,
The earth shall tremble 'neath our tread,
And echo with our shout.

To him that overcomes the foe,
White raiment shall be giv'n;
Before the angels he shall know
His name confessed in heav'n.
Then onward from the hills of light,
Our hearts with love aflame,
We'll vanquish all the hosts of night,
In Jesus' conqu'ring name.[832]

---

[832] "Faith is the Victory," John Yates

Read Hebrews 12:1-13

Hebrews 12:1-2 1 Wherefore seeing we also are compassed about with so great a cloud of witnesses, let us lay aside every weight, and the sin which doth so easily beset *us*, and let us run with patience the race that is set before us, 2 Looking unto Jesus the author and finisher of *our* faith; who for the joy that was set before him endured the cross, despising the shame, and is set down at the right hand of the throne of God.

The Christian life is compared to a race. It is not a sprint, but it is a marathon that is run for a lifetime.   It is imperative that we do not give up along the way.   That is why we run the race with patience (perseverance).   We must lay aside any weights or sins, because those things could slow us down or even stop us. *Nothing* must hinder us in running this all-important race.

For this to be seen in context, we must consider it in light of what came before. The great cloud of witnesses includes those great men and women of faith spoken of in Hebrews 11. Their testimony encourages us to persevere. The same One who was faithful to them, all the days of their earthly race, will be faithful to us in ours.

As we run this race, we keep our focus on the One who stands at the finish line awaiting our arrival, the Lord Jesus Christ.   He finished His earthly race, going all the way to the cross.   He endured His suffering with joy, because He knew was purchasing you, the Church, His Bride! He is the Author of our Faith, the One who began a good work in us[833].   He is also the Finisher of our Faith, the One who will see us through to the finish line. He is the Captain of our Salvation and will guide us safely to our Heavenly Destination[834]!

As I write these words, I think of the words of a little chorus that we can make our prayer today.

<blockquote>
Keep me true, Lord Jesus, keep me true,
Keep me true, Lord Jesus, keep me true,
There's a race that I must run,   There are victories to be won,
Give me power every hour to be true[835].
</blockquote>

---

[833] **Philippians 1:6** Being confident of this very thing, that he which hath begun a good work in you will perform *it* until the day of Jesus Christ:

[834] **Hebrews 2:10** For it became him, for whom *are* all things, and by whom *are* all things, in bringing many sons unto glory, to make the captain of their salvation perfect through sufferings.

[835] "Keep Me True," Nell E. Mayes.

Read Hebrews 12:14-29

Hebrews 12:28 Wherefore we receiving a kingdom which cannot be moved, <u>let us have grace</u>, whereby we may serve God acceptably with reverence and godly fear: For our God is a consuming fire.

Our God is a consuming fire! What fearful words to describe an awesome and holy God. Some of this chapter looks back to when God gave the Law on Mount Sinai. It was an awe-inspiring day. No one was allowed near the mountain upon penalty of death.[836] They did not dare to come close. Though only Moses could ascend the mountain, the people were terrified, trembling with fear, because of what they saw and heard.[837] God Himself descended on Mount Sinai accompanied by fire and smoke and the entire mountain shook![838] He shook the earth that day, but there is coming a day when all of creation will be shaken.[839] A great day of shaking is coming. Are you ready?

How may we approach such a holy God, one who is indeed both fearful and awesome? There is only one way that it is possible. The answer is grace! He says, "Let us have grace, whereby we may serve God acceptably with reverence and godly fear." Because of what Jesus did on another mountain, Mount Calvary, I am able to approach the one who is a consuming fire.

Hebrews 4:16 Let us therefore come boldly unto <u>the throne of grace</u>, that we may obtain mercy, and find grace to help in time of need.

---

[836] **Exodus 19:12 And** thou shalt set bounds unto the people round about, saying, take heed to yourselves, *that ye* go *not* up into the mount, or touch the border of it: whosoever toucheth the mount shall be surely put to death:

[837] **Exodus 19:16 And** it came to pass on the third day in the morning, that there were thunders and lightnings, and a thick cloud upon the mount, and the voice of the trumpet exceeding loud; so that all the people that *was* in the camp trembled.

[838] **Exodus 19:18 And** mount Sinai was altogether on a smoke, because the LORD descended upon it in fire: and the smoke thereof ascended as the smoke of a furnace, and the whole mount quaked greatly.

[839] **Hebrews 12:26 Whose** voice then shook the earth: but now he hath promised, saying, yet once more I shake not the earth only, but also heaven.

Read Hebrews 13:1-14

Hebrews 13:5 Let *your* conversation *be* without covetousness; *and be* content with such things as ye have: for he hath said, I will never leave thee, nor forsake thee.

The word "conversation" as it is used in the King James Version is more than our speech, it is our lifestyle in general. Covetousness, the love of money and things, should never be the lifestyle of a child of God. The tenth commandment says, "Thou shalt not covet," but covetousness is also considered in the first commandment, "Thou shalt have no other gods before me." Whatever we place above Him has become a god to us.

The Lord says, "I will never leave thee nor forsake thee." If you will remember, our teachers cautioned us against using double negatives, because it was not considered proper usage in the English language. However, in some other languages, including the original Greek of the New Testament, multiple negatives are often used for emphasis. Hebrews 13:5, for example, includes not just a double negative, but a quintuple negative in the Greek, emphasizing that he will NEVER, NEVER, NEVER, NEVER, NEVER leave us or forsake us. That is why we can live lives of joyful contentment. The One who will **NEVER** leave us, will **ALWAYS** provide for us!

Philippians 4:19 **But** my God shall supply all your need according to his riches in glory by Christ Jesus.

Read Hebrews 13.15-25

Hebrews 13:15 By him therefore let us offer the sacrifice of praise to God continually, that is, the fruit of *our* lips giving thanks to his name.

The animal sacrifices of the Old Testament are now obsolete, having been superseded by the perfect, once for all time, sacrifice of Jesus Christ on the cross. However, there are still some sacrifices that we are to offer to Him today. For example, we are to offer our bodies (our whole being) as a living sacrifice[840] and here in Hebrews 13:15 we are told to offer the sacrifice of praise.

First, the sacrifice of praise can only be offered rightly in relationship with Him, and as He enables us, for the Bible says that we bring the sacrifice of praise "**by Him**." Second, the sacrifice of praise is something that is offered continually. Praise is not just what we do in church. It is a lifestyle of praise. Third, it is truly a sacrifice, it costs us something, and always involves giving our best, the first fruits unto the Lord.

Think of these truths today as you sing a familiar old chorus taken from this Scripture:

> We bring the sacrifice of praise into the house of the Lord,
> We bring the sacrifice of praise into the House of the Lord,
> And we offer unto You, the sacrifices of thanksgiving,
> And we offer unto You, the sacrifices of praise.[841]

---

[840] **Romans 12:1-2** 1 I beseech you therefore, brethren, by the mercies of God, that ye present your bodies a living sacrifice, holy, acceptable unto God, *which is* your reasonable service. 2 And be not conformed to this world: but be ye transformed by the renewing of your mind, that ye may prove what *is* that good, and acceptable, and perfect, will of God.

[841] "The Sacrifice of Praise," Kirk Dearman

Read James 1

James 1:5-7 If any of you lack wisdom, let him ask of God, that giveth to all men liberally, and upbraideth not; and it shall be given him. 6 But let him ask in faith, nothing wavering. For he that wavereth is like a wave of the sea driven with the wind and tossed. 7 For let not that man think that he shall receive any thing of the Lord.

Godly wisdom is very important. Proverbs 4:7 reminds us just how important, "Wisdom is the principal thing; therefore, get wisdom: and with all thy getting get understanding." Because it is so important, and such a need in our lives, the Lord has seen fit to make an amazing promise. Any of us who lack wisdom, and this is probably all of us, can ask for and receive the wisdom that we need.

When our Father grants wisdom in answer to prayer, He does not give it in sparing supply, but liberally, that is with an open hand. He will never upbraid us or scold us for asking, or for asking too often. He is probably more willing to give wisdom than we are to receive it.

He tells us that we must ask in faith, if we are to receive that wisdom. Romans tells us that faith comes by hearing and hearing by the Word of God. Promises like this one help build our faith so we can ask for and receive what God has promised. Our Lord Jesus Christ is the source of all true wisdom. This old hymn says it well.

Jesus Christ is made to me,
All I need, all I need,
He alone is all my plea,
He is all I need.
Wisdom righteousness and pow'r,
Holiness forevermore,
My redemption full and sure,
He is all I need.[842]

---

[842] "All I Need," Charles P. Jones

Read James 2

James 2:10 For whosoever shall keep the whole law, and yet offend in one *point*, he is guilty of all.

Some believe that they can be saved through keeping the Law and their own good works. If that were possible, one would have to do so perfectly, offending in even one point makes one guilty of the totality of God's Law. In other words, if I have ever lied, I am as guilty as if I were a murderer. If it were possible to do that one would also have to do so continually. Paul said in Galatians, "Cursed is everyone that **continues** not in all things which are written in the book of the law to do them."[843] God's Law proves to us our great need of a Savior.[844] The standard we would have to attain to justify ourselves is the glory of Almighty God, and we have all fallen short of that![845]

Does that mean that works of righteousness have no part in a Christian's life? Absolutely not! The context of this entire chapter is that Christians are not to have "respect of persons," but are to treat others in the body well, regardless of their social status. He goes on to tell us that we are to fulfill the "Royal Law," that is we are to love our neighbor as ourselves.[846] We are told elsewhere that love is what fulfills the law in our lives.[847] Yes, we are justified by faith, but true faith will manifest itself in works of righteousness.

Ephesians 2:7-10) 7 That in the ages to come he might shew the exceeding riches of his grace in *his* kindness toward us through Christ Jesus. 8 For by grace are ye saved through faith; and that not of yourselves: *it is* the gift of God: 9 Not **of works**, lest any man should boast. 10 For we are his workmanship, created[848] in Christ Jesus **unto good works**, which God hath before ordained that we should walk in them.

---

843 Galatians 3:10
844 Galatians 3:24-25
845 Romans 3:23
846 James 2:8
847 Romans 13:8-10
848 A new creation, through being born again! (2 Corinthians 5:17).

Read James 3

James 3:2 For in many things we offend all. If any man offend not in word, the same *is* a perfect man, *and* able also to bridle the whole body.

What we say is a barometer of what is happening on the inside of us. Jesus said, "out of the abundance of the heart, the mouth speaks."[849] He also said that we will answer for every idle word that we speak.[850] James says that if we could live a life not sinning with our words, we would be able to control all the other areas of our lives, but is that possible?

James 3 says that the tongue, though it is relatively small like the rudder of a ship or the bit in a horse's mouth, can have a huge impact. The tongue is like a raging wildfire. Wild animals can be tamed, but the human tongue is untamable. This makes it very clear that we are *all* going to need the help of the Holy Spirit, because we cannot tame that unruly part of our bodies—the tongue--without His help.

My prayer today is one prayed by King David.

Psalm 19:14 Let the words of my mouth, and the meditation of my heart, be acceptable in thy sight, O LORD, my strength, and my redeemer.

---

[849] Matthew 12:34
[850] Matthew 12:36

Read James 4

James 4:14 Whereas ye know not what *shall be* on the morrow. For what *is* your life? It is even a vapor, that appeareth for a little time, and then vanisheth away.

Earthly life is very uncertain, we are never promised tomorrow. The brevity of it becomes more obvious to us the longer we live. Future plans, though not condemned outright in God's Word, should be tempered with the knowledge that only God knows what tomorrow holds.

David prayed, "Lord make me to know mine end, and the measure of my days, what it is; that I may know how frail I am."[851] Also in the Psalms, we find this prayer of Moses, "Teach us to number our days, that we may apply our hearts unto wisdom."[852] All of this makes TODAY and ETERNITY that much more important to us!

> Many things about tomorrow
> I don't seem to understand
> But I know who holds tomorrow
> And I know who holds my hand[853]

---

851 Psalm 39:4
852 Psalm 90:12
853 "I Know Who Holds Tomorrow," Ira Stanphill

Read James 5

James 5:15 And the prayer of faith shall save the sick, and the Lord shall raise him up; and if he have committed sins, they shall be forgiven him.

Is sickness caused by sin?   The answer is both yes and no. Sickness in general, is one of the results of sin coming into the world. There was no sickness before Adam and Eve fell, and there will be no sickness in our eternal home.[854] There are times when sickness *may* be a result of personal sin though, perhaps a result of poor lifestyle decisions.   The Lord tells us in 1 Corinthians 11 that receiving the Lord's Supper in an unworthy manner can even result in sickness. But, it is clearly *not* Scriptural to say that *all* sickness is caused by *personal* sin, because it is clearly not.

In John 9, Jesus and His disciples met a man who was born blind. The disciples believed that his blindness must have been caused by either his own sin or that of his parents.   For it to have been his own sin, he would have had to have sinned in the womb, for he was born blind! To have blamed it on his parents would have been cruel indeed. Jesus made it clear, though, that the affliction was not the fault of the blind man *or* his parents.   Whatever the source of the blindness, when the Lord brought healing it proved to be an opportunity for His power and glory to be revealed!

He is still the Great Physician, able to do more than we can ask or think

Ephesians 3:20 Now unto him that is able to do exceeding abundantly above all that we ask or think, according to the power that worketh in us,

---

[854] Revelation 22:3

Read 1 Peter 1:1-21

1 Peter 1:3-5 Blessed *be* the God and Father of our Lord Jesus Christ, which according to his abundant mercy hath begotten us again unto a lively hope by the resurrection of Jesus Christ from the dead, To an inheritance incorruptible, and undefiled, and that fadeth not away, reserved in heaven for you, Who are kept by the power of God through faith unto salvation ready to be revealed in the last time.

We are reminded of the wonderful heavenly inheritance we have in Christ. We have been named in "the will!" Peter shares some wonderful truths about that inheritance, truths that give us cause to rejoice.

First, we do not receive the inheritance because we deserve it. We receive it, because of His mercy in saving us and bringing us into the family of God[855]. We are God's children now, because of the new birth.[856] Second, that inheritance is incorruptible. Jesus spoke of heavenly treasures that neither moths nor rust can corrupt[857]. Nothing can destroy this inheritance. Third, it is undefiled. Nothing in heaven is impure or defiled in any way, including our inheritance.[858] Fourth, it is eternal, it will never fade away. A million eternities from now, we will still be enjoying it.[859] Fifth, it is *reserved* in heaven for *you*. It has your name on it. I am a child of the King and that calls for eternal rejoicing!

My Father is rich in houses and lands,
He holdeth the wealth of the world in His hands!
Of rubies and diamonds, of silver and gold,
His coffers are full, He has riches untold.
I'm a child of the King,
A child of the King:
With Jesus my Savior,
I'm a child of the King.[860]

---

[855] Titus 3:5
[856] John 1:12, Romans 8:17
[857] Matthew 6:19-20
[858] Revelation 21:27
[859] Ephesians 2:7
[860] "A Child of the King," Harriet Buell

Read 1 Peter 1:22-2:17

1 Peter 2:6   Wherefore also it is contained in the scripture, Behold, I lay in Sion a chief corner stone, elect, precious: and he that believeth on him shall not be confounded.

This Scripture takes us all the way back to Gospels where Jesus told Peter, "Thou art Peter, and upon this rock I will build my church; and the gates of hell shall not prevail against it."[861]   Peter's name means rock, so some have looked at this and said that Peter is the rock upon which the Lord would build His church.   This is where the Roman Catholic tradition that Peter was the first pope comes from.   Was Peter the rock or was the rock his profession of faith on that day, "Thou art the Christ, the Son of the Living God?"[862]

Peter himself answers that question for us here in 1 Peter 2. Jesus Christ Himself is the Chief Cornerstone.   He is the Rock upon which the church is built.   It is not Peter, nor any other human being.[863] Peter and all of the rest of us in the church are building blocks, what he calls "living stones" but Jesus alone is THE Rock!

> The Church's one foundation
> Is Jesus Christ her Lord,
> She is His new creation
> By water and the Word.
> From heaven He came and sought her
> To be His holy bride;
> With His own blood He bought her
> And for her life He died.[864]

---

[861] Matthew 16:18
[862] Matthew 16:16
[863] 1 Corinthians 3:11
[864] "The Church's One Foundation," Samuel J. Stone

Read 1 Peter 2:18-3:12

1 Peter 3:1 1 Likewise, ye wives, be in subjection to your own husbands; that, if any obey not the word, they also may without the word be won by the conversation of the wives;

A believer must never marry an unbeliever. That is contrary to God's Word.[865] What if neither is a believer when they marry, but later one of them gets saved? Peter gives important instructions for the believing wife who finds herself in such a situation.

Those wives with unsaved husbands are to be submissive to their own husbands, not to all men in general. That submission does not mean that the wife must follow her unsaved husband into sin. In that case, she must obey God rather than man.[866] Also, this submission does not indicate a position of inferiority, for the Bible even says that Jesus submitted to His parents,[867] and He was their Creator! Peter later tells us that both husband and wife are "heirs **_together_** of the grace of life." [868] The conversation (godly lifestyle) of the believing wife may preach a far more effective sermon than her words alone. There is a time for words, and there is a time to let our lives speak.

We are reminded of Jesus' words in the Sermon on the Mount.

Matthew 5:16 Let your light so shine before men, that they may see your good works, and glorify your Father which is in heaven.

---

[865] 2 Corinthians 6:14
[866] Acts 4:19-20
[867] Luke 2:51
[868] 1 Peter 3:7

Read 1 Peter 3:13-4:11

1 Peter 3:13-15 13 And who *is* he that will harm you, if ye be followers of that which is good? 14 But and if ye suffer for righteousness' sake, happy *are ye*: and be not afraid of their terror, neither be troubled; 15 But sanctify the Lord God in your hearts: and *be* ready always to *give* an answer to every man that asketh you a reason of the hope that is in you with meekness and fear:

We are reminded that we need not fear anyone.   Who can harm us if we are His followers?   Jesus said that we must not fear them that can only kill our bodies, for they cannot touch our souls.[869]   If we suffer for doing what is right, it should not trouble us.   Peter, like Jesus, said that we should count ourselves blessed when facing persecution for righteousness' sake.[870]

Our attitude when facing these things will cause people to ask questions about our faith and our hope in Christ. We are told to be ready with an answer. The Greek word translated "answer" here is apologia. It means a defense.   The English word apologetics (the defense of the Christian faith) comes from that same word.   That means that, when asked, we should be ready to defend what we believe from the Word of God, not with a sense of pride, but with meekness and fear.

Proverbs 15:23 A man hath joy by the answer of his mouth: and a word *spoken* in due season, how good *is it*!

---

[869] Matthew 10:28
[870] Matthew 5:10-11

Read 1 Peter 4.12-5.14

1 Peter 5:1-4 1 The elders which are among you I exhort, who am also an elder, and a witness of the sufferings of Christ, and also a partaker of the glory that shall be revealed: 2 Feed the flock of God which is among you, taking the oversight *thereof*, not by constraint, but willingly; not for filthy lucre, but of a ready mind; 3 Neither as being lords over *God's* heritage, but being ensamples to the flock. 4 And when the chief Shepherd shall appear, ye shall receive a crown of glory that fadeth not away.

Peter is speaking to those who are the preachers in local churches. The New Testament uses three words to describe that ministry. Those leaders are called elders, those who lead. They are called bishops or overseers, those who have the oversight of a local church. They are called shepherds, or pastors, those who faithfully feed the flock through the careful preaching and teaching of the Word of God. These three words are used synonymously in the New Testament.[871]

These men are to fulfill the ministry God has given them willingly, not because they are forced to do so. Though the Bible says the workman is worthy of his hire[872], that should not be the motivation for what they do. They are not called to be lords and masters over God's people, but to lead them as a shepherd leads his sheep. The Lord promises a special crown to those shepherds who serve His flock faithfully.

1 Timothy 1:12 And I thank Christ Jesus our Lord, who hath enabled me, for that he counted me faithful, putting me into the ministry;

---

[871] We also find these three titles in Acts 20:17-28 Paul is addressing the elders of the church at Ephesus. He tells them to feed the flock of God (serve as shepherds or pastors) the flock of God, over which the Holy Ghost had made them overseers (bishops).
[872] 1 Timothy 5:17-18

Read 2 Peter 1:1-21

2 Peter 1:3-4 3 According as his divine power hath given unto us all things that pertain unto life and godliness, through the knowledge of him that hath called us to glory and virtue: 4 Whereby are given unto us exceeding great and precious promises: that by these ye might be partakers of the divine nature, having escaped the corruption that is in the world through lust.

This is a wonderful Scripture to stand upon and rejoice in. The Lord, by His divine power, has given us everything we need to make it from earth to glory. We receive these things through the knowledge of the Lord Jesus Christ, and we receive that knowledge through the great and precious promises of the Word of God. Thank God for enough heavenly provisions to make it all the way home! We are blessed!

Those heavenly provisions in the Word of God are promised to do two things. First, they are promised to make us partakers of the divine nature, that is to make us more like Jesus. Second, they are promised to help us escape the corruption and sin that is in this old world. I am thankful that He is doing a work in me by His Word! Let's stand on the precious promises today!

Standing on the promises of Christ my King,
through eternal ages let His praises ring;
Glory in the highest I will shout and sing,
Standing on the promises of God.
Standing, Standing, Standing on the promises of God my Savior,
Standing, Standing, I'm Standing on the Promises of God. [873]

---

[873] "Standing on the Promises," R. Kelso Carter

Read 2 Peter 2:1-19

2 Peter 2:1-2 1 But there were false prophets also among the people, even as there shall be false teachers among you, who privily shall bring in damnable heresies, even denying the Lord that bought them, and bring upon themselves swift destruction. 2 And many shall follow their pernicious ways; by reason of whom the way of truth shall be evil spoken of.

Peter warns us that false teachers have been and will continue to be present among God's people. Jesus gave many similar warnings. He said that the presence of false prophets would be one of the signs of the end.[874] Peter said they would bring in their false teaching secretly (privily). That is why Jesus compared them to wolves in sheep's clothing. [875] Paul spoke of Satan and his 'apostles' masquerading as something that they are not.[876]

The false teachings they bring are called damnable heresies, things that can keep people from the truth that will make them free. False teaching denies the Lord. It does not necessarily deny that He existed, but it denies His true identity. It may deny, for example, that He is truly God come in human flesh, [877] or that He rose bodily from the grave. False teachers may be preaching "another Jesus," not the one revealed in the Word of God.[878]

1 John 4:1-3 Beloved, believe not every spirit, but try the spirits whether they are of God: because many false prophets are gone out into the world. 2 Hereby know ye the Spirit of God: Every spirit that confesseth that Jesus Christ is come in the flesh is of God: 3 And every spirit that confesseth not that Jesus Christ is come in the flesh is not of God: and this is that *spirit* of antichrist, whereof ye have heard that it should come; and even now already is it in the world.

---

[874] Matthew 24:11
[875] Matthew 7:15
[876] 2 Corinthians 11:13-15
[877] 1 John 4:3
[878] 2 Corinthians 11:4

Read 2 Peter 2:20-3:18

2 Peter 3:3-4 3 Knowing this first, that there shall come in the last days scoffers, walking after their own lusts, 4 And saying, Where is the promise of his coming? for since the fathers fell asleep, all things continue as *they were* from the beginning of the creation.

Peter warns us that scoffers will come in the last days. Because Jesus has not yet come, they will say that He is not coming. They will claim that everything has been the same from the beginning of time, and it will probably remain the same forever.

Those scoffers forget some important truths. Things haven't continued as they were from the beginning of creation. For one thing, there was a great flood that destroyed the world that was, and this present world will see a fiery judgment some day (2nd Peter 3:5-7). Scoffing at it will not stop that judgment from coming. God lives in eternity and what seems a delay is not really a delay at all. A day with Him is as a thousand years and a thousand years is as a day. (2nd Peter 3:8).

Perhaps the most important reason for what seems to be a delay in Jesus' coming is His longsuffering nature. It is not His will that anyone be lost. He is giving opportunity for people to repent and turn to Christ. We must not be numbered among the scoffers, but among those who are looking for Him.

Hebrews 9:28 So Christ was once offered to bear the sins of many; and unto them that look for him shall he appear the second time without sin unto salvation.

Read 1 John 1:1-2:12

1 John 1:9   If we confess our sins, he is faithful and just to forgive us *our* sins, and to cleanse us from all unrighteousness.

It is said that the English word "confess" comes from two words meaning to "say the same thing."   When we confess our sins, we are agreeing with what God says about them.   We are saying the same thing that He does.   As long as we are trying to whitewash our sin, or compare our sin with that of others, we cannot find the cleansing that He promises.

The Lord gives us several important truths about sin here.   First, we cannot claim to be a child of God, while continuing to walk in sin as a way of life.   He said, "If we say that we have fellowship with Him and **walk** [something habitual, a way of life] in darkness, we lie, and do not the truth."[879]   But, on the other hand, if we claim that we do not sin, then we are also self-deceived or lying, for His Word declares, "If we say that we have no sin, we deceive ourselves and the truth is not in us."[880]   But, if we will continue to walk in the light of His Word, with a repentant and contrite heart, He promises the cleansing of the blood of Jesus.   The blood not only cleanses us, but it will keep on cleansing us, as the tense of the Greek verb indicates!

1 John 1:7   But if we walk in the light, as he is in the light, we have fellowship one with another, and the blood of Jesus Christ his Son cleanseth us from all sin.

---

[879] **1 John 1:6**   If we say that we have fellowship with him, and walk in darkness, we lie, and do not the truth:
[880] **1 John 1:8**   If we say that we have no sin, we deceive ourselves, and the truth is not in us.

Read 1 John 2:13-29

1 John 2:15-17 15 Love not the world, neither the things *that are* in the world. If any man love the world, the love of the Father is not in him. 16 For all that *is* in the world, the lust of the flesh, and the lust of the eyes, and the pride of life, is not of the Father, but is of the world. 17 And the world passeth away, and the lust thereof: but he that doeth the will of God abideth forever.

What does it mean to be worldly? Different people have had different opinions in different times and in different places, and there has not always been agreement. Here, the Word of God gives us three things that are the underlying principles behind all worldly behavior. By world, we do not mean the planet, or its people, but the underlying system of evil under which it operates. In Greek it is the kosmos.

The first underlying principle of the world is the lust of the eyes. It means desiring whatever our eyes behold. It is covetousness. It is the spirit that is never content with what we have. The lust of the eyes says, "I cannot be happy without something more than what I have."

The second underlying principle of the world is the lust of the flesh. That means gratifying the desires of my flesh, regardless of the will of God. It is that attitude that says, "I will do whatever feels good to me," or, "It is my body, I can do with it whatever I please!"

The third underlying principle of the world is the pride of life. Pride was the original sin that cost Satan his place in heaven, and it is a great spiritual problem in our lives today. It is that attitude that says I am the most important thing. I will ever and always look out for number one.

The world is very strong in all three of these areas, but the Lord tells us that we can overcome its downward tug. Our victory over the world comes through continued faith in the Lord Jesus Christ!

1 John 5:4-5 4 For whatsoever is born of God overcometh the world: and this is the victory that overcometh the world, *even* our faith. 5 Who is he that overcometh the world, but he that believeth that Jesus is the Son of God?

Read 1 John 3

1 John 3:1-3 1 Behold, what manner of love the Father hath bestowed upon us, that we should be called the sons of God: therefore the world knoweth us not, because it knew him not. 2 Beloved, now are we the sons of God, and it doth not yet appear what we shall be: but we know that, when he shall appear, we shall be like him; for we shall see him as he is. 3 And every man that hath this hope in him purifieth himself, even as he is pure.

     There is some mystery about the hereafter, what lies ahead for the child of God. John even said, "it does not yet appear what we shall be." In spite of the mystery, there were some things he was sure about. The truth he shares here, is mind-boggling, but it gives us a great desire to make heaven our home.

     Someday, when He returns, we will be like Him. I know that He has saved me, and daily He is sanctifying me, making me more like Jesus. But, when He comes, I will be like Him. On that day, I will see Him as He truly is. I don't think any human being has yet seen Him like that. We will need our new bodies to experience it. While He was here on the earth, he was veiled in flesh[881]. On the Mount of Transfiguration, Peter, James, and John caught a small glimpse, but nothing near His full glory[882]. Later, when John received the revelation, he saw Him in heaven, but still only what his mortal eyes could stand[883]. Just imagine. In heaven, there will be no need for the sun or the moon, because the Lord will be the light of that place[884]. That means His glory is greater, His light is brighter, than the sun in all of its glory. In fact, if we could combine the glory of all of the suns (stars) in all of the universes, His glory would be greater still. It is no wonder that we will need a glorified body to live in the New Heaven and New Earth. These bodies could not stand what we will see, hear, and experience!

We shall see the King! We shall see the King!
We shall see the King when He comes!
He's coming in power, We'll hail the blessed hour,
We shall see the King when He comes![885]

---

[881] John 1:14
[882] Matthew 17:1-2
[883] Revelation 1
[884] Revelation 21:23
[885] "We Shall See the King," John B. Vaughan

Read 1 John 4

1 John 4:1   Beloved, believe not every spirit, but try the spirits whether they are of God: because many false prophets are gone out into the world.

The need of the hour is for discernment. Jesus warned us that there would be many false christs, false prophets, and false teachers in the last days. We are not to be gullible saints, believing everything that we hear.   We are to put everything to the test of the Word of God. The Bereans spoken of in Acts 17:11 had that kind of discerning heart. They received the ministry readily, but they still put it to the test of the Word.   This should be said of every believer. Always check out what you hear from the pulpit, from the printed page, from the Internet, this writing, or anywhere else with the Word of God. It is just as John says here, "Try the spirits."

How do we know that something is from the Holy Spirit, and not the creation of the human spirit, or worse?   As we have said, we put it to the test of the Word.   We also know that the Spirit will always glorify Jesus,[886] will proclaim Jesus as God come in the flesh,[887] and as Lord.[888]   As pertaining to the gifts of the Spirit, we are told to seek after the best gifts[889] and in light of the days that we are living in, discerning of spirits would be one that is needed.

1 Corinthians 12:8-11   8 For to one is given by the Spirit the word of wisdom; to another the word of knowledge by the same Spirit; 9   To another faith by the same Spirit; to another the gifts of healing by the same Spirit; 10 To another the working of miracles; to another prophecy; **to another discerning of spirits;** to another *divers* kinds of tongues; to another the interpretation of tongues: 11 But all these worketh that one and the selfsame Spirit, dividing to every man severally as he will.

---

[886] John 16:14
[887] 1 John 4:3
[888] 1 Corinthians 12:3
[889] 1 Corinthians 12:31

Read 1 John 5

1 John 5:13   These things have I written unto you that believe on the name of the Son of God; that ye may know that ye have eternal life, and that ye may believe on the name of the Son of God.

Once upon leaving a hospital visitation, I said to one that I considered a brother in Christ, "I will see you again, if not here, in heaven."   He was greatly offended by my statement, thinking it was the ultimate in arrogance to assume that any of us could possibly know that we were going to heaven. What says the Word of God, can we know that we are on our way to heaven?   The answer is clearly, YES!"

If you are struggling with the assurance of your salvation, 1 John is a good book to read, because it was written with this in mind, "That we might know that we have eternal life."   Romans 8 says that His Spirit bears witness with our spirit that we are the sons of God.   It is more than a feeling, it is the testimony of the Word of God and the witness of the indwelling Holy Spirit.   As to our feelings,   many years ago Martin Luther is said to have penned these words:

> "Feelings come, and feelings go,
> And feelings are deceiving;
> My warrant is the Word of God--
> Naught else is worth believing.
>
> Though all my heart should feel condemned
> For want of some sweet token,
> There is One greater than my heart
> Whose Word cannot be broken.
>
> I'll trust in God's unchanging Word
> Till soul and body sever,
> For, though all things shall pass away,
> HIS WORD SHALL STAND FOREVER!"

What a wonderful blessing not only to be saved but to have the full assurance in our hearts!

Read 2 John

2 John 1:7   For many deceivers are entered into the world, who confess not that Jesus Christ is come in the flesh. This is a deceiver and an antichrist.

False cults err in their Christology, their belief as to the identity of the Lord Jesus Christ.   There were those in John's day, and in ours too,   that deny the Jesus revealed in the New Testament.   The Jehovah's Witnesses, for example, equate Jesus with Michael the archangel, and call him "a" god (not God come in human flesh, but a god).   As bizarre as it may sound, the Mormons believe that He is a brother of Satan himself.   That is certainly not the Jesus revealed in God's Word!   Universalism teaches that Jesus Christ is just one of many ways to God, when in reality, there is only One Way (John 14:6).

What does God Himself say about beliefs like these?   Jesus said that anyone who tries to come in "another way" is a thief and a robber[890].   John says that anyone who denies that Jesus Christ is come in the flesh is a deceiver and an antichrist.   Paul made it very clear when he said that if any one preaches any other Gospel that they are accursed[891].   What you believe about Jesus is important, eternally important!

1 John 4:3   And every spirit that confesseth not that Jesus Christ is come in the flesh is not of God: and this is that *spirit* of antichrist, whereof ye have heard that it should come; and even now already is it in the world.

---

[890] John 10:1
[891] Galatians 1:6-9

Read 3 John

3 John 1:4 I have no greater joy than to hear that my children walk in truth.

What brought great joy to that great man of God, the Apostle John?   It brought him great joy to hear that his children, probably his spiritual children, those he had won to the Lord and discipled, were continuing to walk in the truth of the Gospel. It would have broken his heart to have heard otherwise.

His daily prayer for them, as he wrote the letter is found in verse 2. He said, "I wish above all things that thou mayest prosper and be in health, even as thy soul prospers."   Some have taken this as a guarantee of health and material prosperity for the child of God. We are not promised that here, but it does clearly show the heart of this man of God. Just as the Father in heaven wants what is best for His children, the man of God wants what is best for them too.

What about you? What are you praying for your children?   Are you praying that they walk in the truth?   Are you praying that their soul prospers, and they daily draw closer to the Lord?   If not, it is time to start making that *your* daily prayer.

Isaiah 54:13   And all thy children *shall be* taught of the LORD; and great *shall be* the peace of thy children.

Read Jude

Jude 1:3 Beloved, when I gave all diligence to write unto you of the common salvation, it was needful for me to write unto you, and exhort *you* that ye should earnestly contend for the faith which was once delivered unto the saints.

The short little book of Jude was written by one of the Lord's half-brothers, Jude the child of Mary and Joseph.[892]   It is a short, but powerful book, giving warnings about false teachers that had crept into the church. Their message could be so deceptive and subtle that some even seemed unaware of their presence.[893]   In light of this, God's people were to contend earnestly for the truth faith, that which had been delivered to them by the Lord and His apostles, that which we now have in the Word of God.[894]   They were to remember the truth that they had heard and they were to build themselves up spiritually by praying in the Spirit.[895] Contending for the faith is an important part of spiritual warfare.   Of course, these things are still very important, perhaps even more important, today!

The doxology[896] in Jude's final two verses gives those of us who contend for the faith great comfort and hope. Times may be difficult in the last days, and false teachers may be ever-present, but our God is able to keep us from falling. Someday, He will present us faultless before the throne.   That is why we offer Him glory, majesty, dominion, and power forever!

Jude 1:24-25 24 Now unto him that is able to keep you from falling, and to present *you* faultless before the presence of his glory with exceeding joy, 25 To the only wise God our Saviour, *be* glory and majesty, dominion and power, both now and ever. Amen.

---

[892] Mark 6:3
[893] Jude 1:4
[894] Jude 1:3
[895] Jude 1:20, 1 Corinthians 14:4
[896] "A doxology is a brief formula for expressing praise or glory to God. Doxologies generally contain two elements, an ascription of praise to God (usually referred to in third person) and an expression of His infinite nature. The term "doxology" ("word of glory") itself is not found in the Bible, but both the Old and New Testaments contain many doxological passages using this formula. Biblical doxologies are found in many contexts, but one of their chief functions seems to have been as a conclusion to songs (**Exodus 15:18**), psalms (**Psalm 146:10**), and prayers (**Matthew 6:13**), where they possibly served as group responses to solo singing or recitation. Doxologies conclude four of the five divisions of the Psalter (**Psalm 41:13** ; **Psalm 72:19** ; **Psalm 89:52** ; **Psalm 106:48**), with **Psalm 150:1** serving as a sort of doxology to the entire collection. Doxologies also occur at or near the end of several New Testament books (**Romans 16:27** ; **Philippians 4:20** ; 1 Timothy 6:16 ; 2 Timothy 4:18 ; **Hebrews 13:21** ; 1 Peter 5:11 ; 2 Peter 3:18 ; **Jude 1:25**) and figure prominently in the Revelation (**Revelation 1:6** ; **Revelation 4:8** ; **Revelation 5:13** ; **Revelation 7:12**)," Holman Bible Dictionary

Read Revelation1:1-19

Revelation 1:1 The Revelation of Jesus Christ, which God gave unto him, to shew unto his servants things which must shortly come to pass; and he sent and signified *it* by his angel unto his servant John:

In verse 1 we find the title for the book, "The Revelation of Jesus Christ."   Revelation is the English translation of a Greek word which means revealing or unveiling.   It is not Revelations (with an s), but the Revelation (singular) of a Person, the Lord Jesus Christ. As we make our way through this book, a book that many find intimidating, we will find that the central character is always Jesus.   It is about Him. Later we will find that the "testimony of Jesus is the spirit of prophecy."[897] It is not about the end times, the great tribulation, or the antichrist, though we will learn about those important truths. It is about Jesus Christ, the King of kings and the Lord of lords!

If you will look for Him, you will find Him revealed in every chapter. We are given specific promises regarding this book. As you read the book of Revelation in the days ahead, expect a blessing! As you hear these words once again, expect a blessing! As you seek to obey what the Lord is speaking here, expect a blessing! We may not yet have full understanding of every minute detail, but we can expect a blessing from reading, hearing, and obeying.

Revelation 1:3 Blessed *is* he that readeth, and they that hear the words of this prophecy, and keep those things which are written therein: for the time *is* at hand.

---

[897] Revelation 19:10

Read Revelation 1:20-2:17

Revelation 1:20 The mystery of the seven stars which thou sawest in my right hand, and the seven golden candlesticks. The seven stars are the angels of the seven churches: and the seven candlesticks which thou sawest are the seven churches.

Often when we find something that seems mysterious in the Word of God, it will be explained if we keep reading. We must always look at the context when reading a portion of Scripture! That is the case with the seven stars and seven golden candlesticks that John saw in his vision.[898] In the New Testament a mystery is something that was once unknown, but has now been revealed, and the Lord reveals the identity of these mysterious symbols here in Revelation 1:20.

The seven candlesticks or lampstands that John saw represented seven local churches. A church is like a lamp, because it is meant to shine light in a dark place. Jesus told us that we are to be like lights in this dark world. Anything that lessens that light is sin. Notice that Jesus walks in the middle of those candlesticks. He is aware of every detail of what happens in every one of His local churches.[899] It is His will that the light shine from every believer and every church.

The stars in Jesus' right hand are the angels of the seven churches. This could be a couple of things. First, it is possible that every church has *an* angel, a guardian if you will, assigned to oversee and protect it.   Also, we realize that the word angel here (angelos) is also the word for messenger. It could be that these "angels" are the pastors of the local churches, those messengers who faithfully bring the Word of God to His people. In either case, it is a great comfort to know that the stars are in His right hand. *He* is responsible for that which He holds!   That, my friend, is a wonderful blessing.

Matthew 5:14-16   14 Ye are the light of the world. A city that is set on an hill cannot be hid. 15 Neither do men light a candle, and put it under a bushel, but on a candlestick; and it giveth light unto all that are in the house. 16 Let your light so shine before men, that they may see your good works, and glorify your Father which is in heaven.

---

[898] Revelation 1:12-17
[899] Revelation 1:13, Revelation 2:1, 5.

Read Revelation 2:18-3:6

Revelation 2:18 And unto the angel of the church in Thyatira write; These things saith the Son of God, who hath his eyes like unto a flame of fire, and his feet *are* like fine brass;

Jesus is described here as the Son of God, the One with feet like brass and eyes like flames of fire.   This is the first time we have seen Him described this way in Revelation,[900] but it will *not* be the last.[901] Eyes of fire indicate that nothing escapes His notice. When we stand before Him at the Judgment Seat of Christ, the nature of our works will be revealed by fire[902].   Perhaps, it will take only one look from His penetrating gaze to reveal all that is in our hearts. In the next verse[903] He tells them that He "knows their works," probably by virtue of those fiery eyes!

Feet like fine brass can indicate several things. It was like *fine* (pure) brass, having come through the fire, emphasizing His holiness. Brass represented strength and power to many in the ancient world, emphasizing His Omnipotence.   He is All Powerful!   Brass can also symbolize judgment, emphasizing that all will stand before Him[904].   His feet were moving toward judgment, but in His mercy, He gave them an opportunity to repent.[905]

Let us never forget that one day we will stand before the Son of God, the One who is holy, the One who is All Powerful.

Hebrews 9:27 And as it is appointed unto men once to die, but after this the judgment:

---

[900] Revelation 1:14
[901] Revelation 19:12
[902] 1 Corinthians 3:13
[903] Revelation 2:19
[904] 2 Corinthians 5:10
[905] Revelation 2:21-22

Read Revelation 3:7-22

Revelation 3:20 Behold, I stand at the door, and knock: if any man hear my voice, and open the door, I will come in to him, and will sup with him, and he with me.

This verse has often been used like this to speak to the unsaved, "Christ is knocking at the door of your hearts, and you must let Him in." Of course, it is true, that we must personally respond to His offer of salvation, but this verse was not written to those in the world, but to those 'sitting' in a local church.

The Church at Laodicea was the last church to which Jesus wrote in the Book of Revelation. Though it was written to an actual local church in the first century[906], it certainly brings a timely message for the church today. Jesus said that they were lukewarm, neither cold nor hot. In other words, their spiritual condition was sickening. They had great material resources. Their 'testimony' was, "We are rich and increased with goods and have need of nothing." Yet Jesus' assessment of their *spiritual* condition was not so positive. He said, "You are wretched, and miserable, and poor, and blind, and naked." They said, "everything is OK." Jesus said, "Everything is NOT Ok!" He was left standing outside the church, knocking, and unheard. However, those who would hear, and open their lives to Him, could still be overcomers, and ultimately rule and reign with Jesus Christ. What about you? Do you hear Him knocking?

Revelation 3:21-22 21 To him that overcometh will I grant to sit with me in my throne, even as I also overcame, and am set down with my Father in his throne. 22 He that hath an ear, let him hear what the Spirit saith unto the churches.

---

[906] Laodicea was in Asia Minor, what is now modern-day Turkey.

Read Revelation 4

Revelation 4:1   After this I looked, and, behold, a door *was* opened in heaven: and the first voice which I heard *was* as it were of a trumpet talking with me; which said, Come up hither, and I will shew thee things which must be hereafter.

This begins the largest of the three major sections in the Book of Revelation[907]. First, John was told to write the things that he had **seen**-- the vision of Christ in Revelation 1.   Second, he was to write of the things which **are**, the messages to the seven local churches in Revelation 2-3.   Third, he was to write of those things which shall be **hereafter**, prophetic things that did not even happen in His lifetime, things that we are still anticipating. That section begins here with Revelation 4 and continues to the end of the Book.

As John is caught up to heaven, many see a picture of what will happen to the church at the time of the Rapture.[908]   If that is so, this trumpet is the same as the one in 1 Corinthians 15 and 1 Thessalonians 4, "Behold, I show you a mystery; we shall not all sleep, but we shall be changed. In a moment, in the twinkling of an eye, at the last trump: for the trumpet shall sound, and the dead shall be raised incorruptible, and we shall be changed....The Lord Himself will descend from heaven with a shout, with the voice of the archangel, and with the trump of God: and the dead in Christ shall rise first.   Then we which are alive and remain shall be caught up together with them in the clouds, to meet the Lord in the air: and so shall we ever be with the Lord."[909]

It is interesting to note that for the remainder of Revelation, until the Lord returns in power and glory,[910] the church is always depicted in heaven while the horrors of the Great Tribulation are taking place on earth.

We know that the trumpet will sound. It could be today.
The question of the hour is this, "Are you ready?"

---

[907] Revelation 1:19
[908] Some do not like the word Rapture, because the word does not appear in the English New Testament.   However, there are other good descriptions such as translation, resurrection, and "catching away!"
[909] 1 Thessalonians 4:16-17
[910] Revelation 19:11-16

Read Revelation 5

Revelation 5:4-5 4 And I wept much, because no man was found worthy to open and to read the book, neither to look thereon. 5 And one of the elders saith unto me, Weep not: behold, the Lion of the tribe of Juda, the Root of David, hath prevailed to open the book, and to loose the seven seals thereof.

Upon being transported to heaven, John finds himself in the throne room! The Lord is holding a scroll in His hand. It is *completely* sealed, seven times over. There are several theories as to the identity of that scroll, but they can be summarized by something found in one of the old commentaries, "The best solution is to see the scroll as 'God's will, His final settlement of the affairs of the universe." This is based on the idea that customarily, under Roman law, wills were sealed with seven seals, each from a witness to the validity of that will."[911] We do know that as those seals are opened, tremendous, and horrifying things will begin to happen on the earth, a witness against a world that has rejected its Creator. As horrible as they seem when we read about them, we know that it is all necessary to bring about God's final plan for a New Heaven and a New Earth wherein dwells righteousness. Since no one, but the Lord, can open that sealed book, we know that He is the only one that bring about that plan.

Stay "tuned" as we make our way through Revelation. We will see what happens as those seals are opened! Meanwhile, even in the difficult chapters, remember there is a blessing for you in this book.

Revelation 1:3 Blessed *is* he that readeth, and they that hear the words of this prophecy, and keep those things which are written therein: for the time *is* at hand.

---

[911] <u>Enduring Word Commentary</u>, David Guzik, quoting William Barclay's <u>Commentary on Revelation.</u>

Read Revelation 6

Revelation 6:16-17 16 And said to the mountains and rocks, fall on us, and hide us from the face of him that sitteth on the throne, and from the wrath of the Lamb: 17 For the great day of his wrath is come; and who shall be able to stand?

As the Lord begins to open the sealed book, judgment begins to pour out on an unrepentant world. The first four seals/judgments are sometimes called the "Four Horsemen of the Apocalypse."   The first, a white horse, speaks of the rise of an imposter, the Antichrist. The second, a red horse, takes peace from the earth.   The third, a black horse, brings devastating famine.   The fourth, a pale[912] horse, brings more death of various kinds. The world system has rejected God, and persecuted His people. As these judgments are coming upon the world, some of those who have been killed by that system are crying out from heaven, "How long until God avenges us?"   Some of what we will see in Revelation is the Lord doing that very thing, avenging His people.

The opening of the sixth seal brings even more terrifying judgments, and one would think the result would be widespread repentance, but that is not the case.   Here we find what has been called a sorrowful prayer meeting. The unrepentant are crying out to the rocks and mountains to hide them, rather than crying out to the Lord, the Rock of Ages. They have a question, "Who shall be able to stand?"   The answer is clear, the only way any of us can stand is in His grace and mercy[913] and the only hiding place is in Him.[914]   In light of this, my prayer today comes from the words of Thomas Hastings' old hymn, "Rock of Ages."

Rock of Ages, cleft for me,
Let me hide myself in Thee;
Let the water and the blood,
From Thy riven side which flowed,
Be of sin the double cure,
Cleanse from guilt, and make me pure.

---

[912] The Greek word is chloros (think chlorophyll), the horse is actually a sickly green!
[913] Romans 5:1-2
[914] Psalm 32:7

Read Revelation 7

Revelation 7:3 Saying, hurt not the earth, neither the sea, nor the trees, till we have sealed the servants of our God in their foreheads.

We saw the sorrowful prayer meeting in chapter 6[915]; an unrepentant world trying to hide from God's wrath. They will cry out, asking, "The great day of His wrath is come; and who shall be able to stand?" The answer to their question comes in Chapter 7, where the Lord speaks of some who will be able to stand in that horrible time called the Great Tribulation.

First, there will be a group of 144,000 Jews, 12,000 from each of the twelve tribes of Israel who will have come to faith in Jesus Christ as Lord, Savior, and Messiah. They will have been sealed by God. It is interesting to note that God says all believers have been sealed by the Holy Spirit.[916]

There will also be many others saved during the Great Tribulation. They are described here as a "great multitude which no man could number of all nations, and kindreds, and people, and tongues,"[917] and as those who have come out of great tribulation and been cleansed by the blood of Jesus Christ.[918] They will have come out of earth's most difficult time, and it is believed that their decision for Christ, most likely, will have cost them their lives.

They will never again face the horrors they endured on earth. The tribulation will be a time of devastating famine,[919] but in His presence they will never hunger again! During the tribulation, the water will be made undrinkable[920], but now they will never thirst again! The tribulation will mean the sun scorching the earth, and those on it[921], but they will never face that scorching heat again! They will have come from a time of great sorrow, but will never again know tears! Most wonderful of all, the Lord Himself will dwell among them, and they will serve Him!

> Soon and very soon, we are going to see the King!
> Soon and very soon, we are going to see the King!
> Soon and very soon, we are going to see the King!
> Hallelujah, Hallelujah, we're going to see the King![922]

---

[915] See the entry for Revelation 6.
[916] 2 Corinthians 1:22, Ephesians 1:13, Ephesians 4:30
[917] Revelation 7:9
[918] Revelation 7:14
[919] Revelation 6:5-6
[920] Revelation 8:10-11, Revelation 11:6, Revelation 16:4-5
[921] Revelation 16:8
[922] "Soon and Very Soon," Andrae Crouch

Read Revelation 8

Revelation 8:1 And when he had opened the seventh seal, there was silence in heaven about the space of half an hour.

Heaven is rarely depicted as a quiet place, but here we find total silence in heaven for a half an hour.   We are not told the reason for the silence, but it seems likely it is a holy hush anticipating the severity of the judgments that are about to come on the world when the seventh seal is opened.   Within that seventh seal are the next round of judgments that will come on the earth.   Those judgments, the seven trumpet judgments, are even more disastrous than the seal judgments of the preceding chapters.   We also see in this chapter that these judgments are linked in some way with the prayers of God's people. Perhaps the judgements are helping to bring about the answer to the prayer prayed by Christians for 2,000 years, "Thy Kingdom Come!"
     Four angels sound their trumpets, and great judgment follows. But, what *will* come from the final three trumpet judgments will be even worse.[923]   When those judgments are falling on earth, I plan on being with my Savior, sheltered in the arms of God.   I hope you are planning to be there too!

Soon I shall hear the call from Heaven's portals,
Come home my child, it's the last mile you must trod,
I'll fall asleep and wake in God's sweet heaven,
For I'm sheltered in the arms of God.
So, let the storm rage high, the dark clouds rise,
They don't worry me:
For I'm sheltered safe within the arms of God.
He walks with me, and naught of earth shall harm me,
For I'm sheltered in the arms of God.[924]

---

[923] Revelation 8:13
[924] "Sheltered in the Arms of God," Dottie Rambo

Read Revelation 9

Revelation 9:20-21 And the rest of the men which were not killed by these plagues yet repented not of the works of their hands, that they should not worship devils, and idols of gold, and silver, and brass, and stone, and of wood: which neither can see, nor hear, nor walk: Neither repented they of their murders, nor of their sorceries, nor of their fornication, nor of their thefts.

Revelation 9 speaks of the continuation of the trumpet judgments that we read about in chapter 8. With the sounding of the fifth trumpet, demonic beings, like locusts, will be released on the earth. Their sting will be so painful that those who have been stung will long for the relief of death, but death will not come. The sounding of the sixth trumpet will bring the release of four more supernatural beings, beings responsible for the death of 1/3 of the remaining population on earth.

One would think such judgments would have people all over the world on their knees in repentance, but that will not be the case. Those who survive these judgements will not repent, but will continue in their sin, sealing their own fate. How wonderful to be living in this day of opportunity, the day of salvation, a day when we can call on Him and be saved from the wrath that is to come.

1 Thessalonians 1:10 And to wait for his Son from heaven, whom he raised from the dead, *even* Jesus, which delivered us from the wrath to come.

Read Revelation 10:1-11:7

Revelation 10:3-4 3 And cried with a loud voice, as *when* a lion roareth: and when he had cried, seven thunders uttered their voices. 4 And when the seven thunders had uttered their voices, I was about to write: and I heard a voice from heaven saying unto me, seal up those things which the seven thunders uttered, and write them not.

What are these seven thunders? Thunder was one of the manifestations of God's presence atop Mount Sinai when Moses received the Law.[925] I am reminded of the words of Job 37:5, "God thunders marvelously with His voice; great things doeth He, which we cannot comprehend." The seven thunders of Revelation remain a mystery, one of those things which we cannot yet comprehend. Daniel was told that some of the things *he* received would be "sealed up" until the time of the end.[926] We certainly do not know it all!

God does indeed have secret things, which He has not seen fit to reveal to us. Some of those things may be revealed to us in the future, but until then we know that He has revealed all that we need to make it to our eternal home in victory. He has given us, through His Word, all that we need for life and godliness[927]. Someone once said, "It is not the parts of the Bible that I can't understand that bother me, it's the parts that I do understand!" Until we know more, we must walk in what we do know.

Deuteronomy 29:29 The secret *things belong* unto the LORD our God: but those *things which are* revealed *belong* unto us and to our children forever, that *we* may do all the words of this law.

---

[925] Exodus 20:18
[926] Daniel 12:9
[927] 2 Peter 1:3-4

Read Revelation 11.8-12.6

Revelation 12:1 And there appeared a great wonder in heaven; a woman clothed with the sun, and the moon under her feet, and upon her head a crown of twelve stars:

In general, the Scriptures should be taken literally. However, there are symbols in the Word of God. When they are used, the Lord will reveal the meaning of those symbols elsewhere in the Scriptures. For example, we know that the woman clothed with the sun in this chapter is the nation of Israel, based on Joseph's dream in Genesis 37:9-11. The child that she bears is Jesus, the One who will rule the nations with a rod of iron.[928] And of course, the great red dragon is none other than Satan himself.

Without going into great detail, which we cannot do in a writing of this length, we can see some basic principles. From the beginning, Satan has known that a human child (the seed of the woman) would "bruise his head," that is, bring his final judgment! That knowledge goes all the way back to the first prophetic word spoken in Scripture— Genesis 3:15. From that moment Satan wanted to destroy the Child, the Seed of the Woman, before He was born. That is why we see so many attempts at the destruction of the Jews. Pharaoh tried to destroy them. Haman tried to destroy them. The pagan people around them tried to destroy them. Sin and idolatry nearly destroyed them. These things were attempts by the one called the great red dragon to destroy the Jews. But, the Lord still has a plan for Israel, most of all that they find salvation in the Prince of Peace. Pray much for Israel!

Psalm 122:6-9 6 Pray for the peace of Jerusalem: they shall prosper that love thee. 7 Peace be within thy walls, *and* prosperity within thy palaces. 8 For my brethren and companions' sakes, I will now say, Peace *be* within thee. 9 Because of the house of the LORD our God I will seek thy good.

---

[928] Revelation 12:5

Read Revelation 12:7-18

Revelation 12:11 And they overcame him by the blood of the Lamb, and by the word of their testimony; and they loved not their lives unto the death.

In these verses, we see that the devil will be cast down to earth, apparently no longer having access to heaven.   He will be very angry, knowing that his time is short. Even now, his demonic minions know that their judgment is coming.   Once, some evil spirits feared that Jesus had come to torment them "before the time.[929]" They knew that their "time" was coming.   The Lord reminds us here, though, that His people can be overcomers even in that time of Satan's last angry throes.

Satan has been the accuser of God's people, but His accusations can be overcome by the blood of the Lord Jesus Christ.   Through the blood of Jesus, our troubled conscience can be purified and cleansed.[930]   He can also be overcome by the word of our testimony.   Testimony is a translation of the Greek word *marturia*, the same word that is translated witnesses in Acts 1:8, "You shall receive power after that the Holy Ghost is come upon you, and you shall be witnesses (marturia) unto me."   You may notice a similarity to our English word martyr, which is also derived from that word. It means one who remains faithful to the end. Notice that Revelation 12 says they "loved not their lives *unto the death*." This is only possible through the power of the Holy Spirit.

Through the wonderful cleansing of the blood of Jesus and the empowering of the Holy Spirit, we are enabled to live victorious lives, not just now, but until Jesus calls us home.

Revelation 2:10 Fear none of those things which thou shalt suffer: behold, the devil shall cast *some* of you into prison, that ye may be tried; and ye shall have tribulation ten days: ***be thou faithful unto death,*** and I will give thee a crown of life.

---

[929] Matthew 8:29
[930] Hebrews 9:14

Read Revelation 13

Revelation 13:1 And I stood upon the sand of the sea, and saw a beast rise up out of the sea, having seven heads and ten horns, and upon his horns ten crowns, and upon his heads the name of blasphemy.

Most of what John has seen so far about future events has centered on what will be happening in heaven. In chapter 13, the scene changes to what will be happening simultaneously on earth. The final evil world dictator will come to power. The Word of God gives him several names and titles, such as Antichrist and the Man of Sin, but here he is, very fittingly, called The Beast.

His empire will have characteristics of other great empires of the past. What John saw can be compared with a vision in Daniel 7, where coming world empires were likened to vicious animals. His kingdom will be like a composite of those previous kingdoms (Babylon, Persia, Greece, Rome, etc.). Someone once said, "This final world empire will have the catlike vigilance of a **leopard**, the slow and crushing power of a **bear**, and the authority and ferociousness of a **lion**."[931] His power, seat (literally throne) and authority are given to him by the dragon, Satan himself, presently called the "god of this world."[932] An unrepentant world will hold him up as a god, worshiping him, which , in effect, is the worship of Satan himself.[933] That evil man will, one day, be revealed. However, I, for one, am not looking for the coming of the Antichrist, I am looking for the coming of the Lord Jesus Christ, and He could come at any moment!

Hebrews 9:28 So Christ was once offered to bear the sins of many; and unto them that look for him shall he appear the second time without sin unto salvation.

---

[931] <u>Enduring Word Commentary</u>, David Guzik
[932] 2 Corinthians 4:4
[933] Revelation 13:4, 8. That worship is encouraged by his second in command, one called the beast from the earth (Revelation 13:12ff) and the False Prophet (Revelation 16:13, Revelation 19:20, Revelation 20:10). His economy will involve some kind of marking system, without which it will be impossible to buy or sell (Revelation 13:16-18).

Read Revelation 14

Revelation 14:6 And I saw another angel fly in the midst of heaven, having the everlasting gospel to preach unto them that dwell on the earth, and to every nation, and kindred, and tongue, and people,

Revelation 14 speaks of three heavenly messengers that will be sent to earth during that horrible time called the Great Tribulation. Our English word "angel" comes from the Greek word "angelos" which means messenger. Three *messengers* will be sent to earth with important communication from heaven.

The first messenger angel[934] flies above the earth proclaiming the Gospel. While the false prophet is encouraging worship of the beast,[935] this angel will call the people to repentance. The Gospel message will go out to every nation, kindred, and tongue, being a final opportunity, and a fulfillment of Jesus' words in Matthew 24:14, "This Gospel of the Kingdom shall be preached in all the world for a witness unto all nations; and then shall the end come." The message of this angel? Judgment is coming! Turn from false worship and worship the Creator[936]!

---

[934] Revelation 14:6-7
[935] See Revelation 13 for more information.
[936] Revelation 14:6-7

The second messenger angel[937] announces the fall of Babylon. Sometimes Babylon speaks of the actual city. Often, though, it speaks of a world system, a system of false worship and idolatry that has its roots in ancient Babylon. Babylon is the birthplace of rebellion against God. The fall of that system will be seen later in Revelation. The message of this angel? Come out of Babylon; judgment is coming![938]

The third messenger angel[939] makes a powerful announcement. If people worship the Beast (the Antichrist) and receive his mark[940], they will be eternally lost, never having rest ever again. In stark contrast to the unrepentant, those who die in the Lord will "*rest* from *their* labors."[941] The message of this angel? Do not take the mark. Do not worship the Beast. Repent, and turn to the only One who can give you rest![942] What a blessing to know that right now, we can find spiritual rest in Him!

Matthew 11:28-30 28 Come unto me, all *ye* that labour and are heavy laden, and I will give you rest. 29 Take my yoke upon you, and learn of me; for I am meek and lowly in heart: and ye shall find rest unto your souls. 30 For my yoke *is* easy, and my burden is light.

---

[937] Revelation 14:8
[938] 2 Corinthians 6:17
[939] Revelation 14:9-12
[940] This is sometimes called the Mark of the Beast. Revelation 13 tells us that commerce will not be possible without the mark.
[941] Revelation 14:13
[942] Matthew 11:28

Read Revelation 14:14-15:8

Revelation 15:3 And they sing the song of Moses the servant of God, and the song of the Lamb, saying, Great and marvelous *are* thy works, Lord God Almighty; just and true *are* thy ways, thou King of saints.

There will be those who turn to the Lord during the Great Tribulation. They are described in Revelation 7:9 as a "great multitude, which no man could number, of all nations, and kindreds, and people, and tongues[943]." They will be killed for their faith, because they will not worship the antichrist, nor take his mark.[944]   Now, John sees them in heaven worshipping the Lord.

Heaven is a place of glorious singing and rejoicing. These "tribulation saints" will be no exception.   The natural response of leaving earth and arriving in heaven will be to rejoice and sing.   It says that they will sing the song of Moses and the Lamb (Jesus).   This is probably only one song, called by both names.   Moses (the Old Covenant) looked forward in faith to the cross and the coming of Jesus, the Lamb of God.   In Jesus (the New Covenant) we look to the cross as a finished work.   It would seem that we will glory in the cross throughout all of eternity!

I boast not of works nor tell of good deeds
For not have I done to merit His grace
All glory and praise shall rest upon Him
So willing to die in my place

My trophies and crowns, my robe stained with sin
Was all that I had to lay at His feet
Unworthy to eat at the table of life
Till love made provision for me

I will glory in the cross, in the cross
Lest His suffering all be in vain
I will weep no more for the cross that He bore
I will glory in the cross.[945]

---

[943] See Revelation 7 for more information.
[944] Revelation 15:2
[945] "I Will Glory in the Cross," Dottie Rambo

Read Revelation 16

Revelation 16:1   And I heard a great voice out of the temple saying to the seven angels, Go your ways, and pour out the vials of the wrath of God upon the earth.

Revelation 16 begins the final series of judgments in Revelation. First, there were the seven seals, then seven trumpets, and finally seven bowls or vials of judgment will be poured out on the earth. These are the most severe of all the judgments.

The first bowl or vial will cause painful sores on those who worshipped the antichrist and had taken his mark.   The second will turn the ocean water into something as disgusting and vile as the blood of a dead man, killing every living thing in the ocean.   The third will produce a similar effect in the fresh water supply.   The fourth will cause the sun to bear down on the earth with a scorching heat, while an unrepentant world continues to blaspheme God. The fifth brings darkness and pain, but still no repentance. The sixth will dry up the Euphrates River preparing the way for the Kings of the East some of the nations that will come against Israel at the Battle of Armageddon.   The seventh will bring terrifying earthquakes, and hailstorms with stones weighing as much as one hundred pounds!

Interspersed in these horrible judgments we find a word from the Lord Himself, a word that we *all* need to hear.

Revelation 16:15   Behold, I come as a thief. Blessed *is* he that watcheth, and keepeth his garments, lest he walk naked, and they see his shame.

Read Revelation 17

Revelation 17:5   And upon her forehead *was* a name written, MYSTERY, BABYLON THE GREAT, THE MOTHER OF HARLOTS AND ABOMINATIONS OF THE EARTH.

Revelation 17-18 speaks of the fall of Babylon, something which has already been predicted in the Book of Revelation.[946]   Babylon is mentioned over two hundred eighty-six times in the Bible, more than any other city besides Jerusalem[947].   Sometimes it speaks of the literal city in what is now modern-day Iraq, or it sometimes represents a false religious or political system.   Many occult and ungodly religious practices had their origin in ancient Babylon.   It is believed that under the Antichrist there may be one massive (and false) world religion.   We see the signs of that today as the claim is made that all religions "worship the same god," or that "all roads lead to God"[948].   Others believe Babylon may "symbolize the entire world system which opposes God."[949]   Perhaps there is an element of each, because we know that the ungodly world system has both religious and political elements, all of which will one day fall to God's judgment!

The Babylonian system is described here as a scarlet woman, a prostitute, that has plied her trade over all of the world.   She is the source of idolatry, wickedness, and abomination of every kind.   Over the generations she has been responsible for the deaths of untold Christian martyrs.[950]   She is described as riding a beast with seven heads and ten horns, showing her close association with Satan himself.[951]   That system is actually what "pulls the strings" politically all over the world.[952]   Born again believers are not a part of that system.   Scripturally, salvation is seen as a deliverance from the ungodly kingdom of darkness and a translation into God's kingdom of light.   If you are a believer, rejoice in your heavenly citizenship today!

Colossians 1:12-14 12 Giving thanks unto the Father, which hath made us meet to be partakers of the inheritance of the saints in light: 13 Who hath **delivered** us from the power of darkness, and hath **translated** *us* into the kingdom of his dear Son: 14 In whom we have redemption through his blood, *even* the forgiveness of sins:

---

[946] Revelation 14:8, 16:19
[947] If you are curious, Jerusalem appears 811 times in the Word of God.
[948] This is the false doctrine of Universalism, the idea that all roads to lead to heaven.   Jesus, on the other hand said that there is but one way to heaven (John 14:6)!
[949] The Complete Biblical Library, Revelation Commentary, Stanley Horton. Springfield, Missouri.
[950] Revelation 17:6
[951] Revelation 12:3
[952] Revelation 17:18

Read Revelation 18:1-18

Revelation 18:2   And he cried mightily with a strong voice, saying, Babylon the great is fallen, is fallen, and is become the habitation of devils, and the hold of every foul spirit, and a cage of every unclean and hateful bird.

Here we continue with God's description of the destruction of the religious, political, and economic system called Babylon.[953]   Revelation 17 seems to speak of the religious element of that ungodly system, while Revelation *18* speaks of its political and economic nature.   Many have become wealthy through this false system,[954] and the governments of the world have benefited from it.[955]   We see frequent mention of merchants and merchandise here in Revelation 18.   The evil world system, called Babylon, certainly has its tentacles in the world economy.   God reminds us that in one hour, that system that has made many rich will come crashing down to the ground[956].   How wonderful to already be living in God's economy, laying up treasure in heaven![957] When what this world trusts in comes crashing down, I want to be standing on Christ, the Solid Rock!

My hope is built on nothing less than Jesus' blood and righteousness,
I dare not trust the sweetest frame, but wholly lean on Jesus' Name.
On Christ the Solid Rock, I stand, all other ground is sinking sand,   All other ground is sinking sand[958].

---

[953] If you did not read the writing on Revelation 17, it would be very helpful to read it first.
[954] Revelation 18:3
[955] Revelation 18:9
[956] Revelation 18:10
[957] Matthew 6:19-21
[958] "The Solid Rock," Edward Mote.

Read Revelation 18.19-19.10

Revelation 19:10   And I fell at his feet to worship him. And he said unto me, See *thou do it* not: I am thy fellowservant, and of thy brethren that have the testimony of Jesus: worship God: for the testimony of Jesus is the spirit of prophecy.

God's holy angels must be gloriously beautiful. This one was so magnificent that John was tempted to bow down and worship him. If the creation is that amazing, just imagine what a glimpse of the Creator will mean! It staggers the imagination to think about it! Angels, like human beings, are mere servants of God.   God alone is worthy of worship!

Amazing things have been happening in this chapter. Heaven is rejoicing at the fall of Babylon, and preparation is being made for the Marriage Supper of the Lamb!   In the midst of these things, this unnamed angel gives us an important principle for interpreting Bible prophecy, "The testimony of Jesus is the spirit of prophecy."   What does this mean?   Stanley Horton once said, "This means that the purpose of prophecy is to bear witness to Jesus, to exalt Him, and to reveal His redemptive work."[959] If we are "rightly dividing" the Word of God, it will always point us to the Savior.

Turn your eyes upon Jesus, look full in His wonderful face, and the things of earth shall grow strangely dim, in the light of His glory and grace.[960]

---

[959] The Complete Biblical Library, Revelation, Stanley M. Horton.
[960] "Turn Your Eyes Upon Jesus," Helen Howarth Lemmel.

Read Revelation 19.11-20.10

Revelation 19:11   And I saw heaven opened, and behold a white horse; and he that sat upon him *was* called Faithful and True, and in righteousness he doth judge and make war.

The return of Jesus Christ in power and glory is certainly a high point in the Book of Revelation. Earlier, He had come **for** His church, an event called the Rapture, Translation, or Resurrection. Now, He is returning to earth **with** His church.   The mounted armies of heaven riding with Him are the saints of all the ages, those who will rule and reign with Him upon the earth! I plan on being a part of that number, and I hope that you do too!

He will set His feet down on the Mount of Olives, the exact spot from which He ascended to Heaven.[961] He will come as the true and righteous Judge and He will come to 'make war,' making short work of the beast (the antichrist), the false prophet, and all those who had participated in their sin and rebellion.[962] He will dispatch an angel to bind Satan and cast him into the bottomless pit for a thousand years,[963] and those of us who return *with* Him, those who participated in the first resurrection (the rapture) will rule and reign with King Jesus for a thousand years![964] Do you remember this old Gospel hymn?

> Then the sin and sorrow, pain and death
> Of this dark world shall cease,
> In a glorious reign with Jesus
> Of a thousand years of peace.
> All the earth is groaning, crying
> For that day of sweet release,
> For our Jesus shall come back to earth again.
> Oh, our Lord is coming back to earth again.
> Yes, our Lord is coming back to earth again.
> Satan will be bound a thousand years;
> We'll have no tempter then,
> After Jesus shall come back to earth again.[965]

---

[961] Acts 1:9-11, Zechariah 14:1-4
[962] Revelation 19:20-21
[963] Revelation 20:1-4
[964] Revelation 20:6
[965] "Our Lord's Return to Earth Again," James M. Kirk

Read Revelation 20.11-21.18

Revelation 21:16   And the city lieth foursquare, and the length is as large as the breadth: and he measured the city with the reed, twelve thousand furlongs. The length and the breadth and the height of it are equal.

Revelation 21 begins to describe our eternal home, the New Heaven and New Earth with the beautiful capital city of New Jerusalem.   It is an enormous city, 12,000 furlongs in each direction, the equivalent of fourteen or fifteen hundred miles.   The city walls are over 200 feet high!   They are not needed for protection, though; there will be no need for that.   Those who live there will dwell in safety. Day or night, there will be no need to shut the twelve "pearly" gates.   The city is illuminated by the One whose face outshines the sun in its glory, the Lord Jesus Christ.

As we read about the glories of "Home" we must realize that John's earthly language could not do it justice. It is far more glorious than human speech can describe. There surely must be sights, sounds, scents, and even tastes that we could not experience without having our new glorified bodies.   The glories of the Savior and Home will not be exhausted in a million eternities!   I love the words of a song a dear evangelist friend, Danny Corey (now already home in heaven!) used to sing.

VERSE 1:
Somewhere beyond the grave, there is a land,
Where Jesus went to prepare, by his own hand,
And for the saved by grace, there is a resting place,
And in a few more days it will be mine.

CHORUS:
Some call it heaven, I call it home,
Some call it dreamin', let me dream on,
Some call it paradise, somewhere beyond the skies,
Some call it heaven, I call it home.

VERSE 2:
Someone said you can't go, back home again,
Things will never be as good as they've been,
I've got good news for you, when heaven comes into view,
One glimpse and you'll know, the best is yet to come.[966]

---

[966] "I Call it Home," Squire Parsons.

Read Revelation 21.9-22.5

Revelation 22:3 And there shall be no more curse: but the throne of God and of the Lamb shall be in it; and his servants shall serve him:

How wonderful to live in a world with nothing remaining from the curse of sin! We join all of creation in literally groaning as we await that day.[967] Sin brought separation from God; cherubim now guard the way to the tree of life.[968] Adam and Eve's fulfilling work of tending and keeping the garden, has become drudgery by the sweat of our brow[969]. In our eternal home, all of that will be forever changed. There shall be no more curse!

No more separation from God; we will have access to His throne. We have all seen the cartoon versions of heaven, white robed beings sitting on clouds idly strumming their harps. Reality will be far removed from that. Adam and Eve were not idle **before** the curse[970], and we will not be idle **after** it has been removed. We will serve Him! All that that means remains to be seen, but I am looking forward to finding out! What about you?

Let's let the word of this song be our prayer today. I want to serve Him now and forever!

I will serve Thee because I love Thee
You have given life to me.
I was nothing before You found me,
You have given life to me.
Heartaches, broken pieces,
Ruined lives are why You died on Calvary.
Your touch was what I longed for,
You have given life to me.[971]

---

[967] Romans 8:21-23
[968] Genesis 3:24
[969] Genesis 3:17-19
[970] Genesis 2:15
[971] "I Will Serve Thee," Bill and Gloria Gaither

Read Revelation 22:6-21

Revelation 22:21   The grace of our Lord Jesus Christ *be* with you all. Amen.

      Revelation 22 contains several "last things" in the Word of God. The final invitation is a call to *come* to the Water of Life and drink freely. When one drinks deeply of that water, he need never thirst again![972] The final promise is from the Lord Himself, "Surely, I come quickly!" With each passing moment, we are closer to that day. The final prayer also concerns His coming, "Even so, COME, Lord Jesus!" That is our Blessed Hope![973]

      It is interesting that the last verse in the Old Testament speaks of the real possibility of God "smiting the earth with a curse,"[974] while the final verse in the New Testament speaks of the wonderful grace of our Lord Jesus Christ!   The Old speaks of the curse begun, and the results of that curse, while the New speaks of Christ removing the curse forever[975].

      I'm glad that God has the "last word"[976]" a word of grace!   Praise Him today, and forever, for amazing grace!

Verse One[977]
Amazing Grace! How sweet the sound!
That saved a wretch like me!
I once was lost, but now am found;
Was blind but now I see.

---

[972] John 4:13-14
[973] Titus 2:13
[974] Malachi 4:6
[975] Galatians 3:13-14
[976] Revelation 22:21
[977] "Amazing Grace," John Newton.   As you can see, there are other, very powerful, but rarely sung, verses to this familiar song.

Verse Two:
In evil long I took delight
Un-awed by shame or fear;
'Til a new object met my sight
And stopped my wild career.

Verse Three
I saw One hanging on a tree,
In agonies and blood
Who fixed His languid eyes on me
As near His cross I stood.

Verse Four:
Sure, never 'til my latest breath
Can I forget that look.
It seemed to charge me with His death
Though not a word He spoke.

Verse Five:
My conscience owned and felt the guilt,
And plunged me in despair;
I saw my sins His blood had shed,
And helped to nail Him there.

Verse Six:
Alas, I knew not what I did,
But all my tears were vain;
Where could my trembling soul be hid,
For I the Lord had slain.

Verse Seven:
A second look he gave which said,
"I freely all forgive!
"This blood is for thy ransom paid,
"I die that thou mayest live."

Verse Eight:
Twas grace that taught my heart to fear,
And grace my fears relieved;
How precious did that grace appear
The hour I first believed.

Verse Nine:
Through many dangers, toils and snares
I have already come.
'Tis grace hath brought me safe thus far,
And grace will lead me home!

Verse Ten:
The Lord has promised good to me,
His word my hope secures;
He will my shield and portion be,
As long as life endures.

Verse Eleven:
Yes, when this flesh and heart shall fail,
And mortal life shall cease,
I shall possess within the veil
A life of joy and peace.

Verse Twelve:
The earth shall soon dissolve like snow,
The sun forbear to shine,
But God who called me here below
Shall be forever mine!

Verse Thirteen:
When we've been there ten thousand years
bright shining as the sun,
to sing God's praise
first begun.

Made in United States
Orlando, FL
21 June 2023